MW00355399

For the Love of ...Christi
Death and Grief
Met by Love and Hope

Copyright 2021 by Susan and Don Cox

Published by Almost Heaven Publishing
6506 Huckleberry Cove
Austin, Texas 78746
512-327-4683

All rights reserved.

ISBN 978-0-578-95923-8

Cover design and formatting by George Zirfas gzirfas@comcast.net

Editorial production by Angela Smith asmith1411@gmail.com

Printed in the United States of America

For the

Love of ...

Christi

**Death and Grief
Met by Love and Hope**

Almost Heaven Publishing
Austin, Texas

This book is dedicated
to all those who have
held our hands
and walked with us
on our grief journey.

Table of Contents

Preface

Why did we write this book?

That's a real good question:

the short and simple answer is Love!

Love for our daughter Christi Lanahan.

Her life was cut short at age 20 on October 26, 1985. The full answer lies in the pages that follow. It includes our personal pain and suffering, trying to make sense out of what happened, and how we are going to survive as individuals, a couple, and a family. At times our lives were overwhelming and hopeless. With great effort we reinvented ourselves and found hope.

Acknowledgements

We will never be able to thank all the people who have and continue to help and support us. We thank God for putting you in our lives. One of the people who encouraged us to write this book is Terri Schexnayder. In 1987 she was working for the advertising agency GSD&M. The big boss, Steve Gurasich, volunteered her to help us get started to create "For The Love Of Christi" now known as "The Christi Center." We guess since he never told her to stop she just kept going to this day! Unlike many well intentioned people who have a lot of good ideas, she was willing to help us with this monumental task. She patiently encouraged us to go back, and go deep. At times this was very painful and emotional. It is safe to say without her love and direction we would have never been able to undertake this book. Besides our own story we felt the need to include the lives and loves of some of just a few of our members. We apologize that we could not include more stories and may consider publishing additional members stories in the future.

We also want to thank Loyce Allen. She and her husband Mike are dear friends and members, having lost one of their sons, Michael, to cancer. Loyce is a retired English teacher and was very helpful with her insightful suggestions for revisions in content along with grammatical corrections to early drafts of this manuscript.

Melanie and Jay Holtz, also members and dear friends, were also very helpful, especially with their technical abilities. They offered their help in memory of their precious son, Matt, who died from a seizure.

A real "God-incidence" occurred when Angela Smith agreed to help us complete and publish the book. We have known Angela and her husband Charles for many years. They were so important to us that the night Christi was killed they were the first people we called for help while we were still at Brackenridge Hospital. They arrived minutes later and were constant companions, holding our hands, for the heartbreaking weeks and months after her death. We feel sure Christi had her hand in guiding us back to them to complete the circle.

1 | The Loss

CHAPTER

A Mother's Loss

I miss Christi's laughter, her love for life, the children she would have had.

— Susan Cox

I learned the true meaning of a mother's love on January 19, 1965, when Christi, my first child, came into the world. She was always a happy person with an infectious smile and magnetic personality. And what a humble person Christi was, always connecting with the people she met with an unconditional love. This was a trait inherited from her maternal grandmother Susan Jane Piper, who from the age of five, lived in an orphanage with her three older brothers after their mother died. Christi was very close to my mother and while attending the University of Texas, Christi sent her a prayer called "Don't Give Up," which we found hanging in my mother's bathroom after she died from a heart attack in May 1988.

Christi loved the outdoors, sports, swimming, reading, and, most of all, her little brother Sean, who was four years younger. As a Girl Scout, she had proudly earned 27 merit badges to pin on her sash. High School Homecoming Queen, head cheerleader, and cum laude graduate of

Westlake High School were just a few of her many achievements. In her junior year at the University of Texas at Austin and about to make the Dean's List, she was on her way to earning many more successes. A member of the Tri-Delta Sorority, she cherished the close relationships she had with her sorority sisters.

Christi and I enjoyed our special mother-daughter talks, going to the movies or shopping, cooking together, and, of course, skiing and taking other vacations with the whole family. In those pre-texting times, we talked all the time on the phone.

On her last phone call to us, Christi asked if we could get together on Friday evening, October 25. After we talked more, we decided it was better to wait until that Sunday so that we would have more time to visit and have dinner together. What guilt we felt later about that seemingly simple decision. That phone call was the last time I heard my daughter's voice, her saying, "Be sure to put baby's breath in your hair for the party, Mom." After midnight on that Saturday, Christi was killed. I don't remember much after we received the call and rushed to the hospital. All I really remember was the doctor standing there, his scrub top stained with blood, telling us, "We lost her."

Now I would learn the true meaning of a mother's sorrow.

CHAPTER

A Dad's Tale

Being a Dad is more than being a Father.

— From a Super Bowl ad, February 1, 2015

Christi was an easy person to love. Everyone who knew her felt like she was their best friend and being her stepdad was no different. To this day, I treasure my last gift from her, a money clip with the inscription: Thanks, Dad. I never had children of my own, so Christi and her brother Sean were a blessing for me. Not that we did not have difficult times adjusting to life as a blended family—we did, but we were always able to work things out. I credit much of that family harmony to Susan; she created a loving environment that nurtured respect and accountability.

Early in the morning on October 26, 1985, around 2:25 a.m. Susan answered the phone. Because of background noise and commotion, she assumed it was a prank call and hung up. A few seconds later, the phone rang again. This time the caller said he was from Brackenridge Hospital and looking for the parents of Christi Lanahan. Susan handed me the phone, saying, "Oh, my God, Don, it's Brackenridge Hospital!" I am sure the caller realized that I didn't grasp the severity of the situation, when I asked him, "Just how bad is it?"

His answer haunts me to this day. "I am not supposed to tell you this, but Christi has been in a terrible accident, and we don't think she is going to make it." Hearing that, I hurried to wake up Sean so we could face the crisis together. Still in a state of disbelief, I did not share the words of the caller.

We arrived at the hospital and identified ourselves as Christi's parents, and suddenly everyone disappeared. It seemed like an eternity before a nurse directed Susan, Sean, and me to a small room. I kept thinking, "I don't like the looks of this." Finally, Dr. Faulkenberry, the surgeon, walked in, still wearing his scrub top splattered with blood. When Susan asked him how Christi was, his head dropped and he spoke the heart-breaking words. "We lost her."

At that point, we entered a black hole of shock and despair. When I asked the doctor if we could see Christi, he told me to wait and to let the funeral home perform their miracles! Later that afternoon, we were notified that Christi's body had arrived from the coroner's office. Susan and I agreed that I should go see her body. First, to make sure it was really Christi, and, second, to determine if it would be possible to have an open casket for her funeral. We still didn't know how she had died, although I assumed she had been in an automobile accident.

It was only after I, along with my trusted friend Charles Smith, viewed her body that we learned the details of her horrific death. She was a pedestrian who had been hit by a drunk driver and dragged underneath a car for over 800 feet. No words can describe my thoughts and feelings. I was utterly broken.

CHAPTER

Surrendering My Rage

Don't worry about forgiving this SOB! That's God's job.

—Father Malcolm Riker

Identifying Christi's body was probably the worst thing I have ever experienced. I tried to cope with her death in the only way I knew how—with alcohol. I still remember the man at the funeral home trying to talk me out of seeing her. I am forever grateful to Charles Smith for being with me at that moment. He asked the man, "What would you do if this was your daughter?" The man had to agree he would want to see his child. I believe it was the right thing that I did see Christi, and that Susan and Sean were spared that.

After seeing her, I was haunted with images of her horrible injuries, dealing with nightmares and seething rage at the man who was responsible. I was angry with Christi's father for the way he parented her after the divorce, and angry with myself for the things I wish I had done or not done while she was alive. In the weeks and months following her death, my use of alcohol went from social-habitual to chronic. I would stand at Christi's grave and ask her for help. Unfortunately, my John Wayne Manual had no chapter on grief.

On top of all this, others around me were dumping their anger on me, saying, "I don't know how you are handling this. If it were me, I would have to kill that SOB!" Or, "Just think how much worse you would feel if you were the biological father." Those painful comments were like pouring gasoline on fire, flaming my overwhelming urge to kill the guy who killed Christi.

Remember, this was 1985 to 1986, long before there were metal detectors in the courtroom. He was out on $10,000 bond and was attending pre-trial hearings as they were scheduled. Thank God, a friend of mine, an Episcopal priest, Malcolm Riker, called me to go look at some real estate. I had helped him acquire some land for a few churches, so we had a close personal and professional relationship. Malcolm was not your typical priest. He was a veteran of WWII in the Pacific Theater, which meant that he had seen his share of death.

He told me he knew I was going to try to kill that guy; in fact, he said I could probably even get away with it once the jury saw the pictures of what he had done to Christi. He also reminded me that, when I died, I would have to face my Creator and answer for the death of Christi's killer. Then, he gave me the best advice anyone could have provided me at that particular moment:

"Don, give this to God. It is too big for you. Don't worry about forgiving this SOB! That is God's job. You just go into neutral, and remember that God is not only all-forgiving, but He is also all-just. This person needs to answer to God—not you—for this."

I knew that Malcolm was right, and that very day, I agreed and made my deal with God to surrender and go into neutral. The man who killed Christi would answer to God—not me.

CHAPTER

How Do I Go on Living

If I had a rose for every time I thought of you, I'd be picking roses for a lifetime.

– Swedish Proverb

On that dreadful October night, while walking with three of her friends near Sixth Street, Christi and Jenny, her best friend and roommate, were run over by a drunk driver and pinned underneath his El Camino. Jenny's body dislodged when the car sped away, but Christi remained steadfast underneath the vehicle, dragged over 800 feet. She was left lying in the street for dead. She died an hour later.

We learned many of the details of this tragedy from the television and newspapers in the days following her death. This was one of the biggest stories in 1985— front page and lead on the 6 o'clock news. Even the media in San Antonio picked up the story. Watching the coverage the

Saturday evening after she was killed, we finally learned the gruesome details of her horrific and nightmarish death. My shock turned to horror.

Hundreds of people crowded the church for Christi's memorial service. I was still so numb that much of the funeral was a blur. I do remember that at one point in the service, the minister looked at me and said, "Isn't that right, Mother?" That hit home. Yes, I am the mother of this lovely young woman we are burying today. A mother, who had to find a way to go on living and had no idea how to do that.

I wanted "The Rose," one of Christi's favorite songs played during the service, and our friend Charles Smith played it on the piano. "The Rose" was also playing when we took family and friends to the Oasis Restaurant for dinner the next night. I felt that this was a sign from Christi letting us know that she was okay and still with us. A few years later as my siblings and I gathered around my mother's casket to say our last good-byes, Don got our attention. "Listen, everyone." We heard an instrumental version of "The Rose" playing. Christi was telling me that her "Gran" was with her.

Many more times throughout the years, I would hear this song just when I needed it the most. Flowers overflowed at Christi's gravesite. She had touched so many lives during her short time on this earth. I didn't know it at the time, so deep was my grief, just how Christi would continue to touch thousands more even in her death. For the burial, I had requested that Christi have baby's breath in her hair, because she loved the flowers.

I never got to see her crowned with the baby's breath. Her injuries were too extensive. The casket was closed.

CHAPTER

Throwing Away the John Wayne Manual

In the John Wayne Manual, you learn to be tough, pull the arrow out of your shoulder, and keep on fighting. Never show the pain or fear!

— Don Cox

On March 20, 1986, I hit the wall. I reached the point of no return. After Christi's death, my life spiraled out of control. I was medicating myself with alcohol and a sedative that had actually been prescribed for Susan. Since she was not using it, I kept renewing the prescription and using it myself more and more to help even me out when I didn't have access to alcohol. Alcohol and drug addiction are progressive diseases. They are most appropriately described as cunning, baffling, and powerful in the Big Book of Alcoholics Anonymous. In my case, I knew that I was on the road to addiction; however, Christi's death and all of the circumstances surrounding it caused me to hit the fast forward button with my disease. In the five months following her death, I lost control of everything. If I slept, I had nightmares reliving how she died. And when I was awake, I was heartbroken trying to console Susan, let alone having to deal with my own grief.

People would ask me how Susan and Sean were doing. No one asked about me, or a few times, if they did, all they wanted to hear was "fine" and "doing okay." Sean, who found himself in the eye of the hurricane of our grief and anger, saw the pills that I was taking, and thinking they were not helping, flushed them down the toilet. By doing this, he saved my life.

I began to go into withdrawal, unable to sleep or keep any food or alcohol down. After a hellish night, I called the AA hotline, and they directed me to the closest meeting, Western Trails, which was run by a treatment center. On my way over, I tearfully asked God to help me and made a promise to do whatever He directed me to do. By six o'clock that evening, I was at the La Hacienda Treatment Center in Hunt, Texas.

When I arrived, I was so sick the attendants could not even draw my blood. What I went through during detox was hell on earth. I kept a journal while I was in treatment, and, occasionally, I look at it to remind myself where I was then. I spent four weeks in treatment there, diagnosed with something I had heard a little about in the 1970s when I was in the Navy. It was called Post Traumatic Stress Disorder (PTSD).

The end result: I threw away my John Wayne Manual and have now been in recovery since March 1986. It is a miracle for which I give thanks to God and Christi on the heavenly side, and Susan and Sean, and many others, on the earthly side.

CHAPTER

A Parent's Worst Nightmare

If you know someone who has lost a child and you're afraid to mention them because you think you might make them sad by reminding them that they died, you're not reminding them. They didn't forget they died. What you're reminding them of is that you remembered that they lived, and that is a great gift.

— Elizabeth Edwards

Immediately following Christi's death, we received a tremendous outpouring of love and support from our families, friends, and many in Austin and some from the surrounding areas who we didn't even know. After a short while, everyone went back to their normal, routine everyday lives. We could not—life as we knew it had been changed forever. Before Christi died, I owned a monogram business with a partner, helped Don with his real estate business as his office manager, and, was in training to be a Jazzercise instructor.

After Christi died, I could barely get out of bed, much less function in these day-to-day activities. I cried all the time, could not sleep, and experienced violent headaches and stomach aches. A tape of how Christi died, guilt of not being able to be with her in her last moments, fear that something would happen to Sean, and intense anger at the drunk driver who had taken her life played over and over in my mind. As her mother, I had nurtured and protected Christi. Why couldn't I have prevented this tragedy that took her life? If Sean was a few minutes late coming home, I would panic, thinking that something had happened to him.

Why did this drunk person choose to drink and drive? Why did this happen to Christi? Why our family? My faith was shattered. Surely, I imagined, I was being punished by God for something I did in my life.

Well-meaning friends and acquaintances, never having experienced a debilitating loss, had no idea what to say to us. They weren't aware of the hurt we felt hearing the comment after six months or a year, "Aren't you over it yet?" I thought that there was something wrong with me because I was still in so much grief. We needed to tell the story over and over again. We needed someone to listen to us as we poured out our grief. We began to wear friends out, and some fell by the wayside. Thankfully, our good friends Angela and Charles Smith were close at hand, always there when we needed them. They walked beside us as we trudged along the path.

Then there were the people who began to avoid us in public. Once I was in the grocery store when I glanced up to see a friend pushing her cart on the same aisle. At first she smiled at me; then, with a look of horror, she realized who I was and turned around to avoid me.

I was a parent's worst nightmare come true. I had lost a child.

CHAPTER

The Criminals' Justice System

The title of this chapter is grammatically correct. It is based on my experience with the criminal justice system.

—Don Cox

Christi was killed by a hit and run drunk driver. Two other men were in the car with him. One was so drunk that he claimed he didn't know what happened. The other man contacted the police once he learned that Christi had been killed. That was how Christi's killer was caught. They had abandoned the wrecked pickup truck across I-35 in East Austin and caught a cab home while Christi lay dying in the emergency room at Brackenridge Hospital.

At first the police charged him with failure to stop and render aid. However, the District Attorney's office realized that he could claim that he didn't know he had hit anyone, and, therefore, get off on a technicality. So, they recharged him with involuntary manslaughter—although there was nothing involuntary about his drinking and driving, causing the devastating event that killed Christi, and fleeing the scene of the crime. In 1985, the maximum punishment was ten years with no minimum amount of time to serve. There was also no such thing as intoxication or vehicular manslaughter. Christi's killer was able to post $10,000 bail and drive away. That's right—they couldn't even take his driver's license!

At this point I was ready to KILL. I started hearing about how weak the juries in Travis County were. Never mind that I had lived in Travis County most of my adult life! This was a highly publicized case. Everyone was asking us or telling us what to do. We didn't know who to trust. The District Attorney's office wanted to talk to us. I held out and told them we would only talk to the head D.A. himself, Ronnie Earle. At first all I heard was how busy he was, etc. I don't consider myself to be a very good poker player so I told the top Assistant D.A. exactly what I planned to do. Susan and I would meet with Mr. Earle in the next 48 hours or I would go to the media. Christi's death had made me fearless. Either you were on our side or against us. There was nothing in between.

Our first meeting with Mr. Earle in his office was one of the toughest experiences of our lives. We later learned that it was one of the toughest experiences for him, as well. We sat across from each other, and Susan began by placing a picture of Christi on his desk. She looked him straight in the eye and pointing at Christi's picture said, "Mr. Earle, this is why we are here today."

What he said after that was compassionate, honest, and direct. The best that we could ever expect would only be a semblance of justice. We all knew that nothing or no one could give us what we wanted—to have Christi back. Mr. Earle committed to giving the best that he could, given the legal limitations with which his office had to work. Susan and I left feeling that we could begin to trust again. The rest was up to God.

Still, several things were particularly hard for me to deal with. The first was being a stepparent. I had no legal right in the case, although Susan and Christi's biological father deferred to me to make what few decisions needed to be made between us, the D.A. and his staff. Second, this case was not ours. It was not the "Family of Christi Lanahan vs. her killer." It was the State of Texas, Travis County, vs. him. The third item was the toughest for me to deal with. I had crossed over from being a social-habitual drinker to a full-blown alcoholic.

There was much speculation that the defense would try somehow to put the blame on Christi in an attempt to minimize the guilt of the killer. I had only one conversation with the D.A.'s office about a possible plea bargain, and we quickly told them we would accept nothing less than the ten-year maximum sentence. Prior to the trial, we were cautioned not to make any public statements that the defense could use against us. When you hear something like that, it only intensifies your pain. Why should we worry about inflaming the jury or him getting a fair trial, when we all knew that he was guilty and deserved far worse punishment for killing Christi!

The trial started in April 1986, about six months after her death. In the criminal justice system, this was speedy turnaround. It is quite common to have to wait a year or more for cases like this to be brought to trial. Since the trial was only about his sentencing, you would think this would only take a day or two. However, all the evidence related to her death and the defendant's life leading up to, and including that night, had to be presented. Christi's biological father and I were determined to stay in the courtroom, especially during the most graphic testimony, so that the jury would know our presence.

We did not look, however, at the pictures of Christi's body passed around in an envelope for the jury to see. I had identified Christi's body a few hours after her death, which sent me spiraling into a deep dark hole of despair that seemed to have no bottom and no hope. I wanted to protect myself from being re-traumatized as this led to my becoming a chronic alcoholic for which I sought treatment about a month before the trial began. The four weeks I spent at La Hacienda Treatment Center literally saved my life.

Looking back at that time now, I realize that I was not only preparing myself for my new life, but especially for the trial. Sitting just feet away from the man responsible for Christi's horrific death, while experiencing such debilitating pain and suffering, was only made possible by my prayers and the prayers of, God only knows, how many other wonderful people.

I still remember at the summation of the trial, Steve McCleery, one of the prosecuting attorneys, put a picture of Christi in front of the jury and sat down. It was the same picture that Susan had put in front of Mr. Earle when we first met. For several minutes, there was dead silence in the courtroom. Then, he said, "We are here because Christi is not." The jury took only a few hours to come back with the maximum sentence—ten years.

We knew that the killer would not serve the full sentence, but were horrified to later learn that only eight months after he was sentenced, he came up for parole! I could not imagine that was even possible or that parole would be considered every eight months until he was released. He fully served his ten-year sentence in two and a half years with credit for good time. The last time he came up for parole, we took a member of the jury with us to let the parole board know what the jury thought of their Criminals' Justice System. In fact, that juror said that the jurors tried to find a way for him to serve more time than the ten years!

As District Attorney Ronnie Earle so aptly said, we can only receive a semblance of justice.

2 | Zebras Finding Our Place in a Herd of Horses

CHAPTER

My Faith Raised Me Up

The painful things that happen to us are not punishments for our misbehavior, nor are they in any way part of some grand design on God's part. Because the tragedy is not God's will, we need not feel hurt or betrayed by God when tragedy strikes.

—Rabbi Harold S. Kushner

In the first year after her death, I tried to think about the good times we had with Christi. For example, a year before her death, we all went to Florida to spend 10 days at Walt Disney World and visit my parents in Saint Augustine. We were all together! However, on October 26, 1986, the first angelversary of Christi's death, I could not avoid the reality. "Oh my God, it's been a year since she died!"

On top of that, whenever I would start talking about Christi and her death, folks would get that stricken look on their faces or change the subject, so I would stop. In the John Wayne Manual, you learn to be tough, pull the arrow out of your shoulder, and keep on fighting. Never show the pain or fear! I realized that I needed to reaffirm or reinvent every facet of my life. I quit almost every outside activity, such as the Lion's Club, the Civic Club, the Austin Woods and Water Club, and any board positions connected with my Realtor profession. All were things that I dearly loved in my previous life before Christi died, but in which I could no longer participate with my untreated disability as a grieving parent.

Like many others, I used to believe that if you go to church, pay your taxes, do a good job at work, and eat healthy—then, a "bubble of protection" would cover you. I could tell by the questions they asked some people still believed that. They were trying to figure out what you did wrong since they always considered you to be like them: a good person. That is why Rabbi Kushner's book When Bad Things Happen to Good People is so powerful. He and his wife lost their young son Aaron to progeria, a rapid-aging disease. His book continues to help so many people who are coping with the death of a loved one. He likens the popular belief about the "bubble" to a kind of faith that is like being in a corral with a bull.

You think, "That bull won't charge me, because I am a vegetarian!" (Which I am not!) The truth is that faith is not there to protect you from the bull; rather, faith is there to pick you up after the bull runs over you. Make no mistake, sooner or later, the bull (life) runs over all of us. Some get run over sooner and rougher, or more often, than others. Rabbi Kushner is quick to remind people that the title of his book is not WHY, but WHEN Bad Things Happen to Good People.

On May 8, 2007, we were blessed to have Rabbi Kushner speak at a For the Love of Christi fundraiser at the Dell Jewish Community Center in Austin. While giving him a tour of our facility, he learned that, besides the death of our children, we had another special connection.

After Christi's death, I went back to reread Viktor Frankl's Man's Search for Meaning, which I highly recommend, especially anyone trying to find a reason to go on living. It is a chronicle of his World War II experience in four concentration camps and how he survived Nazi death camps, while his parents, brother and pregnant wife perished.

I first read it as a freshman at St. Edward's University in 1965. Later, I was privileged to meet Viktor Frankl when he came to Austin to receive the Quest Award from St. Ed's in 1976. When I mentioned this to Rabbi Kushner, he shared that he had been honored to write the forward for the 50-year anniversary edition of Frankl's book.

CHAPTER

Adjusting to a New Normal

We bereaved are not alone. We belong to the largest company in the entire world—the company of those who have known suffering.
— Helen Keller

How long was this pain going to last? The first year after Christi's death, I sluggishly moved through each day. I was dealing with getting her things from college, writing thank-you notes to those who were there for us, and filing out so much paperwork. It was after the trial for the man who killed Christi that my grief really hit me hard.

Every problem in our marriage, our lives, was magnified—either nothing I did seemed right, or it just didn't matter. The hard work of dealing with the wrenching pain of loss left Don and me exhausted with little time for each other. Christi had once told me, "Everyone should be so lucky to have someone who loves them as much as Don loves you." We would have to try to keep it together. Don tried to console me, but he was also in the depths of his own grief and couldn't hold up both of us. We mourned the loss of the same person, but each of us were grieving in our own way. Our son not only lost his sister, he also lost his mother as I disappeared into inconsolable sorrow.

I began to question my very life. Who was I in a world without Christi in it? I would walk by a closet, see her laundry bag engraved with purple lettering, I'm Home, Mom, and would fall into another pit of grief. Literally brought to my knees, I prayed, "Dear God, if I have to live with this pain for the rest of my life, what is my purpose?" As I looked for a reason to go on living, an answer began to come to me: "Help others in Christi's memory, and they will help you."

Don was getting help through his AA program, but I desperately needed help, too. I was made even more aware of the dismal state I was in when Sean asked Don before I left for the California workshop. "What are we going to do if this doesn't work?" Don answered, "We'll just keep trying."

In the summer of 1986, I attended a Elizabeth Kubler-Ross Growth and Transition grief workshop in California. There, I learned techniques to handle day-to-day stress, how to better understand the grieving process, and, how to express my feelings. The focus was on helping us determine what we were going to take with us and what we had to leave behind, such as my all-consuming anger for the drunk driver who had killed Christi. I had a choice to make: I could become a bitter person or better person by reaching out to help others. I knew in my heart which Christi would want me to do.

An opportunity to reach out to another person came this same summer when we met an exchange student from Switzerland, Lars Von Muehlenen.

CHAPTER

Hosting Exchange Students

The more good I do for others, the more I will feel Christi's love.

— Susan Cox

In the summer of 1985, we had a wonderful experience with another student Mosa Al Omran from Saudia Arabia. He spent six weeks with us while Christi visited a roommate's family in Singapore. The year following Christi's death, in 1986, Sean asked us to consider hosting another exchange student, Lars Von Muehlenen of Switzerland.. Given the depths of despair we were dealing with, it seemed like too soon to welcome another exchange student to our home.

We just could not imagine it being fair to anyone moving into our situation. Sean told us he had some friends with whom Lars was living, but that Lars was not happy with this arrangement. He would come over to our house on his own and visit with Sean, Susan, and me. Lars was good for all of us during this time, especially Sean. Sean had no one to share his grief with, and Lars became like a brother to him. It soon became apparent that Lars was a special person, and once we learned more about his situation, Susan, Sean, and I agreed that if Lars wanted to move, he was welcome in our home. Just after Thanksgiving Lars asked, "Is that deal about moving in still good?" We said, "Yes!" and he moved in that day.

Lars became part of our family, and we became part of his. We took him to our place in Ruidoso during Thanksgiving for a skiing holiday. He was a great skier, and he even encouraged Susan to go down the Black Slope! Lars' parents, Hans and Pia, came to stay with us during his graduation from Westlake High School, and they have opened their home in Switzerland to us. We continue to stay in touch with each other. He and his family refer to us as his American parents and Sean as his American brother. Lars is our Swiss son-brother.

Looking back at it now, we think Christi had her hand in helping us find Lars, and later, in June 1988, discovering our dog Angel.

CHAPTER

Driven to Make a Difference

Before I'll ride with a drunk, I'll drive myself.
— Stevie Wonder on "Reader's Digest" poster

Within five months of Christi's death, Susan and I began to work on the creation of a program to encourage individuals, who were planning to drink, to first designate a driver to get them home safely. Susan saw a Reader's Digest ad, featuring blind musician Stevie Wonder. He had teamed up with the Dodge Division of Chrysler Corporation and Mothers Against Drunk Driving (MADD) in a "Don't Drink and Drive" campaign. She immediately began her letter-writing magic to make contact with Stevie and his management team. Success!

We met with Stevie backstage after his Austin concert on July 12, 1986, and had the opportunity to speak to him about our mission. We discovered that Stevie once had his own experience with a drunk driver, who struck his car—an accident that left him with injuries and a scar on his forehead. Stevie was compassionate and generous, and when he reached over to hug Susan, crying as she shared Christi's story, he whispered, "She is always with you."

We received the Stevie Wonder posters from Reader's Digest, and Susan distributed them at Westlake High School for their graduation party in the gym. Our persistence in contacting others about the designated driver idea also paid off. In 1988, the Texas Alcoholic Beverage Commission (TABC) and the Texas Automobile Dealers Association (TADA) endorsed our "Designated Driver" program poster. An estimated 15,000 to 20,000 were distributed statewide. Along with the Be a Friend for Life ... Designate a Driver message, Christi's beautiful photo was prominently displayed. Under her photo were the words:

"For the Love of Christi, January 19, 1965 – October 26, 1985

Later that year, with the help of a sympathetic President Ronald Reagan and First Lady Nancy Reagan, who forwarded our information and letters on to the US Department of Transportation, we met with the president of the National Safety Council in Chicago. The result was worldwide distribution of Christi's picture and her story on their calendar for the month of October, the month she was killed. Since this calendar was circulated to all Armed Forces, we heard from Military personnel from Germany to Japan. The poster read:

Killed By Someone

Who Chose To Drink and Drive

Christine Denise Lanahan

1965–1985

Junior, University of Texas

CHAPTER

Honoring Those Who Were There for Us

The hardest part of this job for me has always been the helplessness I feel in the face of the unspeakable grief that consumes victims of crime ... I can't make their way any easier or their pain any less.

— Ronnie Earle, former District Attorney, Travis County

On October 26, 1986, in observance of the one-year angelversary of Christi's death, we held an event on the LBJ Library grounds to honor those officials and community representatives who were there for us during our tragedy. Attendees included the late Marshall Littleton★, the investigating officer called to the 400 block of Red River after Christi was hit. Travis County District Attorney Ronnie Earle and KVUE-TV reporter Keith Elkins were also recognized for their efforts on our behalf.

For Keith, airplane crashes and other deaths were an expected occurrence in the news cycle. He was trained to cover these stories with a certain detachment; then, he had to cover Christi's death and subsequent trial. "I could not allow myself to get too close to the subject.," he told us. "Until I had to interview the Cox's about their loss of Christi ... then, it all changed for me." Keith became actively involved in our organization, serving on the board and filming a chemical-free graduation party video for Westlake High School seniors.

Also there for us was Edi Moriarty, who worked with MADD, and stood right by my side during the ceremony. From the beginning when Christi died, she was there for me with her love and support, including long-time future work at our center. We presented plaques of gratitude to those who offered their services throughout our ordeal, the trial, and beyond with Don sharing our sentiments, "The recipients had shown not just sympathy, but compassion—meaning they were willing to help. None of these nine individuals knew Christi or our family before the tragedy."

We also used this event to reinforce our Designated Driver program, launched earlier in the year. Officer Littleton stressed in his speech that most people have the "don't think it can happen to you" mentality. On October 26, 1985, we certainly never imagined it would happen to Christi and our family. Turning our attention to the efforts of others was at least one way of helping to soothe our grief.

Little did we know then how our fledgling organization, For the Love of Christi, would come to impact more than 100,000 individuals, directly or indirectly, during their own grief journeys after the loss of their loved ones to any type of death.

★ Marshall Littleton (deceased) is the brother-in-law of Bernadette Ruiz, whose husband, Senior Deputy Sheriff Keith Ruiz, a 13-year veteran, was shot and killed during a narcotic's raid on February 15, 2001. Bernadette and her three sons Matthew, Alexander, and Joshua later received help and friendship through The Christi Center's Kids Who Kare.

CHAPTER

Standing Up for Others

Advocacy would become an important cornerstone of our organization, working on behalf of victims of all types of crime. We would hold the legal system accountable to the survivors and try to change the criminal justice system.

— Don Cox

As our efforts with the Designated Driver program grew, so did our passion to advocate on behalf of others who had lost someone. Christi's death was extremely violent, and we hoped victims of Drinking While Intoxicated (DWI) would gain new rights under HB 878 during Texas' 70th Legislature. We later learned that Christi had been a volunteer for Representative Terrell Smith's campaign and had received a letter of thanks for her efforts to get him re-elected. State Representative Smith supported passage of this bill, but he and other bill supporters met strong resistance. The criminal defense attorneys, many of whom are often legislators themselves, pushed strong lobbying efforts to stop it.

On April 30, 1987, Susan joined close to 100 other individuals connected with the group People Against Violent Crime in the Capitol Rotunda, as part of Texas Crime Victim's Rights Week, to hear state legislators announce the bill's passage. The new law gave victims of violent crimes the right to confront the newly convicted criminal with an impact statement. The impact statement allowed crime victims to make known to the court just how families were affected by the loss of their loved ones. The new law also provided psychological counseling for victims of violent crimes. On the steps of the Capitol that day, Susan stated, "Hopefully, this bill will finally give us a chance to sit in the court and have character witnesses just as the people committing the crimes do."

Christi's death was a huge TV and newspaper story. It made headline news for many months after she was killed due to the horrific story of how she died, being dragged over 800 feet under an automobile. The public realized, as her story unfolded in the news that Christi did not die immediately. Had it not been for the senselessness of the crime and the poor decisions by the hit-and-run driver, this unspeakable tragedy could have been avoided. Instead, his reckless actions knocked down two innocent pedestrians and pinned Christi under his El Camino.

Advocacy would become an important cornerstone of our organization.

3

For the Love of ... Christi

CHAPTER

Seeking a Heart Connection

This is the best bunch of people I wish I had never known.

— Al Cox, who lost his son James Alan Cox in 2007 in a media helicopter crash in Phoenix, Arizona

---

In the beginning, our grief support meetings were sponsored by a minister friend. We met in different homes with individuals and families who were dealing with all types of grief, such as divorce and job loss. However, when it came our turn to talk about our loss of Christi, everyone would shake their heads and exclaim, "Oh, my God! My grief is nothing compared to your grief for the loss of your child!" That may have helped them, but it made us feel even worse. Soon, we realized we needed to be with others who were trying to adjust to life after the death of a loved one.

We began the process of establishing our own new nonprofit, For the Love of Christi, in May 1987. Our mission was to help anyone who was having difficulty adjusting to life after the death of a loved one, regardless of the circumstances of the death or their relationship to the deceased, as well as educate the general public on the needs of the bereaved. Another important aspect of the nonprofit mission was that those who came to us would pay no dues or fees—ever! We felt those who needed our help had already paid too high a price.

We moved into our first office space in the Cielo Center in October 1987. We met new friends who like us had broken hearts, and we shared our stories, sitting on lawn chairs in a circle, a cooler of soft drinks at our side. We started each meeting by passing a little purple glass heart, saying our name and the name of the lost loved one(s) for whom we grieved. These early members served on our board and staff; served as facilitators and on panels for schools, churches, law enforcement agencies; and, helped with workshops and events. They became our dearest friends, and many still remain active to this day.

We began For the Love of Christi with meetings each Monday, dealing with any type of loss from terminal illness to sudden death. But, the organization and need for its grief support just kept growing. It was apparent that we needed to find a larger, safe place to give solace, comfort, and hugs to other Zebras.

CHAPTER

A Home for Good

I had no idea of the depth of services you are offering. I also have no doubt you are here to stay.

— Greg Kozmetsky, RGK Foundation

From 1986 to 1990, Austin was in a bad recession with a lot of office space available. I sought the advice of the other Don Cox, a fellow real estate broker, about office space and he recommended I talk with Steve Gurasich, one of the founding partners of GSD&M Advertising. Our initial conversation with Steve, who had recently lost his brother "Bird" couldn't have gone better. Steve showed compassion for our cause and understanding of our mission.

In October 1987, he offered us an office at the rate of ten dollars a month in the Cielo Center on Capital of Texas Highway. That included access to an amazing advertising team, led by account manager Terri Botik (now "Schexnayder") who helped develop our logo, promotional materials, and special events at no charge. Terri's marketing and personal devotion to our organization has continued, long after she left the internationally-renowned firm. Bob Plunk, who was with Preferred Risk Insurance (now Guide One

Insurance), sent us a check for $5,000. He told us to stay focused on our mission, and we took his advice to heart! We were pleased to know that Bob, Steve, Terri and so many others believed in what we were doing.

When the Westlake building ownership changed five years later, our rent went up dramatically. During the board meeting when we brought up the substantial increase, hands began to fly up. Tee Barbour was the first one of our members who offered to personally pay the rent. Later, a 1993 move two blocks away to Westlake Plaza increased our monthly commitment from $600 to $800, and I knew we had to purchase our own facilities in order to control our overhead and not be at the mercy of a landlord.

A Hancock Drive house came up for sale in May 1996, and I thought it was perfect location for our new center and expanding needs. The first step was to change the zoning status; it was zoned residential and everything else around it was commercial. While we were in the middle of the rezoning, Mrs. Murchison, the owner of the home passed away. As a real estate broker, I know you are usually done when someone dies during a contract. When we went to the funeral home to offer our condolences, we met the daughter Dorothy Murchison, the only child. She told us that her mother was so pleased to know what we were planning to do with her home. She was going to honor her mother's contract.

Thanks to my good friend Richard Crank, we were able to properly rezone the property. Susan and I guaranteed the note after we raised enough money for the down payment. As luck would have it, board members Stephen and Johnna Jones were able to help us. Stephen's family owned a bank in Albany, Texas. When I asked the bank contact Randal Palmore what I needed to do to get approval, he replied, "If Stephen told you to call me, it's already approved."

Community angels were with us every step of the way toward finalizing the purchase of our permanent home at 2306 Hancock Drive!

CHAPTER

Athletes Step Up to the Plate (and onto the Court)

The community has done so much for me and I was looking for some way to pay it back. My satisfaction is in knowing that it's a good cause.

— Kelly Gruber, third baseman for Toronto Blue Jays, and one year ahead of Christi at Westlake High School

From the moment we launched For the Love of Christi, support from individuals and businesses poured out to us. On February 13, 1988, the turnout from so many former sports heroes was overwhelming. Kelly Gruber, a former Westlake High School student with the Toronto Blue Jays, and DPS Trooper Lance Coleman organized the "Sportslink Superstars Basketball Benefit" for our organization. Athletes from around the country, including UT Longhorn and Boston Red Sox player Roger

Clemens, UT Longhorns Donnie Little, and Coach Jim Hudson of the New York Jets signed up to play.

Attendees packed the Westlake High School gym to watch Dicky Grigg, Jerry Hall, Pam Busfield, Ken Oden, and Roger Schultz, along with local and state officials State Representative Terral Smith, Travis County District Attorney Ronnie Earle, Sheriff Doyle Bailey, County Commissioner Pam Reed, City Council member Sally Shipman, who tried their hoop shots at the half-time "mini" game. Local entertainment venues and retailers donated auction items and other businesses stepped up to underwrite the event and its publicity.

Another successful event held later that year to benefit For the Love of Christi was the "Cielo Fall Fun Fair." The fair focused on health, safety, fashion, and music. Held in October 1988, and hosted by our office building landlords, its activities ranged from exploring the Starlight Helicopter for children to an evening fashion show that featured Austin's top designers and merchants. The highlights of the fundraiser were the auction of John Travolta's shirt, which he wore in Urban Cowboy, and an autographed Mickey Mantle baseball.

Over the many years, the generosity of so many has come to us again and again, so that the organization and its amazing staff and volunteers can continue to help individuals for free during their grief journey and as long as they need it. We've never had a lot of money, but always, enough to keep us going.

CHAPTER

Our Own Angel on Earth

On Saturday, June 11, 1988, I was doing something no parent should have to do—visiting my child's grave at the cemetery.

—Don Cox

On my way home from an appointment, I stopped by the cemetery to visit Christi's grave. There, I passed an area that particularly touches my heart—where the babies are buried. Under a canopy over a new grave was a precious young dog, barely more than a puppy, lying in the turned earth of an infant's grave. After giving the puppy water to drink, I wondered what to do. I went on to visit Christi's grave, and then, home to Susan where I shared my story of the little dog.

Susan wanted to see the puppy for herself so we went back. The puppy was still there, so we fed her and agreed it must belong to the family of the infant. The following day we again visited Christi's grave. The dog was gone, causing mixed feelings of disappointment and a confused sense of relief. Before leaving, Susan said, "Let's go by the baby's grave one more time just to make sure."

And, there she was—hot, tired, and covered with fleas, but with the sweet and serene temperament of what we believed was a collie mix. We decided this time that God and Christi must want us to have her. After a good bath and a trip to the vet's, the little dog sported a shiny coat and a new collar. Now we had to come up with a name for her. When our neighbor, Marie Mouer, saw our precious puppy, she said, "What an angel!" Of course, that would be her name—Angel—so very appropriate.

Angel Cox, our new family member, became a vital part of our organization. She was especially good for children who were coping with the death of a parent, grandparent, or sibling, and who had a difficult time expressing their feelings. Angel would nuzzle up to a child and they soon became new best friends. As the facilitator encouraged, "Let's tell Angel how you feel," the child would pet Angel and start talking to her, and healing would begin. Angel was remarkably intuitive. She would gaze up at Christi's photo on the mantel. During one gathering, Angel carefully looked at each person in the room, one by one. A psychologist noted, "This dog has a very special gift."

For more than six years Angel was active as a pet therapy dog with the Kids Who Kare program and other venues. She visited retirement centers and served as a presenter with Don and me at conferences. At one Governor's Conference, she was awarded an honorary Ph.D. (Pretty Happy Dog). Her field of expertise was human compassion.

She passed away in October 2001. Her diploma and photo still hang in our office, and she lives on in our hearts.

CHAPTER

Plant a Tree in Memory of Loved One

Because of your dedication, folks had the chance to show their 'Love Of', that love really does change that special place on Town Lake, now known as Lady Bird Lake, into a sacred space.

— John Giedraitis, former City of Austin Forester

The idea for our annual Memorial Tree Grove, which over the years became one of the most anticipated events, grew from the notion of a living memorial. We were visiting with John Giedraitis, then a City of Austin Forester, who told us about a master plan designed by landscape architect J. Robert Anderson and approved as part of a city bond passed in 1983. The impressive plan included walkways and tree groves, but, since voter approval, the money for trees had instead been spent elsewhere. We suggested that our organization raise donations for trees and the City of Austin plant them.

Mayor Lee Cooke proclaimed the day of October 28, 1990, as "For the Love of Christi Day." On April 21, 1991, we held a ceremony celebrating the planting of 182 trees along Festival Beach at our first event. Little did we know that year would bring a terrible drought. As luck would have it, we had donated a tree in memory of Brock Green's grandson. Brock was a Parks employee who made sure that not only his grandson's tree survived, but all the others, as well. Every weekend, on his own time, he would go there to water all the trees. His grandson's name is on the marker with the other 181 names of loved ones. Brock's gratitude for our gift is just one more example of how those who grieve help one another even though very few knew him or realized how valuable his gift was to us.

New members started asking, "Could I have a tree planted for my loved one?" We continued the program, planting 30 to 40 trees a year as we advanced into Fiesta Gardens on the North Shore; then, moved to the South Shore of Town Lake (now called Lady Bird Lake). We ran out of space when we hit 600-plus trees. Urban Forester Emsud Horozovic, who formerly worked with the City of Austin and had moved to the City of Round Rock Parks and Recreation Department, became our biggest advocate for placing the Memorial Tree Grove in Old Settler's Park in Round Rock.

Presenting the idea to Nyle Maxwell, Round Rock Mayor, and a very compassionate city council, Emsud helped win their approval for the project. At one of the Round Rock Ceremonies, doves were released. The birds took off into the sky, circled, and then headed home. Like the souls of our loved ones when they die—they are with us and then head home. We later released balloons into the blue October skies. In 2014, we planted our 1,000th tree.

One of those honored was six-year-old Zachary who died in 2005. His mother, Michelle, shared this powerful memory about her son:

We have lived so much of our lives in this park that I can't think of a better place for a living memorial to Zachary. He spent countless hours watching his brothers play baseball, making friends, catching ladybugs, and, of course, flirting with girls! Occasionally he would 'run' the bases in his wheelchair, but he was most often found on the field, next to his youngest brother, singing the national anthem and shouting, "Play ball!

CHAPTER

Celebrating Christi and Special Anniversaries

God never said that the journey would be easy, but He did say that the arrival would be worthwhile.

— Max Lucado

As we approached the 10th anniversary of our organization, we looked in the rear-view mirror to see how far we'd traveled on our journey. Though we'd passed many milestones, this one seemed at once an endless highway; yet, only a short distance from that horrendous night of Christi's death. I knew that keeping her memory alive was one of the things that brought us comfort. One of our greatest fears after the death of someone we love is that they will be forgotten. I had chronicled Christi's life from childhood to young womanhood in a scrapbook that I wanted to share with others forever.

The Austin American Statesman had an article commemorating For the Love of Christi's 10th Anniversary, giving Don and me a chance to tell Christi's story and to express what the organization meant to us. As I said in the article, "One of the reasons I have survived is this group, I feel Christi's presence here." The Westlake Picayune also marked the date with a front page article about Christi's life. At Westlake High School, Christi was Head Cheerleader, Homecoming Queen, and she also served on the yearbook and newspaper staff. Graduating cum laude, Christi went on to become a University of Texas honor student and was named to UT "Who's Who" lists.

In the Westlake Picayune article, we invited her friends to honor her memory at a For the Love of Christi reunion at our home. It gladdened my heart that so many of Christi's friends showed up, shared their memories, and told us what Christi meant to them. In turn, I was able to share my scrapbook with them. The much beloved late Toody Bird, director of counseling at Westlake High School, summed up the many tributes by saying that Christi was what one would call Miss Westlake. In Toody's words, "She was smart, beautiful, and filled with school spirit and love." As evidenced by the love at that gathering, Christi was indeed a friend to many.

At the 15th anniversary, we invited friends to tour The Christi Center. Many came and supported us with their love donations in Christi's honor.. We celebrated the 20th on Saturday, October 27, 2007, at the annual Tree Grove Memorial Dedication in Round Rock. The trees planted in the memory of loved ones symbolize the seeds of hope and love spread by The Christi Center. Round Rock Forestry Manager Emsud Horozovic joined Mayor Nyle Maxwell, who presented a proclamation to commemorate the organization's landmark year.

Christi's memory was once again honored. And once again our journey was made easier by the outpouring of love and support of friends and fellow journeyers.

CHAPTER

Songs of the Heart

Where there is a need, I will write a song.
— Patricia Stuart, Ph.D.

Dr. Patricia Stuart, a long-time advisory board member and dedicated volunteer, performed her heart-felt music for several decades at our annual events. As a psychologist, Patricia understands how painful the holidays and beyond can be for those who grieve. She has referred many of her clients to our organization through the years. Her incredible voice comforts those in the room during our annual December Candlelight Remembrance Service, held in the Mabee Ballroom at St. Edward's University. We unveiled her CD, Through a Shred of Light, in 1997 at the 10th anniversary of the service in a room filled with more than 300 people and a Christmas tree covered with purple hearts—each with a picture and the name of their loved one(s).

Patricia performs her songs of inspiration, remembrance and comfort all across Texas, lending her songwriting and singing skills to a wide range of non-profit organizations and social causes. In the early 1990s, another long-time friend and volunteer, Reverend Ron Campbell (who passed away April 11, 2012), brought Patricia to us. Ron once shared the details of their first meeting.

"As we drove by Republic Park after dinner, we saw hundreds of luminaries and heard people singing. I knew it was something special. When we parked, I walked up to the woman playing the guitar and said, 'I am supposed to meet you'."

Patricia later became involved with us and recorded a CD for us, her songs touching people in need across the country but her heart has remained with us in Texas.

Patricia and Randy Frazier, Ph.D., her husband who accompanies her on the mandolin, have given above and beyond in board service and through countless speaking engagements, workshops, and retreats. Patricia demonstrated her passion for our Kids Who Kare program when she helped us win and implement a research grant from the Academy of Recording Arts and Sciences to help children write, perform, and record their own songs of love and loss. These children and their produced songs were later celebrated at a Grammy Award-like CD release party. We gave each child a permanent memorial of their loved one.

I cannot imagine a Candlelight Remembrance Service without Patricia's voice filling the space and touching the hearts of all blessed to hear her.

4

Expanding Our Mission and Programs

CHAPTER

Retreats to Help Cope with Loss

Should you shield the canyons from the windstorms you would never see the true beauty of their carvings.

— Elisabeth Kübler-Ross

As our organization grew through the generosity of so many angels, we sought ways to expand grief support beyond the Hancock Center space. The Elisabeth Kübler-Ross Center had once helped me hold on to my sanity, so I had first-hand knowledge of the power of the *Life, Death and Transition Workshop* held in California. Elisabeth Kübler-Ross wrote an article about our organization in spring 1992, which featured Christi's picture on the front page with the story. She wrote me a letter saying how very proud she was of us.

A few members were able to attend a five-day Kübler-Ross workshop through grant scholarships. Other women have found peace of mind at our early grant-funded Texas retreats in Gruene, Fredericksburg, and

Salado with the help of two amazing volunteers, Loyce Allen and Mary Graf. We also had Women's Retreats for those who have lost children, spouses, siblings, and parents at *Almost Heaven* in Ruidoso, New Mexico, and at *Charlie's Place*, a serene and lovely site near the cool waters of Lake Buchanan, shaded by lush Texas trees.

Charlie's Place was founded in 2004 after Lou and Dave Seideman lost Charlie, their 17-year-old son on Mother's Day in 2001 in a car accident. Their first thought after viewing the property centered on the possibility of hosting retreats for The Christi Center.

Lou and Dave had so many questions: "How could something like this happen to Charlie and to us?" "Why do we feel so guilty—could we have done something different?" "How can we possibly go on with our lives?" They shared they could hardly do anything without crying, which either embarrassed or upset their family and friends.

At the weekly meetings, Lou and Dave met others who shared their grief, and they could talk and cry and even laugh with them. They still don't have all the answers, but they know no one else does either. Their friends at The Christi Center are like family, connected by a personal under-standing of how a loved one's loss can affect the lives of those left living.

Lou and Dave's time with others over the years has been filled with sharing photos and celebrating the lives of loved ones. The retreats have helped them as much as those who have attended. After the loss of a loved one, it's hard to think you'll ever laugh again. But as Dave once said, it's okay to go there, to think about your lost child, but allow yourself to go away, too.

CHAPTER

Kids Who Kare, the Forgotten Grievers

For me, this work is sacred, and very much an honor to be able to witness the process of healing. Because we all at some point experience deep loss, the mission of The Christi Center truly serves as a lifeline of hope for so many.

—Christi Neville, L.P.C., The Christi Center

Perhaps the most vulnerable and confused of those who come to The Christi Center for support are the children who have lost a parent, sibling, or other close family member. They tend to hold in their feelings, as they don't want to be known among their peers as "the girl who lost her brother" or "the boy who lost his dad." As the needs of our organization grew, grief support expanded to serve ages five through twelve, and we established the Kids Who Kare (KWK) program.

Meeting twice a month, KWK serves both children and their caregivers, valuing the importance of addressing the family system as a whole. Dinner is provided at meetings in an effort to bring everyone together over a nourishing meal and to also relieve caregivers of cooking on the evenings they get the family to group. While the adults have their own meeting that supports them, the kids participate in therapeutic activities, which focus on normalizing and educating them on the grief process. This includes coping skills to use in everyday life. Developed by the staff facilitator, a licensed counselor, the age-appropriate activities are designed to be engaging, fun, and conducive to making friends with their peers. Through the childhood language of play and artistic expression, children are helped by many activities to find ways to remember and memorialize their loved one, a cornerstone of healing.

The Memory Jar, for example, is a mason jar they decorate with great detail and pride. They fill it with memories of their loved ones and often tailor the jar for important holidays and anniversaries that might trigger their grief. Mindful exercises are utilized to help the children relax and connect to their bodies, minds, and spirits. Annual outings provide laughter and fun—The Children's Retreat at *Charlie's Place* on Lake Buchanan, or visits to the 7-A Ranch in Wimberley or Northwind Farms, where each child is paired with a miniature horse that they get to groom, walk, and bond with. This healing dose of equine therapy has put a smile of joy on more than one young face.

Volunteers and interns also play a major role in supporting these young grievers. Dave and Lou Seideman have shared so much of their time with these children. What would the KWK Christmas party be like without Lou providing delectable gingerbread houses for the children to decorate, while Dave keeps them dancing around the room to the beat of his amazing band!

Another blessing came when we hired Christi Neville in 2015 as a KWK facilitator. Christi had lost her fiancé Alan, a free-spirited Englishman, while skiing together. He had just moved with Christi to Colorado so that she could attend a graduate counseling program and was hit from behind and killed by an intoxicated skier. Her tragedy can only be described in Christi's own words:

"I went from planning a wedding and future full of dreams, to planning a funeral. For the next few years of my life, I was completely overwhelmed by the many layers of loss. On the outer layer, I was trying to finish graduate school amidst the debilitating effects of post-traumatic stress, and was closely involved in precedent-setting criminal case against Alan's killer. It went to the state supreme court and, eventually, to trial, which resulted in a conviction—three years after Alan's death, of negligent homicide.

"On the inside, I was struggling daily with the depths of grief, yet devoted to learning how to repair a broken heart, broken spirit, and broken dreams. What struck me early on is how little our culture understands grief, and how little permission there is for it. When I was in a more healed place several years down the line, I was inspired to support others in grief, and have continued to learn through a career of hospice bereavement work, leading groups in the community, and private practice grief counseling.

"When, through grace and luck, I later found The Christi Center, it felt like a professional home. I realized what an incredibly valuable resource it is. I'm humbled by the bravery with which these little people try to piece together their worlds, and I recognize the crucial role of peer support. In this setting, they have a safe place to express feelings they are not always able to verbalize, and they realize they are among other kids who can understand their situation. Though some children initially come to group anxious and resistant, they usually leave their first group smiling and asking when they can come back. Here, they realize they don't have to grieve alone, and they don't feel so *different*.

"I do this work for the love of Alan, for the love of many family members I've lost since that time, and for the love of these amazing children."

CHAPTER

The Teen Group

A teen once said to me, "You saved my life." I responded, "No, you saved yourself by getting your butt here when you needed us."

– Erin Spalding, LCSW, The Christi Center

After we lost Christi, we didn't know at that time that Sean's grief over losing his sister during his high school years would be so different from ours. He once shared that his shock at first led him to believe she was not gone. He would wait for her to come home on the weekends just as she always had before. His personal anguish was channeled into how Susan and I were feeling, and then slowly, he went back to his life routine — doing homework, spending time with friends, and taking on chores around the house. Talking about Christi's death was not at the top of his list. The idea of meeting with a group of strangers at The Christi Center would be understandably off putting to the average teen. It's not until they really try it that they get it.

According to Helen Fitzgerald, author of *The Grieving Teen*, "Teen years are already tumultuous years, and the bereaved teen needs special attention. Under the ordinary circumstances, teenagers go through many changes in their body image, behavior, attachments, and feelings. Life becomes even more complex when a father, mother, sibling, or other significant person dies—a shattering experience faced by one child in every ten before the age of eighteen."

Erin Spalding, staff member since 2007, took over the facilitation of our Teen Group in 2010, knowing all too well the often humiliating part of the grief journey that a teenager will experience after the loss of a loved one. When Erin was only nine-years-old, her father died suddenly. She recalled only being known among her peers as "the girl who lost her dad." Today, she is driven by a passion that resulted from her personal loss of both parents—her mother died many years after suffering a stroke. Based on her own personal experience, Erin was able to help guide teens through the roller coaster of emotions they shared at weekly meetings.

"We always do a check-in; for example, we do a 'Rose, Bud, and Thorn' activity. 'Rose' is sharing something positive. 'Thorn' is the negative. And 'Bud' is something in their life, which could go on either way, such as an exam or a first holiday without a parent," Erin said.

The idea Susan and I created about being Zebras among a herd of Horses plays very differently among teens. Erin shared that when she tells that story, adults get it, but teens give it a different take.

"When I share it with youth, their response is so profound. 'But, Erin,' one girl said, 'the horses will see your stripes. That's why they treat you so different.' The fact is you are a teen and the most important thing is your peers. When you are a teen, instead of being just you, you are the girl with the dead brother or the one whose dad died."

We also learned from Erin that when working with teens, one of the things you never say is "I'm sorry." They will answer, "Why? You didn't do it!" A more empathetic approach would be, "I am sorry you are fifteen and you don't have a mom anymore." This shows genuine care and is less generic than what people say when you stub your toe. Our knowledgeable facilitators over the years have gone out to help train others about these sensitivities when working with youth. We have partnered with school districts, various nonprofits that work with vulnerable populations, and case managers who represent various agencies.

The Christi Center hosted teens at very special retreats at Charlie's Place and the Candlelight Ranch in the Texas Hill Country. There, young adults are invited to simply bond and have fun. As with the meetings, at first they don't want to come. But once they take that step and deem you "worthy" of hearing their story, transformation begins. They finally see the value of getting away with others who, like them, have experienced loss. Our organization has helped them find those safe places, and Erin aptly expressed what it was like to be able to witness some of these transformations.

"Something really neat about teens, you get more depth of feeling and insight out of them. With adults, there are so many more walls to break down, but with teens, once you get through that first wall, you are able to help them. I was sixteen when I attended a friend's wedding rehearsal. She thought my tears were because I was happy for her, but, actually, they were because I thought about how my dad would never walk me down the aisle."

CHAPTER

Celebrating Our Volunteers

If you want to lift yourself up, lift up someone else.

– Booker T. Washington

It would take another book to mention all the extraordinary volunteers who serve on our board, facilitate our meetings, serve on panels, help with all the events, mow the lawn, plant the gardens, or give their time to pass out literature at our annual events. Many of them came here after the loss of a loved one and then stayed to help others during their grief journey. Our Annual Volunteer Event honors their endless and untiring love and support. About 80 to 100 volunteers are recognized at these events, and our first *Volunteers of the Year* were Alberta and Luther "Tee" Barbour, who received a plaque designating them such in December 1992. Later, in 2013, we created a special volunteer award named the *Jimmy Shields Lifetime Achievement Award*. Jimmy logged more than 1,400 hours while board president in 2009 and 2010.

Jim Letchworth did not have a tragic loss that brought him to us; rather, he simply believed in our mission and has been with us since he showed up to volunteer in 1992 at our One Westlake Plaza office. We were in dire need of a database program to more efficiently track our efforts—Jim not only created one, but built a website, too. After moving into our Hancock home, he took on the volunteer role of ground management, mowing and watering our lawn. He was honored with Volunteer of the Year two years in a row. He started with us almost 30 years ago and is still helping us today.

Loyce and Mike Allen came to For the Love of Christi in 1996 after losing their 30-year-old son Michael to cancer in September of that year. As they began to regain their footings, the Allens started to volunteer with many of the day-to-day tasks needed to operate the center. They facilitated groups, offering hope to others in return for the love and support they had received after their loss. I came to the realization that Loyce's compassion and skills as a former teacher made her an excellent addition to our small staff. Joining the nonprofit in 1999, she offered comfort to others through her work in leading retreats, serving on panels, and talking one-on-one to those in grief who dropped in to find help. After leaving her staff position in 2004, Loyce continued to facilitate the Wednesday group, alternating with Jean Bazar, who first came to us after losing Sam, her son, in 2007. Like Jim, Jean pitched in when extra help was needed.

Another committed volunteer Pat Moore lost her dad Harold Carter to an unsolved homicide in 1991. Pat and Max Moore served on our board, and Pat now enjoys helping with our events. Since 1992, she has designed a beautiful cake with an angel and the words *For the Love of Christi* for our annual Candlelight Remembrance Service. Pat once said, "For the Love of Christi helped me deal with my anger and denial after my dad's murder … a place to make me feel comfortable to express the way I felt. If it wasn't for Susan and Don, I wouldn't be here."

Amazing organizations, such as The Junior League and Richard P. Slaughter & Associates, also provide support for those along their grief journey. The League members bring extra hands and hearts to help coordinate our annual events, such as the Remembrance Service, and support member sign-ins on Monday nights. Richard P. Slaughter & Associates holds annual golf tournaments for our organization and other nonprofits. Over 150 amazing interns from University of Texas, Texas State University, St. Edward's University, Southwestern University in Georgetown, University of Houston, Texas Tech, University of Southern California, Liberty University, Baylor University, and Louisiana State University have provided endless hours of creativity and support.

After we purchased the Hancock property in 1996, we were soon faced with the dilemma that it was too small to meet our growing needs. However, trying to raise the money necessary to build another building at that time seemed too much for our small donor base. We had the perfect spot—a two car garage and a storage building with a dirt floor. But no one thought our timing to build was right. I was told, "Let me know when you get enough money to get started."

When it came to building the much-needed Annex on Hancock Drive in November of 2000, many individuals made that happen through their generous donations. Among them were Paul and Nancy Korzilius, who lost their seven-year-old daughter Katherine in 1996 and their son Senior Deputy Christopher Korzilius, 32, who died March 18, 2020, while driving to work. He was hit head-on by another vehicle and died at the scene. They provided the seed money for the construction of the Annex, and pictures of their precious daughter and son now hang there. Others like Manual Zuniga gave of their valuable time and talents. He took on the daunting task as general contractor and saw the Annex project through from foundation to roof. We honored Manual at our dedication for his unwavering devotion to the important addition. He is one of those brave hearts who suffered the loss of his father, two sisters, and two brothers within a short period of time—and, eventually, found the energy to give back to make our organization a better place.

I had been in the Navy and for a period of time in the Reserves as a Seabee. I approached my former unit RMCB22, a construction battalion, and asked them to help me with a community service project—to tear down the old garage and do the site work for the foundation. It worked! As soon as that was done, we started getting donations to finish the

Annex. Architect William Massingill designed an attractive multi-purpose building, which now serves our Center so well.

There are no words to express how much these extraordinary and loyal individuals mean to us, but we sure try. Our volunteers tell us that this is their way of giving back for all the love and support they received after their loss of a loved one. Each act of kindness for others has helped them with their healing and provided one more way to honor their loved ones.

CHAPTER

Passing the Reins on to Others

Grief drives men into habits of serious reflection, sharpens the understanding, and softens the heart.

—John Adams

Susan served as executive director of our organization for more than 18 years without pay. Anyone who knows her will tell you that she was totally devoted to this "heart work." When people walk in the door of The Christi Center, they feel the importance of her contribution and how much she has meant to the organization. I was president of the board of directors from the beginning, and I'll bet other nonprofit leaders will relate when I say that I knew when it was time for me to step down from that role. We were still reeling from 9/11, and the tech wreck had hit Austin; both events had impacted my real estate business.

As we approached the time when we were going to develop our first professionally designed strategic plan, I decided I was not the right person to take the organization into the next critical phase. But I knew who was: our vice-president and my good friend George Lane. His experience mirrored mine; however, with his business background and nonprofit accounting savvy from his work at Austin Community College, he was more knowledgeable about what was required for the future.

George and Nat had lost Leslie, their 15-year-old daughter, in a carnival ride tragedy. Just before the ride began, Leslie had said to her nine-year-old brother Tyler, "You are too small to sit on the outside, so trade places with me." As George watched his children enjoying themselves, his joy soon turned to horror as his children were thrown from the Himalaya Ride. Since they had traded places, Tyler survived with minor injuries, but Leslie died that night. Due to negligent maintenance and needed repairs, her death led to criminal charges against the carnival owners. In addition to the local and national news, this incident was later featured on an edition of *Dateline*.

When I decided to step down, I called George and asked if he was serious about something he once said to me, "Just let me know if there is anything I can do to help you." When he said he meant it, I said, "Good, you are now the new president of For the Love of Christi!" A man of his word, he took over for me.

I felt extremely blessed and grateful for those who were going to take over the reins. And now so many dedicated board members, staff, and volunteers continue to take us to whole new levels. I have remained very active with the organization in many ways. My proudest moment as president was being able to purchase and create our beautiful facilities; then, to expand them.

I am also very proud of the fact that we are debt-free. According to financial experts, our organization has always had one of the lowest costs of operating, which allows our small budget to go further.

From my standpoint, one of the greatest blessings of owning the Hancock property is how much it has contributed to the sustainability of our organization.

CHAPTER

Focusing on the Heart Work

The Christi Center taught me how to take one day at a time—actually, one minute at a time.

—Marianne McDonald, who lost her son Dylan in 2006

I realized that I needed more help with all the responsibilities of running our organization. As an unpaid executive director for more than 18 years, I was involved in fundraising, writing grant proposals, leading presentations and workshops, holding support groups in seven schools, planning events, and handling all the administrative duties of our growing nonprofit. Our organization was rapidly growing, more sophisticated technology was being implemented, and, like Don, I knew it was time to step aside.

I wanted to spend more time with those new in their grief and also stay in touch with those from our early days. This is where my heart was when I decided to transition from my long-running term in January

2006. Passing the position of executive director on to someone else would also allow me to spend more time with Sean, now married with a family of his own. Don and I could travel more often with family and friends to *Almost Heaven* and other fun places. I definitely wanted to stay involved with the organization's meetings and retreats, and helping with the many presentations we held throughout the community. My goal was always to help others understand grief and to get the word out on how we help the bereaved.

As I looked back to where we started with the organization, now called The Christi Center, I never thought we would be where we are now. We hold more than 35 meetings a month and have a satellite office in Georgetown, plus an impressive evolution of diverse groups and types of retreats. I feel Christi smiling down on Don and me for all we have accomplished in her memory. She always wanted to help others. I am so proud of how we have helped so many discover healing and new joy in their lives again after the loss of loved ones.

The bottom line is that our pain drove us to do this "heart work," which, in turn, helped us to find new meaning and purpose in our lives. Our nonprofit and its life-changing work for others enabled us to learn how to go on living again, even with our broken hearts. We feel Christi's love with us every day. She is our guiding angel!

CHAPTER

Accolades for Hard Work

You do not have to accomplish great monumental acts in life; just small acts with great love.

— Mother Teresa

The Christi Center has received hundreds of accolades for the work done in our community. Awards and certificates of appreciation from the Austin Police Department Victim Services, the American Red Cross "Heroes of Central Texas," and the Governor Conference's "Best Program of the Year" Award for Texas, among so many others, have arrived at regular intervals since we began the organization in 1987. These special recognitions always gave cause for us to celebrate with our staff and volunteers. Susan and I were also honored with personal awards representing the work of our growing organization—received because of the amazing work of so many others who have helped us through the years.

While I felt blessed to receive the 2005 Lumen Gentuium Award from Bishop Gregory Aymond of the Austin Catholic Diocese, my proudest moment came when Susan was chosen as one of only six women in the United States (and the only one from Texas!) to receive *Traditional Home Magazine's* "Classic Woman Award" in 2009 for her commitment to volunteerism. We were on the way to Minneapolis to visit Sean when Susan received the call. Immediately after, a whirlwind of activity began. In addition to a $5,000 donation to our organization and a great article in the magazine, Susan and I were flown to New York for the Thanksgiving week luncheon at which she accepted her award. As I sat with Sean and Anne, my stepmom, on either side of me, I was so happy to see Susan at the podium, receiving her award from Deborah Norville of *Inside Edition*.

Here was my bride, Christi and Sean's mother, being recognized for her significant *heart work*, which had restored hope, love, and laughter to so many lives. She was being honored for work that so few of us understand or appreciate. This was the woman who had lost her faith in God and who didn't want to go on living with the pain of Christi's death. I fought back tears as I thought of how proud I was of Susan. I knew that she was receiving this honor, not just for her love of Christi, but in honor of all the loved ones she helped, and would continue to help.

Susan was nominated by a member, Linda McCullough, who lost Jay, her 19-year-old son, to a drowning in September 1989. Linda saw the application in one of the *Traditional Homes* magazines and totally on her own, submitted it. To read the article, go to *Traditional Homes* "Classic Woman Awards" 2009.

I will never forget that day and how awed I was by my Susan.

SECTION

5

Reaching 30 Years

CHAPTER

Finally, the Answers to My Questions

May God bless you for channeling your energies to help other families deal with loss. You are not only honoring Christi, but doing the Lord's work.

— Bob Gale, Creator-Writer-Producer, Back to the Future

I was haunted for a very long time, wondering if Christi called my name as she lay mortally injured on the street after being dragged under an El Camino that early morning in October 1985. When she needed me the most, I was not there, and this thought filled me with guilt and over-whelming sadness. In 2007, more than 20 years after her death, I received a call from a woman named Connie who brought some comfort about who was there for Christi when I couldn't be.

Connie told me she had wanted to call me all these years since Christi's death in 1985 when she was working at the Cedar Door Bar at First and Nueces. She said she heard noises outside the bar, and when she stepped outside, saw Christi's body lying in the street. She then shared the full story with me:

A gentleman and his friends were walking in front of Christi and her friends about a block up from the Cedar Door Bar. The men had just crossed the street when they heard a vehicle. When they looked back they saw the El Camino coming. It hit a parked car, which, in turn, hit two girls. One of the men ran to help Christi's friend Jenny, who was lying at the scene of the crash. Jenny was screaming, "Where is Christi?" Another man ran to where Christi lay, 800 feet away from Jenny. As he sat next to Christi, Connie called 9-1-1 and then returned to hold Christi's hand as they waited for the EMS to arrive.

Years later, Connie explained, she and her husband were dining at Jaime's Spanish Village Restaurant on Red River Street when they saw Christi's picture on the wall. Our dear friends and owners, the late Jaime and Teresa Tames, proudly placed Christi's beautiful "Designated Driver" poster at the cash register in their restaurant. Connie asked them how she could reach me. The Tames gave me Connie's number, and finally, after all these years, we connected with one another.

During our conversation, Connie shared that Christi's death had changed her life. She went back to school, taking nine years to get her nursing degree. On that phone call in 2007, Connie shared she was an ER nurse at St. David's Hospital. I will always remember this lady with great love. She will never know just how much her kindness meant to me.

Ron Hanson, the EMS Paramedic who arrived at the horrific scene in 1985 over the years has continued to stay in touch with me. We have served together on panels related to drinking and driving. He stopped by the office again on May 15, 2017, to take a tour of The Christi Center and to meet our staff. During this visit, I was surprised to learn from Ron that Christi had spoken to him that tragic night and told him her name. I had always believed that after that horrendous event, she had never spoken to anyone.

71

Another unanswered question remained for me. Steven Spielberg's movie *Back to the Future* had just come out in theaters before Christi died. She told us it was one of her favorite movies and that we had to see it. We never got around to that until six months after her death on the night before our trial began in April 1986.

We could not believe our eyes when the date that the DeLorean time machine was programmed to go back to the future flashed up on the screen. The date and year on the time machine automobile in which Marty, Michael J. Fox's character lived was October 26, 1985. I couldn't believe it! Why had the director or writer chosen Christi's death date for this movie? I had to know and had wondered about this since her death.

In April 2014, I wrote directly to Spielberg. On June 19, 2014, Bob Gale, Creator-Writer-Producer of the film, wrote his heart-felt condolences. He finally provided the answer I needed.

The
CHRISTI CENTER
Always Here After Your Loss

April 20, 2014

Dear Mr. Spielberg,

I have postponed writing this letter to you for many years, but now I feel this it the time to do it. Maybe this is a God incidence now and you will understand as you read my letter.

My whole life changed on October 26th, 1985 when my 20 year old daughter, Christi, an honor student at the University of Texas, was killed by a hit-and-run drunken driver while walking with friends in downtown Austin, Texas. She was dragged under his car for over 800 feet and died an hour later at Brackenridge Hospital. You can only imagine the nightmare I went through with my husband, Don, and Christi's 16 year old brother, Sean.

During the late summer of 1985, Christi kept telling us we needed to go see one of her favorite movies," Back to the Future". After her death, we were in such shock that we were not able to do anything with our abnormal life. In May 1986, the night before the trial of the person who killed her, we were very nervous so thought we would try to see a movie. My husband noticed that "Back to the Future" was playing as a rerun at a local theatre so we thought Christi was giving us a little sign that we should go to see it. You can only imagine our shock when we noticed that the date, October 26, 1985 filled the whole screen! The same day and almost the same time as her death! Was this a message from our precious Christi?

This connection has always haunted us and, hopefully, you can understand my need for wanting to know why this date was chosen for this movie. I would be so blessed to know your reason for deciding on this date. Please see the enclosed articles about how we are honoring Christi's memory and helping the broken-hearted.

I am praying that I will hear from you, and I thank you from the bottom of my heart for taking the time to read my letter. I am doing this For the Love of Christi and all our loved ones.

Love and Blessings,

Susan P. Cox
Co-Founder of The Christi Center
Christi and Sean's mother (the greatest title I could ever have)

BOB GALE
Creator - Writer - Producer

19 June 2014

Susan Cox
The Christi Center
2306 Hancock Drive
Austin, TX 78756

Dear Mrs. Cox,

Your letter of April 14 addressed to Steven Spielberg finally made its way to me.

First, please accept my sincere condolences over the tragic loss of your daughter. The pain you and your family have suffered is unimaginable to me, and you have my deepest sympathies.

You wish to know how the date of October 26, 1985 was chosen for the movie. I'm certainly the best person to answer that because I co-wrote the script and selected that date. The reason was as follows:

We knew the movie would be released in the summer of 1985, but the character Marty (Michael J. Fox) had to be in school. So, to make it a present day story, we chose a 1985 date in the near future. We couldn't use December because we didn't want to have the town square decorated for Christmas. And September was too close to the beginning of school. Because late October 1984 was our original start date, a late October date meant that the trees would look correct in the movie. The audience would also accept the fact that Marty needed to wear a down vest at night. So we settled on October 25/26, because it had to be a Friday night/Saturday morning for the late night time travel experiment (and not a school night). I did not choose October 18/19 because I was worried it would make the time displays look confusing to have a "19" adjacent to "1985." I used November dates for 1955 to more clearly differentiate 1955 from 1985 on the time displays and in dialog.

I hope that gives you closure on that question. I'm glad our movie brought joy to Christi while she was here with us, and hope that you and your family can share in some of that joy.

May God bless you for channeling your energies to help other families deal with loss. You are not only honoring Christi, but doing the Lord's work.

Very sincerely,

c/o Moss Adams   P.O. Box 24950   Los Angeles, CA 90024

2306 Hancock Drive
Austin, Texas 78756
(512) 467-2600
www.christicenter.org

BOARD OF DIRECTORS
Kathleen McCleskey, *President*
Randy Frazier, PhD, *Immediate Post President*
Suzanne Torres, *Vice President*
Joel Ferguson, *Treasurer*
Kate von Alt, *Secretary*
Susan Cox, *Founder*
Don Cox, *Founder*
John Adams
Joel Ferguson
Pascal D. Forgione, Jr., PhD
Kelli Johnson
Cory Macdonald
Robert McCleskey
Danni Morford
Pete Morford
Suzy Rowley
Jimmy Shields

ADVISORY COUNCIL
Alan Cox
Barbara Cox
Steve Crossett
David Flores
Dorcas Green, Esq
Emsud Horozovic
Phyllis Lacey
Michael Larkin
Cindy McCoy, LPC
Stuart Napier
Dina O'Brien, PhD
Sandra Rebecek
Rev. Dr. Dale Schultz
Terri Schexnayder
Richard Schott, PhD
Dave Seideman
Lou Seideman
Beverly Straub, CPA
Garry Vacek, CPA, Esq
Bishop Joe S. Vásquez
Nick Voinis
Charlotte Winklemann

July 5, 2014

Bob Gale
Amblin Entertainment, Inc.
100 Universal Plaza
Bungalow 477
Universal City, CA 91608

Dear Bob,

Your compassionate letter touched my heart deeply. Thank you for taking the time out of your busy schedule to let me know how the date was chosen for the movie, "Back to the Future."

After 28 years, my prayer has been answered. I will never forget how you lifted my heart with your letter which helped me to feel Christi's love.

Thank you from the bottom of my heart and may God continue to bless you with His love.

Love from my heart to yours,

Susan P. Cox

Susan P. Cox
Co-Founder of The Christi Center

P.S. If you ever make it "Back to the Future" (as in Austin), we would love to meet you!

CHAPTER

Serving a Wider Community

You go there for help and then you realize part of the healing process is the fact that you have survived. Your story is testimony to others and you give them hope. You can keep the story of your loved one alive.

— Jimmy Shields, former board president and long-time volunteer

The Christi Center meetings and programs grew and grew as word continued to spread about how we could help those in grief after the loss of loved ones. We serve, directly and indirectly, an estimated 100,000 individuals. Phone calls to our organization often increased after newsworthy tragedies, such as 9-11. Reporters covering the news would ask, "Where do the survivors go for help?" and often the answer was The Christi Center.

Our dedicated board, staff, and volunteers carried our message about hope and healing, often sharing their personal stories of grief, to a variety of organizations throughout Central Texas. The Christi Center had become the model program in Texas and beyond, and we were only too glad to share what we had learned with other groups. Many of our members were traveling from Williamson County to The Christi Center in Austin. The increased demand for our services in that county led us to open a satellite office at the Georgetown Community Resource Center in the fall of 2010.

The Christi Center's expansion to Georgetown was driven by a core group of supporters who were committed to furthering our vision of a community where no one has to grieve alone. Expansion is a challenge, and because Georgetown is a different place, it wasn't just a matter of replicating services from Austin—we had to have buy-in from key members of that community. From the beginning, Barbara and George Brightwell played a key role in the successful expansion of our services, and we are so grateful to have them as allies. Dedicated volunteers and philanthropists with unwavering commitment to the Georgetown community, the Brightwells had a strong sense of the need for our services and what relationships would help support those. They provided information, advice, introductions to key individuals, and funding support to help plant the seeds for programming. A key connections made was to Georgetown Health Foundation and the newly established Community Resource Center where our organization would co-office with other nonprofits. This shared space not only offered affordable space in Georgetown, but vital connections to other nonprofits doing work in the community.

Working hand-in-hand with the Brightwells were Jimmy and Mary Shields. The Shields' heart connection with the organization began after the loss of Amy, their 21-year-old daughter, in a car accident in 2004. They went on to serve as board members and as facilitators in Georgetown. Additionally, their priceless personal commitment, which raised an estimated $10,000 through their "Friend to Friend" letter-writing campaign, helped our nonprofit flourish.

Sandi and Larry Rebecek joined our group in January 1999 after the loss of Jake, their 19-year-old son, a Texas A&M student who died in a car accident. This amazing couple has contributed so much to us—they served on the board, helped with the KWK and Teen retreats, and painted the new annex. And like the Shields and others, they have been a positive force in their fundraising efforts. They also facilitate group meetings in Georgetown. The pretty Christi Center Heart sign that hangs in front of the Hancock home was designed and handcrafted by Larry.

In June 2011, another dream came true when we held the dedication for the 1,506 square-foot, two-story addition to the Hancock center. Envisioned by architect William Massingill, Tom Green, PE, renovation guru John Ward, and myself, the additions included a conference room, staff offices, a brightly colored KWK room, and a cozy library-meeting room. Through the generous gift of $200,000 from the Greg and Dawn Crouch Family Charitable Fund, this much-needed space became a reality. The new addition is named in the Crouch's honor, and when we broke ground the year before, we gave Greg the honor of uprooting the first shovel of dirt. Others who worked long and hard on the expansion included:

> Austin Renovations – John Ward (for the love of Johnny)
> Austin Seamless Gutters
> Casa Mechanical Services
> Chasco Constructors, Ltd.
> Designer Floors of Texas, Inc. – Ron Ferguson
>   (for the love of Brandon)
> Bill and Markie Duncan
> Gemini Mechanical Services, Inc.
> Greenearth Engineering, Inc. – Tim Zhang, PE
> Gretchen's Painting - Gretchen P. Johnston
> Hector Seijo (for the love of Nicole)
> Ikea
> Jose I Guerra, Inc. – Reese Hurley, PE
> Level Best Foundation Repair
> Lola Wright Foundation
> McCoy's Building Supplies

Tami Migl, PE
Pete Morford, PE
PG Architects, Inc. – William Massingill, AIA NCARB
Prince Plumbing - Oscar Prince
Chris Schexnayder, RAS
Jimmy Shields Painting Company (for the love of Amy)
Tom Greene & Company Engineers, Inc. - Tom Greene, PE,
     John Davidson & Greg Maxwell

Over and over again, as we moved toward 35 years for our organization, angels from the community were there to assist us and open new horizons for The Christi Center to better serve those in grief throughout Central Texas.

CHAPTER

Moonlight and Memories: Celebrating 25 Years

All of our services are open-ended and free of charge. It can be 10 years later and someone can come back to see us.

— Cara Fox, former executive director

Cara Fox joined The Christi Center first as a part-time development director in November 2010. She moved to part-time Executive Director in October 2011. Under her dedicated leadership, the staff expanded The Christi Center's programs and outreach efforts. Her grant-writing talents and passionate presentations resulted in important funding to continue the organization's important heart work. She helped guide the name change from For the Love of Christi to The Christi Center. Cara worked closely with long-time volunteer and writer Terri Schexnayder and designer Milburn Taylor to create a new logo and tag line: *Always Here After Your Loss*. And, Cara greatly extended the organization's critical messages through advanced social media presence.

As the organization approached its 25-year anniversary, Cara, staff, and volunteers orchestrated special events to celebrate the landmark birthday. Reunion Potluck Dinners brought together members, volunteers, and staff who had served since 1987. Those who had not been to the Hancock center in a long time were delighted to see the additions, discover the magical healing garden in front of the building, and the soothing meditation pond in the backyard. And, of course, many old friends had the chance to reconnect and reminiscence about the early days.

The "Moonlight and Memories" party, held October 6, 2012, at Hill's Café was chaired by Barbara Cox and Kate von Alt. We tapped into the creativity of Phyllis Lacey and Janet Brown who decorated for many other special events for The Christi Center. Their candlelit centerpieces of country chic burlap designs graced each table. On that perfect fall evening, the sounds of The Rocket 88s filled the air as guests dined on tasty cuisine and took photos. Through Cara's personal contacts, Music Doing Good, a Houston-based nonprofit, donated a musical video about The Christi Center that they had written and performed. It was one of many highlights of the event.

Don and I were surrounded by so many people who cared deeply for us and the organization. We were especially touched that Sean and his wife Michelle traveled from Minnesota for the celebration. We felt blessed by the outpouring of love, knowing that hundreds of individuals had made sure it was a night we would never forget.

Due to Cara's mother's terminal illness, she resigned as Executive Director in January 2015. Later, after her mother's death, Cara returned as our part-time development director. Lara George was promoted to Executive Director from her position as a part-time director of community engagement in February 2016. The smooth transition between these two bright, dedicated women guaranteed continued future success for The Christi Center.

CHAPTER

Healing Through the Arts and Gardening

Nature teaches you that death is normal, a natural part of life. Through gardening, you reduce stress, and are filled with a sense of wonder, well-being, and hopefulness.

— Angela Carver, member

We have watched so many passionate volunteers come together to create permanent beauty at The Christi Center in honor of their loved ones. Their contributions have been appreciated and given solace to many others. Examples of these lasting gifts are the two serene garden spots that best express this love and community. The healing garden is nestled under the large tree out front. In the back of the Hancock home, a quiet, running steam fountain provides a peaceful place for our members to meditate on sweet memories of their loved ones.

Angela Carver lost Sean, her four-year-old son, to a drowning in 1989. She led the creation of the healing garden, reminded how the many hours she had spent tending the little garden on his grave, filled with orange (his favorite color) flowers, had helped her cope with his death. She decided to recreate this place of healing at The Christi Center. A garden, Angela said, is "a place for restoration, meditation, sanctuary, and a place to heal." On September 29, 2011, we gathered with volunteers from Little Helping Hands and the families of Bazaarvoice to turn the rich soil and compost donated by Keep Austin Beautiful into a sanctuary of native plants and wildflowers.

What better way to calm oneself and connect with nature than sit by a tranquil running stream fountain, listening to the sounds of water rushing over the stones. Chung and James McArdle dedicated the garden in October 2011, in memory of their son Terence. His parents said Terence is that running stream—always there, always listening, and always ready to playfully splash a little water on you. The inscription on the rock beside the fountain, written by Terence on Mother's Day 2001, reads:

I will always love,
No matter where I am,
Or how old I've gotten

Healing came through the arts, as well. When launched in 2014, the Heartstrings Art Show showcased the powerful works of members of our KWK and Teen programs, and art from adults who had found The Christi Center. On canvases, filled with emotions from the blackness of death of a loved one to the lightness representing the hope and new joy eventually found, the artists share their grief journeys with us. The Art Show was the brainchild of one of the interns Sheena Yazdandoost. Sheena and Victoria Valles, then the KWK Coordinator, put together the top-quality event in under three weeks. In 2015, Finn Lowden, a Westlake High School freshman, decided he wanted to do his Eagle Scout project with The Christi Center. When he saw the art that kids and teens had made and heard some of the stories behind those paintings, he decided putting on the Art Show would be his project. He enlisted the help of classmates at

Westlake High School, friends from his Troop, and individuals through his parents' connections to organize, publicize, and produce the second Art Show. Finn continued to support the Art Show into its third and fourth years, serving as a volunteer coordinator.

Our "Second Stage" programs, held on the second Monday of each month, provide even more avenues for expression and healing through the art, writing, and yoga workshops. Our mission remains as it always has been: We offer hope after the death of a loved one by providing support networks, community education, and therapeutic activities that are free, peer-based, and ongoing. We are grateful to those living angels who make these programs possible.

CHAPTER

It's Okay to Cry: Our Men's Retreats

By giving back, by helping others along the way, grief has been transformed into my greatest experience of personal and spiritual growth.

— Glenn McIntosh, volunteer facilitator, Survivors of Suicide Group

Most men of my generation were raised on what I call the *John Wayne Manual*. The only problem is that the manual has no chapter on grief. The most common result of this mentality is that after losing a loved one, many men tend to self-medicate or stay angry, or both. One of the many things at The Christi Center that I am most proud of is the large number of men who actively participate in the program. I believe that is largely due to the number of our support groups and retreats held just for them. These retreats give men an opportunity to drop their guard and share their issues and feelings in a trusting environment under the guidance of caring facilitators.

I will never forget our first retreat in Ruidoso in February1989, facilitated by the late Larry Bugen, Ph.D., who helped save our marriage. The late Reverend Ron Campbell led the next retreat in 1990. He knew Christi when he was the vice principal at Westlake High School. Next, Reverend Laren Winter facilitated the sessions for several years before moving to Colorado. Currently, Randy Frazier, Ph.D., serves in that role and has led many retreats since he joined the board years ago. He is a real brother to me and to so many of our members. Randy has a special way of connecting with the men.

Every year in June, we hold a Men's Retreat at *Almost Heaven* and at the homes of the Lanes and McVeys in Ruidoso, New Mexico. Jim McVey came to The Christi Center after the murder of his 39-year-old son, Jim Jr., on February 24, 1994, in Fort Worth, Texas. His son had been abducted in what police believe was a gang-related initiation, and the crime remains unsolved to this day. Jim and Beverly became involved in the support group meetings and then started participating in the KWK retreats. The McVeys and the Lanes, along with us, shared the blessing of having second homes in Ruidoso by donating them for the annual men's retreats. This helped keep the costs down for the eight to 12 participants who attend. We typically drive and share the cost of gas and food.

Sadly, Jim died on August 9, 2018. The only consolation was he died while visiting his favorite place in Ruidoso, New Mexico, with his wife and soulmate Beverly at his side.

At the men's retreat, each day we have one or two sessions where we take turns sharing our stories. We laugh a lot and also take time to cry – not easy for most men, especially in the early stages of grief. Along with lots of rest and relaxation, we make time for special things you wouldn't ordinarily associate with a grief retreat—going to the horse races, golfing, hiking, bird watching, fishing, taking naps (almost daily). Or just sitting outside to take in the beauty of the mountains and enjoy the fresh air and cool weather.

As men, we have learned that these retreats enable us to return home and take better care of ourselves and others, especially our families. As Randy and I continued to remind the men, "The one selfish thing we must do is to take care of ourselves first in order for us to be able to take care of others." It's a bit like the message you hear on a plane about putting the oxygen mask on yourself before trying to assist someone else.

During each retreat, we go to visit our member Teresa Thompson's church in Cloudcroft, New Mexico. Teresa lost her three young children Illian (5 years), Ivan (7 years), and Sasha (9 years) to homicide in 1989. She turned her unspeakable losses and grief into creating a beautiful stained glass window for her church—a smiling Jesus with her daughter on His lap and her sons on each side of Him. Their eyes seem to follow you as you move about. As Teresa said, "Of course, He's smiling. He's with *my* children."

I once thought she wouldn't make it, but now, she and her art minister to the men on our retreats. Her stained-glassworks can be found in churches throughout the Southwest.

CHAPTER

Remembering Christi

Christi was always telling me to laugh and laugh out loud. I was so shy and afraid that someone would notice me that I would not laugh when something funny happened. I would just smile. All of the friends I had before her swore that they would get me to come out of my shell—she is the one that succeeded!

— Robin Scoggins, Christi's high school classmate

First of all, I never thought I would live this long after the loss of Christi. I think about her and Sean every day. I think about what she would be doing now—if she were still alive—married, with children. I think about what we would be doing together, the laughter, and trips we would be taking. When I see young children, it brings back memories of Christi at that age. I love kids and when I can hug them, I always say, "Give me a kiss on the cheek." I am reminded of the kisses Christi once gave me, and I can relive that moment. It brings me joy, but then it hits me! I won't have that ever again with her.

After her death, the first thing I thought about in the morning was Christi, and Christi was the last thing I thought about before going to bed for another sleepless night. Her laundry bag, the one we gave her for college, still hangs in a closet. The monogram, *I'm Home, Mom,* reminds me of her when she was home, doing her laundry—now, it means she's home in Heaven. Upstairs in our office closet, I have her junior and senior year prom dresses and Westlake High School cheerleader outfit. This is not for the whole world to see, but for me alone — to go back to the times she wore these, how it made me feel, knowing the fun she had when she was alive. When I touch them, I have what I call a "Christi moment." I close my eyes and say, "Christi, give me a hug. I love you, Don loves you, and your brother loves you, and we all miss you." I can say that, and no one is around to scold me, "You should be over that by now."

After all these years, I finally know how to talk about Christi to other people. Wherever I go, I run into someone who has experienced a loss. For example, once at Walgreen's buying cards, I opened my wallet at the checkout and the cashier saw Christi's photo. She said, "She is beautiful. Is that your daughter?" After saying it was, I listened as she told me about her sister who had recently died. She was comfortable enough with me, so I told her about Christi's death and that my daughter and her sister were now together. It's up to us to let others know our loved ones should never be forgotten.

I now know how to talk to people so that they won't be upset. When asked questions like, "How many children do you have?" I answer, "I have two, Sean, my living son, and my daughter who is in Heaven." It's not as awkward for them when I then ask," And how many children do you have?" Once, I could not stop crying and I was also very angry. People did not realize how hurtful it was when they spouted common platitudes: "She is in a better place," "It was God's will," or "You still have another child." What parent has a disposable child? What about those who have lost an only child?

Little by little, I began to understand that these people, despite the hurt they caused me, really did care. It's just that they had never experienced such loss and didn't know what to say. My job is to help them learn how to talk to people in grief so they will use words that are supportive and not inappropriate, such as, "It's been a year, why aren't you over it?" I am going to continue to talk about Christi, share the beautiful album I created from the day she was born to the day she took her last breath. The connections Don and I still have with many of Christi's friends touch our hearts deeply.

Each year since 1986, I have received a Mother's Day card with a sweet note from Christi's friend Denise Dellana Tharp. One year Denise told me that since she is now a mother, she understands the love a mother has for her children. We hear from Jenny Dedrick Krengel, the friend who was with Christi on that dreadful October 26, and Robin Snodgrass Scoggins, another of Christi's dear friends.

Yes, I still have grief attacks. But I have stopped thinking about how she died and now focus on how she lived — the good memories. I stopped asking *Why?* because no answer ever came. I know the more good I do for others, the more I will feel her love. It's okay for me to be mad, it's okay for me to grieve, but slowly over time, I've found ways to let go of that anger. I know my faith has helped me.

When Don and I visit her grave, we tell her how much we love and miss her. We ask her to look after us and Sean and his family, to give love to my mom and dad, my brother Sammy, my sister Nancy, and nieces Janel, Kimberly, Shari and Debora, Don's mother and dad, his sister Reenie, his brother and sister-in-law Jack and Sharon Cox, and to our sweet dogs Angel and Lucky. It helps me, when I think about Christi and all our loved ones embracing each other for us. I also ask for more signs. When I see heart clouds or find heart-shaped stones, I know it's her way of telling me, "Hi, Mom. I'm with you and I love you."

Hearing the song "The Rose" when I least expect it reassures me that Christi is always with me. Like the time Don and I were in Kauai in 2011 after Sean's wedding in Maui. We were dining at the Hyatt Restaurant, and I had a sudden grief attack. I was so happy for Sean and Michelle, but it hit me that Christi should have been there for her brother and his bride. I started crying—I am sure others thought Don and I were having an argument! As Don tried to find out what was wrong, he suddenly said, "Do you recognize that song?" I listened closely to the tune being

90

played on a ukulele. It was "The Rose." How many times have you heard that — "Somewhere over the Rainbow" on a ukulele, maybe, but "The Rose?"

When I get my signs from her, whether it be "The Rose" or a cloud in the shape of a heart, it's no coincidence—it's a "God incidence." I don't care if the sign was real or not. Whatever helps me. No matter how many years pass, Christi is forever 20-years-old to me – always there, always present.

CHAPTER

Surrendering to a Higher Power

Ask Jesus what he wants from you and be brave!
— Pope Francis

Since Christi's death, I have hit 40, 50, 60, and 70. I call these *zero birthdays*. Each decade that has passed is more than just a zero birthday. They are significant passages for me. Besides the normal aging challenges, I am still trying to learn how to anticipate and deal with my feelings of grief and loss for Christi. Each decade accentuates the fact I will not have her in my old age. I missed her graduating from college, getting married, having children of her own, and even grandchildren. These things can affect you both emotionally and physically.

In October 2017, getting ready for my 70th birthday, I took a stress test and I went beyond the time they wanted me on the treadmill. I went from out-of-breath and proud of my endurance to being asked if I had ever had a diagnosis on my aorta. I could tell by the look on the doctor's face that she was concerned. A few days later, I had a heart catheterization. I came out of that procedure and Dr. Levy said, "You are not going to Spain to celebrate your 70th birthday." Two days later, never leaving the hospital, I had my aorta and aortic valve replaced, along with two bypasses.

I feel less anxious now about approaching that landmark date. I have also learned to deal with the predictable grief moments, such as when I hear stories about tragedies like ours. I used to think tragedies just involved DWI, but now understand that there are so many other ways in which parents lose their children by sudden death and terminal illness..

In a healthy way, I have learned to be helpful and hopeful. I am often asked, "How do you do this without burning out?" I do it by taking trips with Susan to see Sean or other family members. Or I get back to nature, especially at our second home *Almost Heaven*. There is also a reward side to this heart work. Even though you see people in their darkest moments, you also see them when they begin to heal. Over the many years we've been at this, we've seen the rewarding proof that The Christi Center has saved and enhanced countless lives. I also learned how to find balance in my life. In *Chariots of Fire*, there is a scene where they are trying to talk one of the main characters into running on Sunday. He refused because it went against his religious beliefs—it was apparent that running was an extension of his faith.

My St. Edward's University education with the Holy Cross Brothers was best expressed by Father Basil Moreau. He believed, "The mind should not be educated at the expense of the heart." I realize this grief work is an extension of my faith.

The reality of losing a child is that you still wake up and still have the same responsibilities as you did when they were alive. Deep depression and even the will to go on living are normal issues for the bereaved. In my vocabulary, I call it the "Aw Fuck Its" when nothing seems to have any meaning. St. John of the Cross wrote about "the dark night of the soul." Everybody, no matter how spiritual they are, deals with it. Mother Teresa talks about it in a *Time Magazine* article, and even Jesus had to face His dark night in the Garden of Gethsemane. So, yes, I still have occasional "dark nights of the soul."

Christi's death drove me to that darkest of places where I hit the wall. It was "do or die" time for me. Today, I talk to Christi about the things I need help with, and I thank God often for all I have been given.

CHAPTER

Pilgrimage to Heal Hearts

Tears of loss are shared, memories are brought up to life with joy, and comfort is gained by knowing you will never walk alone on this journey.

— Kate von Alt, loss of her son Garrett, 15 years old

In October 2017, we celebrated 30 years of our debt-free nonprofit organization—quite a remarkable achievement! The Christi Center has been so successful, inspired by our mission and the decisions that thousands of dedicated individuals lovingly and strategically made over the years. Created after Mother Teresa's model, our programs are available for free to anyone who has lost a loved one. Our belief is that what we do is not worthless, but priceless! Our help is not limited to persons who have experienced one type of death, but is there for anyone, always, regardless of how your loved one died. The Christi Center, open to all, no matter what your faith or religious beliefs, is one of the few places that truly practices "heartfelt love."

Most importantly, we reached the 30-year landmark because of the people who have touched our organization through their volunteerism, giving so generously of their talents, time, and treasures every step of the way. Without the dedication of our staff, board members, facilitators, and endless volunteers in so many capacities, those who came to The Christi Center would never have found the caring, nonjudgmental, and safe place they so desperately needed. You will read more about some of these members in the final Chapters, but a particularly poignant one concerns a group of mothers brought together through our organization after the loss of their sons. It demonstrates the bonding and longevity that we constantly witness at The Christi Center.

Elda Arellano, Danni Morford, and Kate von Alt took the 500-mile pilgrimage, Camino de Santiago, the Trail of St. James, in 2014. On their journey in Spain, the women discovered a very different reaction when they mentioned that they were there to honor their sons, Jesse Arellano, Travis Morford, and Garrett von Alt, who had died. Unlike so many times in their day-to-day lives, when the subject of their sons' deaths came up in conversations, this time, "People didn't turn away from us," Danni said. Instead of expressing discomfort, fellow pilgrims along the Camino de Santiago embraced the women and often prayed with them. Kate explained the healing magic of their journey:

"As soon as a parent is 'born', so, too, is constant worry and concern for your child (children). Are they safe, healthy, fed, lonely, sad, happy? As strange as it might seem, this worrying does not suddenly end after their death. Both the biological and heart connection proceeds far into the mysterious beyond. Keeping with this thought, it might not be surprising to learn that many from The Christi Center talk about their kids (and loved ones) meeting up with one another on the 'other-side' and together work some incredible connections in support of their grieving loved ones remaining on Earth," shared Kate. "Our wondrous and healing journey along the Camino de Santiago is a perfect example of our boys' working some magic from the other side for the love of their moms."

We are grateful that Danni, Elda, and Kate, wonderful women who have given so much to our organization, found another safe and beautiful place on which to continue their grief journey and strengthen their already deep friendships.

CHAPTER

Always Here after Your Loss

The only people who can understand what you are going through are those who have been through it themselves.

— Susan Cox, Austin American Statesman, 1995

As we begin each meeting sitting in a circle at The Christi Center, Don and I welcome everyone. While holding a little purple glass heart, I tell everyone in the heart circle, "We are sorry for what brings you here, but you have come to a very safe and caring place where you can share your thoughts and feelings." Then Don poses his challenge: "I have a $100 bill for anyone who says anything that shocks us!" So far, no one has collected it, but a few have come close!

I start the meeting with, "My name is Susan and I am here for the love of Christi, my parents, my sister, my brother, my three nieces, and several friends, and I am also here for the love of your loved ones." I pass the heart to the person next to me who says his or her name and the name of the person or persons they are here "for the love of." After we pass the heart, I ask everyone to stand, hold hands, and close their eyes to do a breathing exercise. Then we open our eyes to offer each other a handshake or hug before we break into groups according to the type of loss—child, spouse, parent, sibling, other relatives, or friends. Since the beginning of our organization in 1987, the number of individuals in and around Central Texas who have been touched by The Christi Center through the weekly meetings, retreats, and outreach programs, has surpassed 100,000.

The first thing you must realize after the death of a loved one, is that you must be able to talk about and share your grief, your anger, your frustration—whatever you are feeling—with someone. Our purpose is that simple: To provide a space, facilitated by some of the most amazing individuals you will ever meet, who will listen and understand, because they have also experienced deaths of loved ones. We are here to listen. Thousands who have lost a loved one to any kind of death have found help. Eventually, they also discover a peace with the help of our weekly meetings and annual events. Our current Executive Director Lara George has beautifully led efforts to take us into the next 30. Lara joined the Christi Center in January of 2012 as administrative assistant, and her talents quickly moved her to the executive position.

How Lara found her connection is best explained by her:

"I previously had been with several other nonprofits, and had left my most recent position to allow my husband and me to take a career opportunity for him in Treviso, Italy. When I returned, I spent some time looking for my next job. Meanwhile, our family building plans were coming to an end. In the process of navigating the infertility and pregnancy loss world, I had taken advantage of some online peer-support, so I was comfortable with loss and all the emotions that go along with it. Once I interviewed with Cara, who was then Executive Director, I was excited by the energy at The Christi Center and thought it would be a good place to work. The part-time aspect was also appealing. Little did I know that the job would soon take over a lot more of my life! As I later transitioned from interim ED to that role officially in February 2016, I was very fortunate to have Cara by my side as Development Director."

Lara helped launch our new School Grief Support Network in schools in August 2016. In the first school year we served 24 kids with one-on-one counseling. Since 1987, our grief support network has greatly expanded to many more places, touching so many more hearts. We find a common thread among our members of all ages, who have experienced all types of losses. They tell us, "If it were not for The Christi Center, I would not have made it."

On the following pages, our facilitators and members tell in their own words their painful and inspiring stories. They will take you on their journeys leading to healing and renewed hope as they learned to live with their loss of loved ones by honoring and remembering them.

Austin Facilitator Stories

CHAPTER

Elda Arellano

Loss of Son Jesse to Drug Overdose

I lost my son Jesse, my only child, on November 30, 2010, to a drug overdose. He was an amazing, beautiful child, just 21 years old, just starting his life. Jesse lived at home with me at the time, and for that I am so thankful. Our love and respect for one other was constantly expressed, every day until his last. But Jesse dabbled in drugs and we tackled the issue, as we were both educated about the disease of addiction. (I came from a background of addiction in my family.)

Jesse kept a beautiful verse of an ancient Sanskrit poem in his wallet—it's how I describe my precious son. He had this warm indescribable love for everyone and a peace within him that was so radiant. You know when you meet someone whose presence brings peace and calmness? That was the gift Jesse carried. I will begin his story with this poem to give you a brief synopsis of Jesse:

Look well to this day
For it is life
the very life of life
For yesterday is but a memory
And tomorrow is only a vision.
But today well lived
makes every yesterday a memory of happiness
and every tomorrow a vision of hope.

—ancient Sanskrit poem

My wonderful memories of Jesse, his spirit, and this poem is how I try to hold myself together, knowing his love is with me each day. I found Jesse at home the day he died. We were going to have lunch together, and as I left for work, he reminded me, "Don't be late!" He knew my tendency for running five to ten minutes late, and he had plans after lunch. When I found him later in his room, something told me it was an accident. Now that I think about it, God and Jesse were providing a subconscious message, "Mom it was an accident." I can hear this message to this day.

After his death, I went through all the "should've" and "would've," but today, I am at peace with all of it. Yes, I continue to this day, wanting him back, but that is what the grief journey is all about—always missing him, always wanting him back. I then return to the calmness, knowing that he is with me and knowing that God is holding Jesse tightly with much love. I have become a more spiritual being, and, as a Catholic girl, had to find ways to cope with grief. I had to find my "new normal," my new purpose in life after Jesse's death.

At Jesse's funeral, Father Bud gave his homily, asking us, "Jesse only lived with us for 21 years, so how do we keep his spirit alive?" A message from God through our priest. Jesse was such a great kid and knew the Bible more intimately than I did. I asked God to lead me in ways to keep Jesse's spirit alive. Jesse and I had conversations about death before his—that if he died before I did, would I please spread his ashes across the tree tops on the 360 Bridge and Mopac Bridge? He told me that he wanted to run across the tree tops. So I began searching for a place on the Greenbelt to place a City of Austin bench in Jesse's honor. I went on a hike with my significant other David and Ashley, one of Jesse's girlfriends. We found the perfect spot, located at the 4.5 mile Greenbelt marker. The city representative, who assisted me, said she would not normally allow a bench in a flood zone area, but something came over her as we talked on the phone. She just had to honor my wishes on the exact location of this bench. Now dedicated to my son, the beautiful plaque reads: *To my Beloved Son, Jesse Arellano, Jr. May your spirit run amongst these tree tops. Your love exceeds all!*

As I struggled with my grief, I started paying more attention to things around me that were signs from God. I was a runner—for many years a marathon runner—and I love nature. When I thought I was going to lose it, I would go for a run and start talking to God. He would respond with a sunset,or the number "320" kept showing up. I wondered why. David had planned a trip to see the Chicago Cubs for us. And would you believe my flight to Chicago was #320! On that same flight, sitting in a window seat, I saw from the clouds an image of my son's face—clear as can be— reflecting on the fold-out tray in front of me. From his beautiful black wavy hair to his mustache to Jesse's smile so vivid and vibrant. I am not the type of person who likes to bring attention to myself, very private, but I started sobbing uncontrollably. When I finally stopped, I thanked God for this beautiful gift. I now understood why that number kept popping up right after this gift unfolded right before my eyes.

After the loss of a child, you still have to function within society. You tell yourself, "Get it together!" I began to muddle my way back and began to think of ways to celebrate Jesse's life. Keeping his spirit alive is still to this very day one of my missions, and I always celebrate his birthday and *Angel Day* on November 30. The signs from Jesse and God began unfolding so clearly. There are now many gifts of those that I receive—one is to attend a seminar led by Paula D'Arcy, a best-selling author who had experienced the grief of losing a child. I did not know who she was at the time, but something led me to that retreat. Paula began to give her presentation and disclosed her shift after losing her husband and her only child—trying desperately to find herself. How she began to ask what was her purpose in life? When you lose a child, you are raw, searching for answers. Your emotions are uncontrollable, and you wonder why. Everyone's grief is different. In my journey, I was a fragile soul and couldn't understand why life continues and mine was at a standstill. I was just sitting in my grief.

Later, in 2014, I went on the Camino de Santiago, the amazing journey that St. James traveled in Spain, with Kate von Alt and Danni Morford, other mothers who had lost their children. We decided to walk in memory of our boys. Talk about signs—it was sign after sign. It was as if our boys were walking with us. After this amazing hike in Spain, I began to shift. They advise after a loss, "Don't make any changes for a year." But I needed to smile again. I asked myself, "How do I begin to let a little happiness in my heart again?"

I held a finance position at *Texas Monthly* and needed to have more contact with people outside the office. I began praying about this change, and a sales position came open. An amazing vice-president of sales asked me to apply for it. I prayed and decided to let go of my fears and take this position. I trusted in God to move forward. Kate asked me to be on The Christi Center board. I felt I was in this other world looking out, and I wanted to give back to others. Whatever speaks to me, I do it, whatever it is. You are lost, you are gone, and your life has just changed forever. For me, in helping others, I just need to find a small opening of happiness, however that may look. I will trust in God to show me and guide me to this happiness. I began facilitating at the Christi Center in 2016. As a Hispanic woman, we finally started a Spanish-speaking group in 2017. I believe in giving hope to others who have lost a loved one by sharing my message and listening to those who need to know they are not alone in their grief journey. You know Susan and Don! They just want to help anyone who is traveling along this road.

Jesse, nicknamed "Jesse James," used to say, "Mom, Mom!" when he wanted my attention. How I miss these calls from my beautiful son. He was a lover of so much—the piano, guitar, and film. His first degree major was Philosophy—such a deep old soul. Recently, I cleaned my desk drawer and came across one of his class papers in which he wrote about the death penalty, using his religious point-of-view to debate about it. He wrote that the "Ego Society" felt that they can control this act when it is not ours to control. This is why I know in my heart this young man was truly a gift to me. Jesse's love will never die. My entire being misses this boy. So I must continue my journey, filling my spirit with LOVE, HOPE and a small bit of HAPPINESS. And ... keeping Jesse's spirit alive.

Jesse once said to me, "Mom you are so 'black and white' but there is gray in this world." I never really understood his meaning when Jesse was with me in this world. Now today, I see the gray, the silver linings, and I will always remember those words he said to me.

CHAPTER

Janet Brown

Loss of Son Joshua to Colon Cancer

I raised my only son Joshua as a single mother for most of my life. I was always a "Here's the problem — now, fix it" person; just forge ahead and I will take care of it. That was the same dogged determination and focus I used when, in October 1998, I was told that Joshua, my 25-year-old son, had stage four cancer and only twelve months to live. "He is not going to die," I told myself. "Just find the right venues for this chemotherapy and radiation, and take good care of him—he will be cured — even though the doctors told me otherwise."

The next two years were a series of surgeries to remove the tumors, radiation and chemotherapy treatments, and then traveling to other medical centers—Chicago and Dallas among them – that offered clinical trial treatment programs. Before his first surgery, Joshua wanted to live with his roommates, go out with his friends, and live his life as normally as he could. Eventually, my son, never sick and always so independent, finally turned to me and asked, "Can I come stay with you?" As was my role during his growing up years, I was his primary caregiver; I took care of insurance, doctor's appointments, any and all of his daily needs. Then he got worse, then better, and then worse again. When I look back, remembering how he looked, I was definitely in denial.

When the doctors said it was time for Hospice in late 2000, I again questioned what that meant, because I knew he wasn't going to die. The hospice nurses came to our house and gave me pamphlets on things to look for as death approaches. After they left I threw it all in the trash. On October 4, 2000, as I sat with Joshua all alone, he took his last breath. I just sat there saying this was not how this was supposed to end.

I called the chaplain from St. David's hospital. We had gotten close to her during Joshua's illness, and I wanted to let her know that Joshua had died. She came over and called hospice. Suddenly my house was full of friends making plans for the funeral. Then they had to take Joshua's body to the funeral home. After numbly moving through all the whirlwind of the funeral "busyness," I was faced with trying to live my life alone without Joshua. So began my eight long, miserable, unintentional years of *stuffing down* my grief.

My family does not talk about death, and they approach it with an attitude of "They are gone—that's it." I lost a sister in a 1984 car accident, and we never discussed it. When I thought about how I was the only person I knew who had lost a child, it never occurred to me that my mother had lost a child, because I lost a sister. I returned to work the next week because I wanted everything to go back to normal. Little did I know that I was going to have to start living a "new normal" life without my only son.

I learned to compartmentalize my life. At work, I would pretend that everything was okay. But when I got in my car to drive home, the tears would come. I would cry all the way home, and then I would start over again the next day. I didn't know what else to do. Many good friends disappeared from my life or would tell me, "You just have to pray or work" or some other *have to.* Two years after Joshua's death, I started to get physically sick with panic attacks and symptoms of having a heart attack. When I went to the ER, they said I wasn't having a heart attack, but the result of too much stress in my life. When I told the medical team that I lost my son, their response was "Ah, that's it!"

Not a single person suggested I might need to talk to someone. I started taking anti-depressants and after eight long years of silent suffering and medications, my doctor suggested I go to Hospice Austin and talk with a therapist. I was eligible for six free sessions since Joshua used their services when he was ill. After pouring out my broken heart in these sessions, my therapist suggested I go to The Christi Center for additional help with my healing. I thought to myself, "What? I'm not well yet?" I just wanted to feel better. I wanted a magic pill to make all the pain go away.

I went the following Monday to The Christi Center and met Susan Cox, who was so understanding and compassionate. I also met other moms who had lost children. It was comforting to know that I was not alone. At first, I didn't say a word about how it had been eight years since Joshua's death. Surely, they would kick me out since I wasn't *new* to loss, as so many other mothers in the room were. I eventually opened up and shared my story, and no one judged me. In fact, I learned so much at the meetings. I had wondered about things like "What do I do with his pictures or his clothes?" Others were asking all the same questions I had for eight years... but now I had the answers. Marianne McDonald, for example, had made a quilt out of her son's t-shirts. I had one made, too, from his shirts, and the queen-sized patches of Joshua's memories rest on the bed in my spare room. I saved all the buttons and made a button bracelet. I'm finding so many things I had hidden from sight after he died, emotionally and physically.

The mothers also talked about how they celebrated their child's birthday or *angel day* by releasing balloons into the air, or shooting their ashes from a cannon, or parachuting out of an airplane. I had never done anything in memory of Joshua and always wondered, "Was I supposed to forget him?" Now I am learning from the other mothers how to remember and honor Joshua's life. These questions never stopped for eight years, until I found The Christi Center. I can understand why mothers who have lost a child and do not get the support for their grief can think they are going crazy. I'm still learning about the grief process every day from The Christi Center. The one question that everyone asks is WHY? Well, I have learned that there is no answer.

I began my volunteer efforts for the organization slowly by stuffing envelopes and doing other general projects. It was nice because it gave me an opportunity to share stories with the other volunteers about ourselves and our children's lives. I then volunteered as a facilitator for the loss of child group, which met on Monday evenings, and I also co-chaired the events committee for a few years.

I can say I am a little more at peace and take the time to concentrate more on Joshua's life than on how he died. Like the funny things he did as a child or foods he liked. I used to think I couldn't think about those things because that would make me sad. Now, I allow those memories to come. Months after Joshua died, I found three letters that he wrote to me, telling me I was the best Mom in the world, and how sorry he was to be putting me through his illness. He wrote, "So glad to have you at my side. We will get through this together. Everything is going to be fine." If I want to have a good cry, I will get those letters out, and seeing his handwriting brings him closer to me. You always want to know you were a good mom!

I do have a light at the end of the tunnel. When Joshua was 20 and unmarried, he became a dad. Although it wasn't what he planned, we did the best we could to handle the situation. Now, more than 20 years later, I have a grandson who is such a blessing in my life.

CHAPTER

Cathy Collins

Loss of Teenage Boyfriend Brice and Brother Steve to Homicide; Parents Luther "Tee" and Alberta Barbour to Cancer

My first real sense of loss came when I was 15-years-old. My boyfriend was shot off of South Congress at a place called the Pig Stand. I was completely devastated and changed that day without realizing the pain or understanding the feelings of grief and loss. There were no counselors in school or grief groups, and I had to deal with those feelings in many negative ways. Little did I realize that I had experienced trauma deep inside of me and began to make bad choices because I just didn't want to feel the pain. There were no victim's services or counseling available for me. There was no Christi Center at that time.

As I moved into adulthood there was still the memory always present about the first loss. I was married for 20 years and had four wonderful sons. I thought life was good until January of 1990. My only sibling was murdered in his home. I found out while fixing dinner on a live simulcast of my brother's body coming out of his home on a gurney. A memory that I will never forget, and neither will my boys. There was no proper notification given and no victim's services person at my parent's home or mine.

The next day my parents and I went down to the police department to speak with several investigators and meet with a Victim's Assistance counselor. We were all in a state of shock, and very little made sense. The one thing I do remember was that we were given the name of an organization called "For the Love of Christi." After meeting with Susan and several other members, we began to understand the journey that we were in store for. I remember leaving and thinking that my parents were going to be okay. That is all I wanted to know because it was so hard on them. Susan and Don explained what to expect with the criminal justice piece of my brother's death. They were there for us every step of the way.

My brother left a daughter who was six-years-old along with his four nephews. I immediately began bringing the three oldest boys and my niece to the Kids Who Kare program. It made a huge difference in their lives, being there were other kids who had lost family members. My parents got very involved with the group, and I am so grateful for all the help they received from Susan and Don. I was able to attend some meetings, but it was very difficult because nine months after my brother's murder, I was divorced. I began volunteering whenever it was possible for me to be a part of the organization. I was asked to be on panels and share my story. My mother died within five years of coming to her first meeting. She had full-blown cancer and died within three months. Our family was supported by the entire Christi family and friends. Several years later my dad passed away suddenly. Susan and Don were by his side at the hospital. Without their support, I don't know how I could have made it.

I was lucky enough to come on staff part-time when my youngest son was in high school. I got very involved with the crime victims people who had lost siblings, parents, and children. I was able to mentor under Susan and learned everything I needed to know about the grieving process. With these tools, I began facilitating a mixed loss group for people who had lost children, parents, siblings, grandparents, other relatives, and friends. Eventually, I increased my hours since I was beginning to do more outreach and speaking.

It was a calling I believe in, and not a day goes by that I don't show gratitude for the gifts I have received from this organization and my closeness to both Susan and Don. I facilitate many groups, and I believe due to my losses, that I can relate to those new members who walk through our doors. I still do my Mixed Loss Group on Monday evenings, a Crime Victims Group two Tuesdays a month, and an Overdose Group on the other Tuesdays. I meet with the parents, grandparents, and relatives of our Kids Who Care group while they meet with Christi Neville. This is a very special group to me because of my boys who attended the early groups and knowing what a difference it made in their lives.

I do several outreach groups in Austin. I meet twice a month with Veterans at the VA and have outpatient groups at Austin Recovery for men and women once a month. I worked with Communities in Schools with middle school youth dealing with loss and am currently working at Pederas Middle School. Once a month I facilitate a Crime Victims Group that meets in Georgetown at the Georgetown Resource Community Center. My title at the center is Crime Victims Advocate, and I have a passion for this population.

Since I have walked those steps, I understand the layered grief that occurs and how often the system fails victims and their families. I am there for court accompaniments, police interviews, pre-trials, meetings at the DA's office, and helping the families with any questions they might have after the loss of their loved one.

I truly have that "dream job," and I look forward to working with new members and giving back to others all that I received from meeting Susan and Don and honoring Christi.

CHAPTER

Laura Cooper

Loss of Son Wiley Joseph Stillborn at 37 Weeks

On November 28, 2008, my life changed forever. That Thanksgiving Day we learned that the child we had tried for two years to conceive had no heartbeat at 37 weeks gestation. To this day we have no explanation of what happened. The shock and pain were indescribable. We delivered and buried our son, Wiley Joseph. I was his mother, and yet, no one could see my motherhood. No one could understand how much you could love a child who never took a breath. No one, except someone else who had been through it, too.

In 2008 there was little in-person support in Austin. Though The Christi Center was there, I felt like I needed to be able to share my grief with those who had been through perinatal loss. My support came in the form of online forums, blogs, and books. I met some amazing mamas online, but I longed for local community support.

In 2010 my daughter was born. She knows all about her big brother who came before her and who made me the mother I am. Wiley showed me the depth of my love and taught me how to be a mother. We celebrate his birthday every year by visiting the cemetery and having cupcakes together—my daughter blowing out the candle for Wiley. We take a trip each Thanksgiving — in the beginning our escape from the holiday, and eventually the way we could come together in remembrance as a family. But the 10th anniversary was a little different.

In 2009 I knew that I wanted to get involved in pregnancy and infant loss support as a way of honoring Wiley. One of the online forums I had been a part of was Share Pregnancy and Infant Loss. With the help of friends and family, I attended a training to learn how to be a support group facilitator for perinatal loss. When I returned to Austin, I was determined to get a pregnancy and infant loss support group going before Wiley's 10th anniversary.

In the process of trying to get a group started, I called The Christi Center. I told Lara what I was trying to do and met with her and Erin to talk about starting a support group at the center. They said they had always wanted to have one but had not been able to find a facilitator. After completing The Christi Center volunteer training program, the twice monthly Pregnancy and Infant Loss Support Groups started at The Christi Center in September 2018. I can't tell you how proud I felt to honor my son in this way and to try to provide community and support to others who have experienced loss. The group is chugging along, and I am working with other loss organizations to find ways to spread the word about The Christi Center group and other resources available locally for perinatal loss.

Every other Tuesday at The Christi Center I find that no matter how many people show up, I feel energized and connected to Wiley and to the parents who come in and share their stories.

CHAPTER

Mary Graf

Loss of Husband Kenneth to Pancreatic Cancer

My husband Kenneth died of pancreatic cancer in 1990. I was living in Houston at the time, working as a facilitator for the Center for Attitudinal Healing. The Center had groups supporting people dealing with catastrophic illness. Although for years I had been a facilitator for one of those groups, as my husband's health declined I found myself in a dual role, one of facilitator and participant. Hospice had a six-week group, but at its end, five of us needed more support. One of the women in that grief support group suggested we continue with our weekly meetings at various individuals' homes. I latched on to every source of support I could find—not just those that were specifically for grief. In the first few years, it was like the light switch was always on—doing everything I could to keep as busy as I couldn't stay still.

These things were meaningful, and it was not that I couldn't stand to be alone. In addition to joining several women's groups, I went to many workshops in an attempt to figure out my purpose. I needed to talk and didn't want to wear the same people out, so I kept rotating around the different Houston women's groups. When I returned to Austin in 1993, where I had gone to the University of Texas and had a huge family, I was still doing a lot of spiritual searching, and I became more involved in my current church. My sister Irene had recently lost her husband Melvin to cancer, and someone from the funeral home had recommended For the Love of Christi. Irene took her 11-year-old son to the Kids Who Kare program, which really helped him with the loss of his father. I met Susan Cox when I went to the meetings, and she extended an invitation to join other women to their New Mexico home for a retreat over Memorial Day weekend.

But, with my position as a school counselor, that was the time I was always trying to get end-of-year things such as grades and schedules finalized. I went to several meetings with Irene, but was so overwhelmed with moving and dealing with my transition that it was a while before I returned to For the Love of Christi. It was at the 1996 summer retreat, which I finally made, that we talked about my joining the organization as a facilitator.. At the time, the organization's Monday groups were growing, and there was a need for more meeting space. Susan suggested that we move the Spouse's Group to Sundays. After several years, the popularity of the Sunday afternoon group declined, while the demand for it on Monday increased, and the group went back to meeting on Mondays.

Over the months, you could watch the chemistry forming, and there were special relationships developing within these groups. Sometime in the early 2000s, this one special group, who felt they were further along in their grief, felt a bit restricted as they wanted to move on, but did not want to be insensitive of those new to grief and/or The Christi Center. A new group, *Moving On*, was created on the second Thursday of the month. *Moving On* is not a time line thing—there is no set time line for one's grief—but more fluid in what people want to bring up at the meeting, not as narrowly focused as the other sessions. For example, some want to explore their purpose, and others may want to talk about getting out there and meeting people. Some of our topics would be very jarring to those new to grief, such as talking about getting into a new relationship. That is a long process, and some who have lost their spouse eventually get to that place, while others do not. One woman in my group discussed exploring her career horizons. "If my husband were alive," she would say, and then talk about security and other complex issues she faced with his death.

Currently, I facilitate both *Moving On* and two other spouses groups and have a rich network of friendships and strong family ties. In addition to my volunteer work at The Christi Center, I have become very involved in committees and leadership positions in my church. Although I am not in another relationship, I have found meaningful purpose and direction in my life. I realized after my husband died how important it was for me to have a safe place to express what I was feeling: to not be judged or to be away from people who might think that I was crazy or had lost it. When I became aware of The Christi Center, I knew I had to help provide that service. I am grateful to be able to use my training as a counselor for this purpose.

CHAPTER

Phyllis and J.R. Lacey

Loss of Daughter Christina to an Automobile Accident

Your life, as you know it, can change in an instant. Mine did on June 11, 2008. Christina, my 20-year-old daughter, was in an auto accident. She was a senior at Texas State University. Christina was a kind, compassionate, and fun-loving soul. She loved life and lived it to the fullest. Christina had many goals. She wanted to graduate from college before she turned 21 (she was within six months of completing that goal), get her MBA, and start her own business. She was such a motivated young lady.

Two days after Christina passed away two friends who had lost children came to see me. They brought pamphlets from The Christi Center. They told me I needed to go to this place to get help with my grief. Three weeks later my husband and I made our first visit to The Christi Center. I realized that dealing with the loss of my daughter was not something I could do without help. In the beginning of my grief journey I experienced many emotions: panic attacks, anger, sadness, loneliness, confusion, hopelessness, and physical exhaustion. I couldn't eat, sleep or breathe. I didn't think I would survive; nor did I want to. It was just too painful. My life was forever changed.

In coming to the Loss of a Child Group, I realized that the other moms felt the same way I did. Suddenly, I didn't feel so alone in my grief. The Christi Center was a place I could talk about all my feelings and emotions. No one would judge me. The members just listened. They listened to me tell my story over and over again as I tried to process this tragic event in my life. Other members would recommend books to read on grief. Someone suggested journaling. I still journal today as a continued part of my healing. My new life felt so abnormal and strange. I wanted my old life back. I learned through others at The Christi Center that I would have a "new normal." Seeing other members who were farther ahead in their grief gave me hope that I would make it too. As time went on, I continued to look for other tools to help me on my grief journey, along with The Christi Center.

About two years after I started at The Christi Center I was asked to serve on the Events Committee. I began helping with the Remembrance Service, Tree Dedication, and other events at The Christi Center. I also organized a group to walk in the First Night Austin Parade downtown. In 2011, I was asked to be on the Advisory Council. I also went through training to become a facilitator for The Loss of a Child Group. In 2012, I became a co-chair of the Events Committee, and, as of now, I still hold this position. I also began to serve on panels at the University of Texas, for DPS (Cadet training), and Crime Victim Services training. I have served as a Christi Center Representative at the Twin Creeks golf tournaments.

I am forever grateful to Don and Susan Cox for starting The Christi Center. I have seen so many people's lives saved and many being able to reconnect to life again after their loss. I continue to volunteer at The Christi Center and facilitate. I want to be there for others who share this loss and pain. I do this, too, in HONOR of my daughter Christina. I know this is what she would want me to do: *Be there for others.*

Since Christina died, I have had other losses — both of my brothers, my mother-in-law, father, mother, and several close friends. The Christi Center has been there for me through these losses, as well. I have visited other loss groups at The Christi Center, and it has given me time to reflect on my grief for my other loved ones. In the last twelve years, the rawness and sharpness of the pain have softened over time. Thankfully I don't feel those feelings as acutely as I did in the beginning. It's so important for others who are just starting their journey to hear these words from the more seasoned members. It gives them hope that they will make it.

There's not a day that goes by that I don't think of Christina and talk to her. It's how I continue to try to cope with her physical loss. Some might think it sounds crazy, but at The Christi Center you learn that whatever brings you comfort is okay. Christina is a constant companion. She lives on through me. I continue her legacy because she can't, and I believe she won't be forgotten anytime soon. The bond between Mother and Child is forever. The love never ends.

CHAPTER

Beata and Tadeusz Liszka

Loss of Son Peter from a Skiing Accident

Peter was born in Poland in 1974, and at 19 years, he was brave, responsible, funny, good-looking, and incredibly gifted. The funny part was, of course, from me, and the math and physics genius was definitely from his dad. Before we came to Texas, Peter won all the math and physics competitions he entered. Following in our footsteps, he was an excellent skier, too. His top achievement in this field was a trip with his ski club to ski in the high Alps.

In 1990 his dad was offered a postdoctoral position at UT, and Peter really wanted us to move to Austin. It was, at the time, the computer science capital of the world. Believing that MIT was in Peter's future, I agreed. Peter attended the LBJ Science Academy and was their star in all math

122

competitions. After only one year in the United States, he was ranked the number one student in Texas by AHSME. Everybody loved him for his shy smile and humility despite the many achievements.

When an opportunity arose with the youth group of St. Theresa Church, he went on a skiing trip to the Wolf Creek Ski Area in Colorado. It was his first time to ski in the U.S. To make a long, horrible story short, Peter died in a skiing accident on the third day of this trip on March 17, 1993. It was an accident that NEVER EVER should have happened!

After his death, someone told me about the For the Love of Christi organization for grief support. When I entered the room on the day I finally decided to attend, Loyce came and gave me the first of their never-ending hugs. I went to one or two meetings, but couldn't make myself go back. I didn't think it was likely that anyone could truly understand how it felt to lose a child. How little I knew! I immersed myself in my work and was busy trying to maintain a sense of normalcy for my eight-year-old daughter.

A few years later, one of my close friends lost her son in a car accident. I told her about The Christi Center, and she became very active in helping to organize fundraising events. When she asked me if I would be willing to help, I said "Yes." It had been almost ten years since Peter had died, but Susan still remembered his story and recognized me. I was so touched! I decided I was finally ready to come back and let myself grieve. I found comfort from the other mothers who cried and laughed with me. I was home.

I began helping to organize events and then felt ready to start facilitating groups. It is my privilege and honor to offer my experience and time to help other people in pain after having lost a loved one. The Christi Center is a refuge for all the despair, tears, and unspoken words— because we know.

CHAPTER

Cindy McCoy

Loss of Husband Dennis in Airplane Crash

I lost my husband, Dennis Patrick McCoy, 28, in a private plane crash in Brownwood, Texas, while on his way to work one day in April 1985. I was only 29-years-old, and, suddenly, the single mother of two young children ages 14–months-old and 4-years-old. In so many ways, because of the tragedy of my young husband's death, I felt older than my parents, and even grandparents. I had this enormous pain in my life, my heart, that nobody close to me had experienced before.

I stumbled through my painful loss at first by learning to accept help and receiving meals from family and new friends. I learned to be able to share the pain with those who would listen. I began to read self-help books, as well as grief and loss books; there were not many back then—especially for young widows. I looked for counselors or groups specializing in grief; there were none that I could find.

I remember feeling so very alone and, on so many days, not wanting to go on. My mother – only 55-years-old — suddenly died of a brain aneurysm a year and a half after my husband. I remember crying big time in the middle of the night or in the shower, not understanding why God would let all of this happen. However, I knew I needed to give my two girls security and confidence that their worlds would be all right. Thankfully, my children made me "want to heal," and I received much needed support from my family and my husband's family to be able to go on.

Six months after Dennis died, I learned of another young death on the nightly news. Her name was Christi Lanahan, and her story was so tragic that I remembered it, knowing she also had a Mom and Dad and family somewhere who were grieving for her. Her life and death really affected me when, only two years after hearing of her death on the news, I learned on the news that her parents were starting an organization called For the Love of Christi. It greatly impressed me that Don and Susan Cox, her parents, were able to open their nonprofit while still in tremendous pain, heartache, and chaos. Their endeavor not only impressed me, but encouraged me. I would have joined their group, but thought it was only for those who had lost a child. Sadly, it was my mistake.

As I moved through my own pain and grief, friends and family were there to take me out for fun when I did not want to go; shared the holidays with me; and made travel plans, which helped all three of us tremendously. I eventually met another young widow with a little girl the same age as my oldest daughter. We became the best of friends, and I learned just how helpful it is to be able to share with others who have been through a similar experience.

I continued to look for counselors who had been through a similar grief experience, but I was unable to find one. Eventually, I discovered a wonderful Christian counselor who was able to explain to me that I could have the best comforter and healer in the whole universe, and that His name was Jesus Christ. Even though I was already a believer, I surrendered everything in my world, especially myself, my children, my husband, friends and family, and all my earthly belongings and my pain. I took myself off the throne of my life and put Jesus on the throne and started taking Bible studies. I was "Born Again!" In my Bible studies, I began to heal and gained wisdom to raise my children. I have never been the same since. True JOY returned to me!

I remember thinking on the worst day of my life—Dennis' memorial service—that if I ever survived my pain, I would love to help others through theirs. I just did not know at the time what that looked like. But God knew. I eventually felt led to go back to school to get my Masters in Professional Counseling. Looking for an internship, I again discovered For the Love of Christi, now more aware of all the multifaceted groups and programs they provided. I did part of my internship there and really enjoyed working with the groups and getting to know and love Don and Susan. They have become another part of my family, and I can count on them for anything. I only wish that after my loss of Dennis, I had this type of program that Don and Susan were led to open.

Even though I eventually opened my own private practice, I stayed on with The Christi Center, helping to facilitate groups, especially the Loss of a Spouse Group. I served on panels and as a member of the board of directors and advisory board, and assisted with the Kids Who Kare program. It has been such an honor and a huge blessing to help others in grief. I am in awe of what Don and Susan have created in order to serve God and to help others in their grief. They took their own pain and deep love for their daughter Christi, their empathy and compassion for their family, friends and others, their courage and wisdom in following God to help bring comfort to others in pain. They both started this program, thankfully, which will hopefully last long after we are gone. I am so very grateful to them for following their hearts and creating this organization in memory of their sweet Christi.

Even though I am now a retired counselor and no longer facilitate at The Christi Center, I am still in a ministry for helping widows at my church. I am also having fun being a "Cici" to my eight wonderful grandkids whom Dennis blessed me with! I am really enjoying life with my girls and their husbands, my family, and friends. I have discovered that you keep receiving blessings when you share your story and your heart with others. It gives them hope in their grief. God is so good, and I'm so grateful to Him for all His blessings and for loving me and my family, for Don and Susan, and for The Christi Center.

CHAPTER

Marianne McDonald

Loss of Son Dylan Graves to a Truck Accident

Dylan Graves, my son, my only child, the light of my life, died in a truck accident at the gate of his apartment complex on May 22, 2006. Dylan is forever 19 years old. My life became two parts—before May 22, 2006, and after May 22, 2006. I went back to work at the Department of Family and Protective Services one week after Dylan's death. I had worked my entire life, and I didn't know what else to do. I would come home for a couple of hours every day at lunch to write thank-you notes and cry. Writing thank-you notes was all I could do for Dylan, so I wrote some fine thank-you notes and included pictures of my Dylan. Someone who came to my house after Dylan died left a piece of paper, and all it said was The Christi Center with a telephone number.

About two weeks after Dylan died, I called that number. Whoever I needed to talk to wasn't in the office, and I was asked to leave my phone number so the person could call me back. I said "No," because I was going back to work, and I knew I wasn't capable of having that conversation at work. The next day I tried calling again, and the person I needed to speak to was in a meeting. It's hard for me to explain the stress of making that phone call to The Christi Center. After the third try, I left my name and number. I remember when Susan Cox called me back on a Friday. She told me about Christi and asked about Dylan. Susan said she was leaving the next morning going to Ruidoso on a Mother's Retreat. She said the following week she was meeting with another mother who had recently lost a daughter and asked me to come. So I made my first trip to The Christi Center for that meeting with Susan, Mary Shields, and Nancy Thayer. Never in my life did I ever think I would be in a room, one of four moms whose kids had died.

I became a regular at the 11:00 a.m. Wednesday meetings facilitated by Susan and Loyce Allen. One Wednesday, Nancy told me she was going to go to the Monday night meetings. Hell, I didn't even realize there were Monday night meetings! Because I was in such complete shock, I guess. I started going to meetings on Monday nights and Wednesdays. I went to the meetings for about two years. I won't say it felt good, but it was comforting to be around other mothers. One meeting they needed a facilitator and I said I would do it, and that was the beginning of my facilitating. (I did attend facilitator training after that.)

By then, I had planted a tree for Dylan at The Christi Center Tree Grove in Round Rock; purchased a stone for Dylan in the Rock Garden at The Christi Center; and, had leaves painted on the wall in The Christi Center library for Dylan, my Mom, Dad, Aunt Dot, and Uncle Bill. I volunteered at every Christi Center event—tree plantings, Remembrance Ceremonies, and event committee meetings. Other mothers who had lost their kids around the time Dylan died became my best friends.

Since then, I have continued to become friends with mothers not as far along in the process as me. That is the beauty of The Christi Center— finding people with whom you can connect. After facilitating for many years, I recommended that we start a monthly Thursday meeting for mothers who were farther along in their grief journey. Those mothers don't need weekly support, but do have things that come up about their kids that they want to talk about. We would meet at The Christi Center for about an hour. Then we would go to a restaurant to eat and continue our discussions. We all help each other.

I have always been a little different than other mothers. I use curse words at meetings. I am angry that Dylan died, but that's not the reason I cuss. And from the first anniversary of Dylan's death (Dylan Day), I have done something out of the ordinary because I know Dylan wouldn't want me sitting at home being sad. The first year I went skydiving. Never in my life did I ever plan to do that, but I thought Dylan would think it was funny. My tandem partner's name was Dylan, but that wasn't planned. From that first year, The Christi Center members have always been involved in Dylan Days. We've been rafting and tubing on the Guadalupe River, gone to New Orleans and Florida, and to New York to see the medium George Anderson, scuba-dived, been hot air ballooning, and parasailing.

Dylan Day in 2015 was not a day, but a journey. A group of us — Barbara, Leslie, Gail, Susan Trammell, Beth, Hal and I — walked 113 kilometers (70 miles) of the Camino de Santiago in Spain (otherwise known as the "Way of St. James") to receive the Compostela, the official certificate of completion issued by the Cathedral in Santiago. Susan and Tommy Trammell were going to The Christi Center when I started going, and Barbara and Al Cox and Hal came after I did. Barbara and Leslie were walking with me and Hal on the famous *bad day* where we walked 17 miles. I took my shoes off and refused to go another step. Hal convinced me to put my shoes back on, and Barbara and Leslie both encouraged me. Susan Trammell was an inspiration to us all and was the most prepared to walk the 94 miles.

We walked for the love of Jimmy, Dee Ann, Tommy, Lynda, and Dylan. Those Angels all got their Camino passports stamped and received their Compostela. Each of us received our Compostelas on May 22, 2015, the ninth anniversary of Dylan's death. We actually walked 94 miles (not 70 as our guides claimed) in seven days, and it nearly killed me. I don't believe in coincidences and I will always be grateful to Barbara for putting the trip together because of Dylan's death anniversary during the time.

129

We did not come up with the Camino idea ourselves. The summer before Kate von Alt, Elda Arellano, and Danni Morford — other Christi Center moms — walked 500 miles for the love of Garrett, Jesse, and Travis. I knew there was no way I could do that, so when Barbara found a trip that was shorter and arrived in Santiago on Dylan's angelversary, I knew it was for me. I still don't know how Kate, Elda, and Danni were able to do what they did, but they have my total admiration.

I learned in 2006 that it takes a village to survive the loss of a child. Susan and Don and The Christi Center will always be a big part of my village. Without them, I would not be here today.

CHAPTER

Glenn and Mary McIntosh

Loss of Daughter Caitlin to Suicide

January 5, 2000, was the worst day of my life. At the time, Caitlin, our 12-year-old daughter, was being treated for depression. She couldn't sleep at night and was having a hard time adjusting to sixth grade. I remember the doctor saying, "This will do it," as he prescribed Paxil. That drug didn't work, so the psychiatrist then gave her Zoloft along with Zyprexa, Depakote, and some others. They put Caitlin on a cocktail of six to eight psychoactive drugs, which drove her completely crazy! The tragic thing is that Caitlin's death came ten days before she was to enter a sleep study program, which we believed would have helped her.

We had taken all the precautions at home to make sure she didn't harm herself—locked windows, removed sharp objects from her reach, and even slept on a mattress in front of her bedroom door. This was the first week of the second semester, and school had started on a Tuesday. She had gone to class, dozed off, and was having nightmarish dreams/hallucinations, a known side effect of SSRIs. Under the 504 Plan, a student can go to someone if not feeling *safe,* and Caitlin exercised her rights with the school counselor. The next day, the last day of her life, her teacher sent her to detention because she had not turned in her class work from the day before. This was a straight-A student who wanted to be a horse doctor and was never in trouble. For her, it was the last straw. She went to the girls' restroom during break and hanged herself.

What saved my wife and me after Caitlin's death was knowing that there was a police chaplain from Cedar Park at the school. The body had to be whisked away to the coroner's, and we were unable to see her until the funeral. The chaplain came to our house that night and said, "You will be surrounded for a while, but there will be day when you will need help, because people will go back to their own lives." He gave us the name of The Christi Center, and when everyone did return to his or her life, we called the organization.

As I worked through my grief and anger at those at the school and others who did not save her, there was also the guilt. We had no idea in the early days that the medication she was on drove her to do what she did. I know without a doubt now that if she had not had those drugs in her, she would not have taken her life. During those first days, we were dealing with such confusion and bewilderment. Everything seemed so surreal. I was wandering around in a daze, and my wife Mary couldn't get out of bed, so we had to plan the funeral in our bedroom. We had another daughter, and, somehow, we found the strength to keep going. Our grief was so intense that we were blindsided by so many triggers—a smell, a sound. For me, it was seeing Caitlin's friends come by and thinking, they are going to grow up, go to college and marry, and my daughter is not going to be able to do that. It was not just the pain of losing Caitlin, but the loss of her potential. She was supposed to bury us, I thought. Caitlin drank milk all day long, so we would put gallons in the cart at the grocery store, and then remember, "Oh, she's not here." Our other daughter is lactose intolerant.

A transforming moment for me came at her memorial ceremony in February. We held her funeral in January, but it took us a while to prepare for the special tree-planting ceremony on the church property the following month. Songs were planned specifically for the event, and friends came from as far away as California to be in attendance. When I started to place Caitlin's ashes in the hole at the bottom of the tree, a strong gust of wind came up. Her ashes blew everywhere, and some landed on my blue jeans. I remember thinking, "Okay, she doesn't want to be put in there."

Later that night, walking outside, I was suddenly hit by another February date. I rushed into the house, found where Caitlin had kept her important notes in her notebook, and there was her note about Jimmy, the bass player in Bare Naked Ladies, her favorite band. He was performing that very evening with his brother at the Cactus Café! We had gone to a BNL concert in November 1999, arriving four hours in advance to grab a front row seat. We were waiting by the back door to get in when Jimmy stopped unloading the equipment, came over to us, and talked to Caitlin. He told her he would be playing in Austin again in February 2000—the night of her memorial—and she had written the date in her notebook.

I didn't change my clothes, got in the car, and drove to the Cactus Café concert. As I listened to the music, a voice in my head repeated, "I want to live, I want to live, I want to live." I got into the music that night and realized that up to that point I was in such shock I didn't know I wanted to live. I didn't know what I wanted. I looked down, saw her ashes on my jeans, and started brushing them off, so Caitlin could be there, too! It was definitely a milestone in my grief recovery.

Mary and I went to the regular Monday night group at The Christi Center for people who had lost children. But when we mentioned suicide, some members would recoil, as if to say, "Oh, my child didn't die *that way!*" We eventually went to Don and Susan, suggesting the need for a special group for those who had lost someone to suicide, and a new group was formed. As a professional counselor, Mary used her expertise to facilitate the newly formed Suicide Group. We opened with the statement: "Let's focus on the good things about our loved ones."

133

We definitely shared our sorrows, but also wanted to focus on the positive and how to move on after such a horrific loss. Since 2003, I continue to facilitate these meetings, which have helped so many others during their grief journey.

CHAPTER

Dolores and Horacio Segovia

Loss of Son Homero to Driver Under the Influence of Drugs

In 2015, we lost our 23-year-old son Homero when he was driving to work and a driver under the influence of drugs crossed the center lane and hit Homero's car. He died at the scene. We became members of a specific type of grieving family—those who have lost a loved one to a crime. After receiving information about The Christi Center from the Department of Public Safety, we reached out to them for support. Without knowing it, Horacio and I both called the center the same day. He remembered feeling an instant connection with the person he spoke with on the phone. So we decided to go to the meeting together.

We attend the Monday night Loss of a Child group, as well as the Crime Victims group on Tuesdays. They are an important part of my support network, because someone took my son, and it's a different kind of loss. The people in these groups understand exactly what my husband and I are going through. Fellow members support me, so that I can freely talk about the person responsible for Homero's death and also share my feelings on dealing with the justice system—an experience unique to these members! Everyone is so free of judgment, especially when I want to talk about something I have already talked about, and that is okay.

The Christi Center supported us by connecting us with other families who had similar losses; preparing us for what would happen at the trial and inviting us to attend a similar trial; and being there with us through a plea agreement process. Cathy Collins, The Christi Center's intake specialist and crime victim advocate, was there for us every step of the way. They gave me hope and became my family. They support me in a way that no one else can. This is not a place I signed up for, but it is a blessing that this place exists.

As we continue to heal, we eventually gave back to The Christi Center, supplying food for a Crime Victims' potluck and speaking on a panel for the Travis County Sheriff's Office. As native Spanish-speaking persons, we have helped several families in our group with translations. My husband once said about a family he helped, "They didn't feel like they could ever come out of the dark, but after three meetings, they were starting to see the light."

We do our best to support others at The Christi Center to let them know they do not have to grieve alone.

CHAPTER

Beverly Shirley

Loss of Husband Ed after Surgery

Dear Ed,

I've been asked to tell my grief story—our story. This story begins at the end. It was Wednesday, August 15, 2012, and I hoped you would be going home from the hospital the next day. You'd had a routine shoulder replacement, but there had been problems with your blood oxygen level, so the hospital kept you a couple extra days. I was late leaving my office, wrapping things up so that I could take a few days off to be home with you. As I rushed into your hospital room, the nurse redirected me, saying they had moved you in preparation for discharge. Three doctors had all signed off on the release. I bopped into the new room, ready to congratulate you on your progress, but saw you asleep in the chair. I sat down quietly to wait for you to wake up. Only you never did.

In a breath, a heartbeat, or, more accurately, failure of a breath and heartbeat, my world changed. Helpless to quell the storm of events that blew through my life, I fell, headlong and unprepared, into my grief journey. My world was reeling, unreal, surreal. How was I to manage? How many times did I take a deep breath, set my resolve and say, "I can do this," and steel myself to do the necessary tasks that were so unimaginably hard?

I drove to the cemetery office to pick up your ashes. I took our car, the boxy little maroon vehicle full of character. When we bought it, I decided to name it Gertie. You laughed and thought it was cute that I named the car. Others, depending on the circumstance, thought of me as understanding, efficient, tough, strategic, thoughtful, dedicated, determined, stubborn—but never *cute*. Only you thought of me in that way. Thus, a part of me is buried along with you. Taps played on being frivolously *cute*. That was hard.

I bought a guest book for the funeral. Matthew was scheduled to move into a new apartment that weekend, and I was scheduled to help. The move date could not be changed. Sometime between lugging boxes, directing movers, and papering shelves I escaped to the stationary store to get a tastefully simple book for funeral guests to sign. Your vibrant, joy-filled life had provided so much action, so much color - flashes, spins, flips, and turns all part of your zest for life. But the stationary store didn't have tie-dyed guest books for funerals. Tastefully simple, it wasn't right. It wasn't you. It wasn't fair. It was hard.

I sang "Amazing Grace." In fact, I sang a lot of songs. Our faith holds that death is new life, so I wore baptismal white. The mass started with a trumpet blast and "Ode to Joy." '... Ever singing, march we onward victors in the midst of strife. Joyful music lifts us sunward, in the triumph song of life.' We ended with 'I'll fly away, oh glory. I'll fly away in the morning. When I die, Hallelujah, by and by, I'll fly away.' Singing, clapping, smiling, while my withered heart limped through. That was hard.

I saw your ashes lowered to the ground. That happened later in October. Fall was turning to winter, green to brown. Plants were going dormant, life and death in a tug-of-war. There was a caterpillar, fuzzy with orange dots, almost impossible to tell head from tail, crawling along the drying blades of grass on six little insect legs. Soon it would shroud itself in the dark of its cocoon, in its sleep transforming itself into flashes of color and grace until, in the light of spring, it would emerge. I picked it up. "Oh, dear caterpillar of promise. I hold the image of your future, your transformation, your new life. But your life I will not share." That was hard.

And then, in the stillness that followed, I cried. Red nose, red-rimmed eyes, salt traced down my cheeks. Sobs and silence, a bottomless ocean of tears. And then I stared, exhausted, listless, motionless, and numb. Events thundered around me as waves surround a raft floating in a storm-tossed sea, raising it up, throwing it down, buffeting and spinning the fragile heap. Gulping the salt, the brine, not caring whether I sunk into the inky darkness, nevertheless I remained afloat.

And then I faked it, tucking grief away where no one could see and no one would know; there would be no awkwardness or avoidance. But when I was alone, I took grief out and turned it 'round and 'round slowly, feeling where it was smooth and where it was pitted; breathing in its scent as earthy and fresh as the newly turned soil that covered your grave; watching its surface change from colorless, to dark, then painfully bright then colorless again. And, then, GRIEF moved in.

Usually when something moves in, it fills up an empty space. Not so with grief. Grief drills out a space, a hole, a void. And so I was emptied and alone with the cavernous specter of grief. Alone? With my great wealth of caring family and friends? I had so many helping hands – my family so strong; my friends so warm. But grief was a wall, and I had to knock out the bricks, one hammer-strike at a time, to let the caring seep through. I had to want to break down the wall. I had to learn how to break down the wall. I had to never give up breaking down the wall.

And so, with time, my journey has evolved—sometimes plodding and sometimes sprinting, crawling through dark caverns, climbing to rugged peaks. I am a different person on a different path than I'd previously traveled or planned. I've had much to learn, to unlearn, and to relearn. Among my friends are the caring spirits that I found at The Christi Center, a safe place to grieve and heal. Here we come together, to share with each other, to support each other, to lift up and carry one another forward, to provide hope. We share dedicated time in a space and place that is undemanding, nonjudgmental, safe.

As a facilitator for the Loss of Spouse Group, I am committed to fostering a caring, sharing, strengthening, safe space for persons to move forward, to positively explore their sorrows, purposes, and hopes in the context of their changed worlds.

So, Ed, the beat of life continues. Sometimes the cadence is off. Sometimes the rhythm falters. Still, beat by beat, my heart has the strength to carry on, to help where I can, and to always hold you dear.

Love,
Bev

CHAPTER

Marlene M. Smith

Loss of Son Brian (Undetermined) and Husband John to Cancer

I first came to The Christi Center in December 2007 after the death of my son Brian. He was found at a campsite, Boggans Flats in Colorado, on Sunday, October 14. A hiker spotted him lying there, freaked out, and left him to go back to her home. She must have thought about it and eventually called the authorities. They were not sure it was human.

Brian must have felt bad, stopped the Jeep, and dragged himself over to the creek. The ignition was still on, it had run out of gas, and the battery was dead when they found him. Brian's face was in the water, but not the top of his head. His glasses were beside the vehicle, and they could see his footprints. I don't know if he realized he was dying. Did he say, "Mama, help me!" or "God, help me!" Did he die immediately? I have wondered and asked these questions so many times.

The autopsy was not conclusive, but it could have been his heart. My husband came from a family in which everyone had heart problems — perhaps, passed down through the generations? Brian also had a lot of financial problems before he left Austin, so maybe the stress was too much? Once, in late September, before he died, Brian's hernia ruptured while loading his things into a Salvation Army truck. He had corrective surgery at Seton September 24 to 27. After his death, I asked for those hospital records, but found no mention of heart problems. No high blood pressure, no irregular heartbeats. Nothing.

Brian had worked at the Stonebridge Inn in Snowmass, Colorado, several times before in exchange for room and board. He worked at the front desk; set up banquet tables, shoveled snow, and helped in any area he was needed. But this time upon his return, the Personnel Department wanted to see his Social Security card before he could go to work at the Inn. He must have lost or misplaced it. We don't know if he was on his way to the nearest SS office or was coming back, but he had camping equipment in his Jeep. More unanswered questions. Brian was healthy, I thought. He had a mountain bike and rode it often. His death was so unexpected, and he was only 53.

There are several things I am thankful for with my son's tragic death:

> It had not snowed—if it had, his body might not have
> been found until spring.

> The animals did not get him.

> He had email addresses and phone numbers in his wallet,
> so the authorities were able to find his family and friends.

I contacted a psychic-medium several years after Brian's death. He asked me to "forgive" him—that he had been stubborn. I told him I did and asked him to "forgive" me, too. It has been a terrible adjustment to know that Brian is not here anymore. The Christi Center has helped me so much in so many years to cope with my loss. Coming to The Christi Center was the most important thing that I did after Brian's death. At one point, when I was journaling my feelings, I mentioned that I wanted to go into the garage and turn on the car ignition, so that I would not have to deal with my grief, anger, frustration, and sadness. I was angry at God for taking my wonderful caring and artistic son. But The Christi Center got me through that, and I will be forever grateful.

That is why I wanted to return something to help others who are so grief-stricken and sad. I see myself at that earlier time. My pain and sadness will never go away, but it has lessened since 2007 when I lost my son.

When Brian died in that October 2007, all the grief I had suffered after the loss of my husband John in 1980 came flooding back. It was crazy the way that grief worked—I couldn't believe it! John began to have back-aches around Thanksgiving of 1979, using a heating pad during our visit with family in Alice, Texas. Then, at Christmas time, we cancelled an evening out with friends, because he was not feeling well. He woke me up one night moaning in his sleep.

I called the next day to make an appointment with Dr. Journeay's office for tests. He made an appointment with an urologist who was not available soon enough to do the tests. On February 27, John, who was a 20-year Air Force NCO, asked me to drive him to the hospital at Bergstrom Air Force Base. When we arrived, the doctor on duty said he could not help him, but instead called Dr. Journeay's emergency number. We then headed to Seton ER on 38th Street, where we met Dr. Journeay. It was around midnight. I got John registered and into his room and went home.

It took four days for the hospital medical team to check everything. Finally, Dr. John Schneider, the urologist, gave us the news. John had cancer of the bladder and kidneys, and it had spread through his whole system. It was a death sentence. Chemotherapy might take the swelling down, but it would not cure John. We went with only one treatment, because he was so miserable. I spent the whole night going to the small hospital kitchen, making coffee, and taking it to him. It seemed to be the only thing John could handle.

His sister Hope and I took turns staying with John so that he would not be alone. One or two nights, Brian came to stay with him. They had a good time I was told, laughing and telling jokes. I am glad he had that time, and maybe John forgot his pain for a while. I wanted to take him home, and he wanted to go home, but Dr. Journeay didn't think I could manage. My husband was six-foot, four and half-inches tall and weighed 180–190 pounds. A nurse told me about a "hoist" that would help me get him out of bed and into his wheelchair. The American Cancer Society loaned us a bed, wheelchair, and several other items that I would need. So after 33 days in the hospital, I took John home on March 31.

That night, as I sat next to his bed, John asked me several times, "When is it going to be over?" I had to answer that I didn't know. But, I did pray that God would take John so he wouldn't have to suffer any more. The next morning, I went into the bedroom to give him his medication, and I could not wake him. My mother, who was visiting us, could not find a pulse. I called Dr. Journeay. He came to the house and certified John's death.

Brian and I had to select a coffin at the funeral home. That was scary, going into that room filled with all the coffins! They did not have a size to fit John, so they had to bend his legs to get him into one. I planned to take his body back to Chicago for burial in the family plot. There were so many things I had to do: plan a viewing in Austin; make reservations for Brian, my daughter, and me to accompany the body; get information on the Chicago funeral home, and see who was going to meet us at O'Hare to transport John's body to the funeral home.

I think I was numb going through all that. It was Holy Week in Chicago, and we were not sure that the grave diggers would work on Good Friday or Holy Saturday. But everything worked out, and he was buried that weekend. It was cold in Chicago. Sitting at that gravesite for just a little while made us cold, too.

Months after his burial, I dealt with the endless paperwork of bills coming in, insurance claims to be filed, and the probate of the will. It was six months before I finally realized that John was really gone. We moved around so much while he served in the Air Force for overseas duty, he was often gone for weeks at a time. After he died, I kept thinking he would come home like he always had before.

There was no grief counseling back in 1980. I found a psychologist who helped me and my daughter. She was talking about killing herself to be with her Dad. Laini was "Daddy's Little Girl." I tried to devote more time for her. We went to Disney World in Florida for a week, took a trip to the Rio Grande Valley where my mother lived, and shopped and went out to eat. Brian moved home, and that helped. He was there to do the things that John had done around our house.

I missed John so much, just his presence, having someone to talk to, the companionship. Now I was alone, and I knew Brian and Laini would be leaving home at some point to live their own lives. The thought of being alone scared me. I was laid off from work a week before I put John in the hospital. I waited about seven months after his death before I started looking again, and I got another job. That helped. For Thanksgiving and Christmas of 1980, I had my whole family—Brian and Laini, Mom, sister and her husband, brother, nieces, friends—for dinners and sleepovers. That helped. Everyone says, "It takes time." That's true, but you still miss them.

CHAPTER

Deana and John Ward

Loss of Son Johnny, Jr. to Drug Abuse

My story began on September 7, 2007. We lost Johnny, our 18-year-old son. Johnny had been struggling with drugs off and on since he was thirteen. Up until age twelve, he was the happiest, sweetest boy you could imagine. Something happened in puberty, and, unfortunately, we couldn't figure out how to help him. His dad found him in his car that hot September day. If memory serves me, it was 107 degrees that day, so no telling how hot it was in the closed car. We had not heard from him in over 24 hours, which was not like him. He would always stay in touch. His Dad said that Friday morning that he was going to find him. Of course, it was not what we expected. We wanted to bring him home, get him help, and deal with the situation. It was the ultimate loss.

How that day changed my life forever. I felt like I died that day myself, and, of course, part of me did die. I would never be the person I had been before Johnny died. My life would never be the same. I didn't know what to do, how to live my life, or even breathe. I had never felt so alone. It didn't matter how many people I was around, I felt completely alone. There was a deep hole in my heart and in my life.

John and I came to The Christi Center twelve days later. I had never been a group person; I am very private. But I knew that I could not do this by myself. I knew that I needed help from those who were going through the same thing, had the same feelings, and understood all the issues that come with losing a child. How it changes your whole life and all of your relationships. Nothing is ever the same again.

What I learned from The Christi Center is that in time you learn how to live again, how to be happy again. It is never the same, but there can be joy in life again. I didn't believe that when I first started. I could see that the ones that were four to five years into their grief journeys were in a much better place, but I didn't think that I would ever be that person. I would just be miserable and dead inside for the rest of my life. How could I be any other way, I just loved my son too much to ever be happy again. I was going to wallow in tears, guilt, and regret for the rest of my life. And, hopefully that life would not last too long. I wouldn't do harm to myself, but I thought I would just cease breathing.

Well, lo and behold, I did not die. I went to The Christi Center on Wednesdays for a while and then started on Monday nights. Sometimes I would go to both meetings. I don't know what I would have done if it wasn't for The Christi Center. The love that I found there was exactly what I needed to get me through. I have heart connections and friendships that are stronger than any I could have ever imagined. Losing a child breaks down all barriers. It doesn't matter how they died, how old they were, how much money, or how little you have. Doesn't matter what kind of car you drive, what your religious beliefs are, or the color of your skin. We are all in this together for the long haul, and we have to help each other.

I am so grateful to Susan and Don for founding this group and for continuing it for so long. I am grateful for the tremendous love they have for Christi—the reason this group is here. I thank Christi every day for that love. I am grateful to the facilitators that were there for me. It would be easy to say after all these years, "I am in a better place now; I don't need to go to meetings." In fact, there is a time when you are feeling better. Going to a meeting, hearing the new and devastating stories rips your heart out and takes you back to day one, but as I have continued to go, I have gotten past that. The new stories break my heart, but now I just want to help those newly bereaved parents. Show them the love that was given to me. That love is what pulled me through. It also helps me see how far I have come.

I started facilitating in 2011, four years into the journey. I continue to do it because I know that new grieving parents need to see a glimmer of hope — hope that they will get through the unbearable heartache that they are going through. I want to give them the love, friendship, and compassion that were given to me. I want them to know that I understand what they are going through, that I know how miserable and lost they are. They need to know that all the feelings they have are okay; they hurt like hell, but they are normal feelings. They aren't crazy or any crazier than the rest of us.

The "new normal" is what we have to find. We all have to figure out how to accept our lives and understand that we will never be the same. We will always miss and cherish our children, and they will always be a part of us. It is certainly a comfort to have people who truly understand and help you through that long uphill trek. It is the hardest work you will ever do.

We are blessed with a beautiful daughter. Rikki is two years older than Johnny. She is now an only child. Rikki and Johnny should have grown old together. They should have been able to share all of life's momentous occasions, such as graduations, marriages, babies, and losing their parents. We should never have had to bury our son. Rikki, at 18, should not have had to bury her brother. When we lost Johnny our family dynamics changed drastically, and it took us quite a while to figure out how to be a *new* family. People say that they don't know how to deal with or parent their surviving children. You don't at first—everything you knew and were before was wiped away. There really is a "new normal," and it does take some time to learn how to live the New Life that you never wanted.

148

So, a big "Thank You" to Christi, Don, and Susan, all the wonderful people who work at The Christi Center, and all the facilitators and friends who have helped me find my way.

7 Georgetown Facilitator Stories

CHAPTER

Nona and Doug Allen

Loss of Son Aaron to Motorcycle Accident

Our son, who was our only child, was killed in a motorcycle accident on February 10, 2015. He had just turned 29. He was our everything and our reason for living. I went through a divorce while I was pregnant with him and was a single parent until he was four. This was after years of infertility, major surgery at eight weeks of pregnancy, and a minor stroke during childbirth. He truly was my miracle baby! Then I met and married a wonderful man who loved Aaron as his own. He became my son's father. We loved hanging out as a family and traveling. Our house was always the hangout for Aaron and his friends, as they were growing up. In adulthood, he and his friends and their young families still came over every weekend to swim and hang out.

When Aaron was killed, my husband and I knew that we could not survive without help. One of the places suggested by the Victims Services lady was a place named The Christi Center. We knew about The Christi Center because many years before, we were raising foster boys, whom I had taught. Their father had died a few years before they came to live with us. When they came to live with us, their aunt insisted that we take them to the children's group at The Christi Center. I am ashamed to say that at the time I knew nothing about The Christi Center, other than they helped people during grief. I felt like the boys were doing fine. And taking them there was just one more thing on my busy plate. I only took them for a short time. I did NOT get that grief can be paralyzing.

My husband and I began attending the loss of a child group, at The Christi Center three weeks after Aaron's death. I was a total mess. Almost suicidal. When we signed up, the facilitators asked us to please come to three meetings before we made a final decision about attending regularly. The very first meeting we attended, I was totally overwhelmed and really did NOT want to hear that I would survive. I left thinking I would not go back. My husband insisted that we try it again. That second meeting, I listened to another mom who had also lost an only child. She seemed to be struggling as much as I was. She was a little bit into her grief journey, and she seemed to be able to put into words how much she was hurting. By listening to her, I started making my first connection. We also learned at that second meeting how differently men and women grieve. We credit this with helping us stay in our marriage. By the third meeting, I felt I had begun to connect to several of the moms. I began clinging to the fact that these moms KNEW how I felt and what I was going through. At that point, my husband could not attend any more meetings because of his work schedule. But he encouraged me to keep going. And after every meeting I attended, he would ask me how group was and what did I learn. I would share with him what I was learning, and I think it really helped him deal with his grief.

I found myself living from Monday to Monday just so I could go to group. I learned that even though I did not want to survive, I would, just not like before. With time, I began making deeper connections. In other words, I began making friends. Friends that I could call at any time of the day or night, who would listen to me as I cried and talked about my son. Friends who did not judge my grief. Friends, who TRULY understood how I felt. I continued to go to The Christi Center every Monday evening for several years. I KNOW that I would not still be here if it had not been for these other grieving parents who would share their feelings and the wonderful people who worked there.

As time went on, one of the things that I realized was that I wanted to give back. I became the participant who could talk about my feelings and experiences. I discovered that it felt good to help others navigate this complicated journey. For those reasons, I decided to become a facilitator myself. My hope is that by sharing my own grief journey, I can begin giving newly bereaved parents some hope and help them feel more normal by letting them know I empathize with them.

We will FOREVER be grateful for The Christi Center. We want to give a special thank you to Susan and Don Cox. They have shared with us their precious daughter Christi, their grief journey in losing her, and their wonderful vision for helping others. Thank you from the bottom of our hearts!

CHAPTER

Keri Davila

Loss of Sons Kenny and Paul to MRSA Staph Infections

On March 6, 2008, I got that phone call at 4:00 a.m. that no parent ever wants to get. My 25-year-old son Kenny was in the hospital in Dallas, and I needed to go there. I didn't understand the severity until they told me I needed to come immediately. My son had an abscessed tooth and it led to bacterial endocarditis and MRSA, which went through his bloodstream and attacked his heart. Through a series of unfortunate events, he didn't get to a hospital for treatment until it was too late. His heart could no longer pump the blood to distribute oxygen to his organs, and they began to shut down.

My precious son was placed on morphine about 30 minutes after I arrived from Killeen. I never got to hear his sweet voice again. As he FOUGHT to live, his family and friends sat vigil with him. He died on March 11,

155

about 5:30 a.m., after I had gotten into his hospital bed and told him that Jesus and his grandparents were waiting for him and that I would see him again. His breathing up to that point had been very labored and loud. It seemed that he was waiting for our reassurance that we would be okay before he could go. His breathing seemed to become easier, and he quickly went to be with the Lord.

For those people who have walked this horrible path, you know that you spend the next months just walking through the motions of life. I did what I had to do to survive. I lived in denial, hoping that one day I would wake up from this awful dream. Paul, Kenny's 22-year-old brother, struggled with his brother's death. He kept saying that it should have been him. He wanted to fix me, and I wanted to fix him but we were both broken.

Paul moved to Kerrville, where he started *DJing* and was just starting to feel like he had a future. He had a base of friends who showed him that he could have fun and laugh again. Paul got bitten by a spider on his leg, and it got infected. We went back and forth to the doctor and they treated him with antibiotics. I asked if he had MRSA and he said "Yes," but they had it covered. I trusted them. On Thanksgiving Day in 2009, 20 months after his brother had died, Paul was admitted into the hospital in San Antonio in critical condition. The infection had migrated to his spine, and he became paralyzed. The doctors stated that he needed surgery to clean out the infection and that he would need to go home with a central line and probably get six weeks of IV therapy.

I just knew that God would not take both my boys. I had no fear that he would not survive. Sitting alone in the surgical waiting area, I heard "Code Blue, OR 1." My first thought was, "I wonder how many ORs they have." Soon my son's doctors appeared and told me that he had gone into cardiac arrest, and they couldn't get him back.

At this point, both of my precious children were gone. My joy in life was gone. I walked through the motions in life, but I prayed daily that the good Lord would take me. My only concern was that I didn't want my mother to feel the pain that I was going through; I made a deal with God that I just had to live one day longer than my mother. I had to find a way to live until that point.

I went to a Hospice grief group in Killeen but left less than satisfied. I searched and found a group called Compassionate Friends out of Georgetown, and I went to a meeting. It helped to talk about my boys, but it still wasn't what I needed. Lisa Walters, another mother there who had lost her daughter Lindsay the previous March, told me about The Christi Center that had just started a group in Georgetown. I started going in January 2010.

On the second and fourth Mondays of every month, I find myself getting into my car and driving to Georgetown. I live about an hour from there. It takes me longer in winter because of the darkness and having to dodge the deer and other critters. I often think on those Monday mornings that I don't need to go, but come 5:00 p.m., I'm in the car headed to Georgetown. Many of these nights, I don't really want to talk about anything, but I want to be there to show our new people that you can survive the loss of a loved one. I can't say that the group made me my old self again, but they showed me that my thoughts, feelings, and behaviors were normal, and they walked with me down the path of grief.

I no longer felt alone. When I had those days when all I wanted to do was cry or yell or be angry, there was someone there who I could talk to. These people are now an extension to my family. They have walked this journey with me and shown me that I can survive until the good Lord tells me it is time to meet with my boys again.

I took the training to help facilitate groups because I wanted to give back what Don and Susan Cox gave to me – the hope that you can find joy again in your life. I need to show others, that although this is a group that no one wants to be a member of, it is a group that I am thankful that I have in my life. God bless my dear friends from The Christi Center. God bless Don and Susan Cox. They saved my life. They have shown me that I can feel joy again.

CHAPTER

Betty and Harry Huf

Loss of Son Todd to Pickup Accident

It was May of 1997. I was anxious, nervous, and excited to be moving my parents here from Virginia so I could help my dad care for my terminally ill, handicapped mom. My husband was only too happy to include them in our lives, and our grown kids lived close by and would be able to help us out. We became very busy remodeling our detached garage into an apartment for them. On May 11, Mother's Day, I received a call from my friend Karen. Her son had committed suicide in their home the day they were coming back from a vacation. The horrors were just beginning.

We worked late into the evening on Saturday, May 24, coming in for supper after 10:00 p.m. Afterwards, some stayed to finish a game of three ball. As my son Todd went back to the game room, he said, "Got $3.00 on the pool table—going to make *big bucks!*" I laughed and said, "See you tomorrow—breakfast at 10:00." All my children were happy and healthy, and I would soon have my parents here to live close to me. Life was good. As I usually did, I asked the *Angels* to surround my loved ones and keep them safe. I went to bed, happy and content. In the morning, I was startled awake by my daughter-in-law screaming, "Todd's dead!"

My nightmare had begun. Life as we knew it had ended—the pain and misery began. Todd, the son that I grew up with, the first baby who I had at 17, had been killed when his pickup truck left the road. As I focused on taking care of my parents, I was desperately trying to live without him. Several months into the horrible nightmare, still unable to function, I was just going through the motions—trying to work, trying to help my dad take care of my mom. Not eating, not sleeping, wanting to die. Then my friend Karen and I decided to try the grief support group at The Christi Center.

She had heard about this resource through Victim Services. One Monday evening in August, we went together. Well, we went to the parking lot—and cried. We stayed outside for about an hour and then left. The following week, we went again and sat in the parking lot and cried, leaving again after about an hour. On our third trip, we were sitting in the parking lot trying to convince each other we needed to go in, crying (and a little cussing and yelling), when after a few minutes, someone knocked on our window. Startled, we rolled it down, and a sweet lady (we found out later her name was Loyce) asked, "Are you ladies going to come in?" Guess you know we didn't have a choice. Our *journeys* began—the healing, love, and lifetime friendships.

My mother's health continued to decline, and she was placed on hospice care in March 1999. Two weeks after my brother Richard had been to visit her and say his goodbyes, he died in an automobile accident. Now there was new grief. I had become my mother's main caregiver, which left little time for me to attend The Christi Center meetings. Also, about a year after her son died, Karen moved to Oregon to escape the daily reminders of his death. My mother lived until March 2001—another loss.

In July 2001, I was sent to the hospital, thinking that I was having a heart attack, only to find out that it was a panic attack and nervous breakdown. In September, I started going back to The Christi Center and continued to go. This I will do for the rest of my life. Now realizing that *this* is what saved my life, I began helping out when we opened the center here in Georgetown. I went through the facilitator training and now am helping the new broken hearts who attend. My life will always include time for my grief and for others who are beginning this life of nightmares. I will *never* be able to understand how anyone can walk this journey alone.

More than 23 years ago, Susan and Don saved my life—along with all the help from the family at The Christi Center. I can only pray that I am helping someone else.

CHAPTER

Elaine Miller

Loss of Husband Roland to Suicide

On a recommendation from my pastor, I called For the Love of Christi in the spring of 1999. My husband of 14 years had taken his life in November 1998, but he was not found until late December of that year. My three children, ages 13, 11, and 6, and I were in shock and grief, barely keeping things together. When I phoned For the Love of Christi, a sympathetic, compassionate volunteer listened as I blurted out my situation. She asked a few questions, but mainly let me share my story and the struggles I was experiencing. She told me about a spouse's group that met on Sunday afternoons at their house on Hancock Drive.

In a few weeks, I gathered the courage to walk in the front door and attend my first group. That first time I listened and cried for the hour and a half that it met. It was such a relief to be around others who had lost a spouse. I wasn't losing my mind, and I was going to be able to survive this horrible loss. Most Sundays I spent part of my afternoon at the house, telling and retelling my story. Very slowly the pain and sorrow began to fade as I walked this journey with others.

The Christi Center had a group for children who had experienced loss. Volunteer social workers from University of Texas and St. Edward's University helped with these groups. They split the kids into two groups – teens and younger ones. My two older children found comfort in being with others who had lost a parent. It was the only place where they didn't feel weird for having only one living parent. My younger one enjoyed the activities and games the group played. He didn't share much but felt very comfortable with the other kids.

My family attended groups at The Christi Center for about six months. It was a place where we felt loved and accepted while our healing process began. It was a warm and caring place that enabled us to gain a little peace as we walked our grief journey.

Many years later I went back to graduate school for a Master's degree in counseling. The Christi Center was one of the first places I contacted about doing my internship there. I got to spend almost a year giving back to the place that had helped my family so much. Working with grieving people has been a joy at The Christi Center. It has allowed me to come alongside those who are hurting and give them hope for a new life; different from the old, but one that can be as rich as before the loss. Currently, I lead a spouse's and suicide group in Georgetown.

The Christi Center is a special place. It offers love, support, and hope for those who are suffering the loss of a loved one(s).

CHAPTER

Natalie and John Perry

Loss of Son Blake to a Four-Wheeler Accident

February 24, 2008, was a day our lives were forever changed. Memories are now a before or after that day. A date in time that should have had no importance to our lives is now one of the most significant. It's the day Blake, our sweet boy, passed from this earth into heaven. Blake was a 20-year-old man home on leave from the military. He had been deployed for five months prior to the accident. Our son had enjoyed riding his 4-wheeler for many years. They day of the accident, he lost control of a 4-wheeler and collided with a parked wrecker. The following days are every parent's worst night-mare, and we were living it.

Planning a funeral for our sweet son was something I never imagined having to experience, but we were doing just that. Family and friends were there to help us as much as they could, and for that I will be forever grateful. However, they would eventually return home to their families and their own lives. They would kiss their children goodnight and hug them a little tighter, while my family went to bed with a hole in our hearts. We couldn't wake up from this nightmare. We were just going through the motions, but not really living. Knowing we needed to find help, our daughter had given us the name of a local Austin support group for grieving parents, For the Love of Christi.

Three months after Blake's death, John and I attended our first Monday night meeting. We sat in a room with three amazing couples: Don and Susan Cox, Jimmy and Mary Shields, and Tommy and Susan Trammell, each of them knowing our pain, as they, too, had suffered the loss of a child. We shared our story of Blake's life and tragic death. As we talked, not making sense at times, they listened and felt our pain. They understood the hurt we felt, the loss we were experiencing. These couples gave us hope going forward in the days, weeks, and months that followed. They were there with open arms on the days we didn't know if we would make it. They taught us to be gentle with ourselves because grief takes a toll on you emotionally, physically, and spiritually. So, every Monday night we went to our support group for the next two years. I felt like this group was my lifeline and I needed these friends' love and support to make it through another week without my sweet angel. This is how I survived week to week.

The Christi Center is a safe place to discuss all that you are going through. Knowing that others have similar issues with coping but are still able to give support to one another at the same time, you realize that you are not going crazy. You bond with one another and form very close relationships with each other, giving each other hope. The days became a little less difficult through a process that brings about change ever so slightly over time, a process, I am sure, that could have never happened without all the love and support from the people at The Christi Center, especially Don and Susan.

A few years ago, I decided it was my time to give back to other parents. I took Erin's class and became a facilitator for The Christi Center in Georgetown to offer hope and support for new parents entering these doors for the first time.

CHAPTER

Deborah and Michael Peterson

Loss of Son Timothy to Cardiac Arrest Caused by a Blood Disorder and Liver Complications

Our son Timothy passed away at the age of 29 on August 6, 2012, due to cardiac arrest caused by a blood disorder and liver complications. Tim spent the last week of his life in the Transplant Intensive Care Unit at the Memorial Research Hospital in San Antonio, Texas. Michael and I were at his side when he left this world.

A colleague of Michael's, who had lost a daughter, told him about The Christi Center. Three weeks after Tim's passing, we decided to attend a meeting at the Georgetown location. Although, we were still in shock from the loss of our son, the one thing we remember was the gentleman who spoke of his daughter's passing in days (which were over 3,000). On our way home, I kept thinking, I hope this isn't what I will be doing for the rest of my life. At our first visit, Jimmy told the group to attend at least three meetings because group dynamics change; in 2019, we are still attending.

As a result of attending many meetings since that first one, we have learned that there is life after loss. At the onset of our journey, it was very difficult to speak about Timothy, and our memories were focused on the day he passed away. As we attended more meetings, it became easier to speak about Timothy while in groups with similar losses. Our memories of him have changed to the happier times in his life, which we share with our three daughters and five grandchildren.

Dave and Lou Seideman help grieving members by offering a weekend stay at Charlie's Place on Lake Buchanan for a men's retreat twice a year and a mother's retreat in the spring along with retreats for spouses, teens, and Kids Who Kare. Additionally, Don and Susan Cox, George and Nat Lane, and Jim (now deceased) and Beverly McVey offer the use of their homes in Ruidoso, New Mexico, for retreats to help in the grieving process. I have taken classes to become a facilitator, and I'm now in the position where I'm able to assist others who are traveling down their own grieving journey.

Timothy was our oldest child, and we also have three daughters. We asked them to add to our story based on their perspective as his sisters.

Heather, our oldest daughter, was at the hospital when Timothy coded for the second time. She was a new mother of a 4-month-old girl.

I was there at the very end with my parents when my brother Tim passed. I was trying to pretend that this wasn't really happening, trying to stay strong, and be present for the sake of my parents. In the days following, I had my husband to lean on. He had lost a brother years before and was very supportive. I made a vow to myself and my family that we would spend every chance we could together, to never let any reason keep us apart. I vowed to never, never let anything come between us, no fight, no argument. This has been very tough at times, seeing as how we are all very strongly opinionated women, but we all made that commitment to each other and have kept it. We are closer now than we have ever been. My family knows that life is too short and could change in an instant. There are times I get sad and miss Tim, especially when I think about how much he would have loved my kids and how they are missing out on such a great person. One Christmas, I made all the kids a book with pictures of Tim doing the things he loved and we bring it out from time to time and talk about him. One day we will all see him again, and I can't wait!

Michelle, our middle daughter, and her 5-year-old son Kdyn moved back home just as Timothy did a few months earlier. Tim frequently took Kdyn fishing or to visit with some of his friends' kids.

I was on my way to San Antonio when I got the call from Dad, a moment I will never forget. Trying to piece together the reality that my brother was really sick, how this could have happened, and how I was going to tell my son. The week leading up to his funeral, I remember telling my son that sometimes God needs the ones we love in heaven more than we do here on earth. The next few weeks/month were rough. Kdyn was really close with Tim, and having to explain that his uncle wasn't coming back was harder than I thought, so we visited his grave a lot, having picnics, talking and just remembering his big heart and sweet soul. As the months went on and the reality set in, the visits got shorter, and I was slowly accepting it. There are times I feel bad because I have accepted that he is gone, but I know now that we have the best guardian angel. Now, almost eight years later, there are times I get sad, but I remember all the fun we had and all the memories our family shares. My sisters and I keep Tim's memory alive and talk about him with our children. He would have loved them, and they would have adored him. We are all very close and are always here for each other for everything. Best support system there is—FAMILY!

Ashley, our youngest, lives in the panhandle of Texas with her husband and two children.

I would never have thought my last words to my brother would be "See you on the flip side. I love you!" Apparently, my subconscious was more in tune with what would happen in the days proceeding. You won't forget where and what exactly was consuming your day when you get the call that ends it abruptly. As Mom always says, everything happens for a reason. At that point in time I questioned *why*, but would have my eyes opened in the weeks to come. My husband and I had been trying to start our family for almost two years at my brother's passing. Lo and behold, within the same month we conceived our first daughter—not how I would have liked it, but again, everything happens for a reason. I would have loved for my children to meet and know the brother I grew up with. He would have a ball picking on them just as he did us girls. My oldest sister has done a great job keeping the promise she made us, to always be there for each other. The three of us will always be there for each other, no doubt. Till we all see you on the flip side, Tim, we love you!

CHAPTER

Sandi and Larry Rebecek

Loss of Son Jake to an Automobile Accident

Our journey began on December 17, 1998. Our youngest son, Jacob (Jake), was a 19- year-old freshman at Texas A&M. Until that day everything in our world felt almost perfect. Jerod, our oldest son, was a firefighter, and Larry and I were enjoying being parents of an Aggie. Jake was ecstatic over being away at college. He was there with many of his high school friends, but had also met many new folks. But, then ...

Jake came home for semester break on Tuesday, December 15. He and five friends were leaving the following Thursday, December 17, for their annual ski trip. That morning, we got up early to see them off. Larry was dropping him and a friend off at the home of Jake's best friend. I gave him a kiss and a hug and reminded him to *be wise*. In his most sarcastic, yet joking, tone he said, "OK, Mom, I won't kill my friends today." Little did I know that this was the last hug, the last kiss, and the last time I would hear his voice or see him. Approximately 10 hours later, the right rear tire on the Ford Explorer that Jake was driving blew out. He lost control of the car and it flipped over multiple times. From what we understand, he was killed instantly. Although the other two boys in the car were injured, they survived.

In mid-January 1999, we went to College Station to clean out Jake's dorm room. It was hard to believe that we had moved him into that room just five months earlier. A few days later, we walked into The Christi Center for the first time. We were welcomed by Judy Cooper, Mike and Loyce Allen, and, of course, Don and Susan. We immediately felt at home. It was like we had been traveling in a foreign land and finally found a place where the same language was spoken. The people at The Christi Center understood us. They helped us understand our "new normal," and we attended meetings faithfully for several years.

Eventually, we were asked to serve on the board and also trained as facilitators. Facilitating is our main way of giving back and offering hope to those parents who continue to walk through the door. We have also helped out with the Kids Who Kare and Teen retreats, painted the annex, helped with fundraising efforts, and Larry designed and hand-crafted the heart sign that hangs in front of The Christi Center Hancock Drive building in Austin.

We still have our bad days, but they are not near as often or as bad as they were early on. When a bad day rolls around, we can lean on each other, but also know there is a community of zebras we can call on who will listen and offer a hug. We don't know where we would be had we not found out about The Christi Center. As Sandi has said, "The Christi Center is the best place for the worst possible reason."

December 18, 2017, marked a new chapter in our lives. On that day, Jake was gone from the earth longer than he was on it. We felt the emotional strain of that day, but we knew that our Christi Center family would be there to help us through that day and all the days that follow.

171

CHAPTER

Mary and Jimmy Shields

Loss of Daughter Amy to an Automobile Accident

On October 17, 2004, we lost Amy, our 21-year-old daughter, in an auto accident in Nacogdoches, Texas. We had been planning for her college graduation celebration, but instead we began to plan her funeral. At her visitation, a couple we had never met before handed Mary a note with information about The Christi Center. They were Kathy and Bob McCleskey, whose daughter Shannon had died five years prior to Amy. Three weeks after the death of Amy, we contacted the McCleskeys and told them we needed help. This couple brought us to The Christi Center in Austin that November.

The day we walked through the doors of The Christi Center, we did so as two very confused, depressed, and broken human beings. We heard laughter and thought we were in the wrong place. Little did we know that the people we heard laughing were just farther down the road on their grief journey. These people, especially Susan and Don Cox, became our family's lifeline. We discovered that first evening that we would not have to walk alone in our grief journey. The Christi Center is a safe place where we could share our worse feelings, fears, and frustrations. Over time, we found HOPE for the future, and the ability to again experience JOY in our lives.

Two years after our arrival at The Christi Center, we were both trained as group facilitators. We also were honored to serve as board members for this wonderful organization. For five years, we traveled from Georgetown to Austin for the weekly support meetings. We also brought new members with us. We would leave Georgetown by 6:00 p.m. in order to arrive before the 7:00 p.m. meeting start time. Many nights we were not home until 10:00 p.m. or later. The distance and time kept many others from receiving the various grief support services. In 2010 The Christi Center began offering adult grief support services in Georgetown. We are blessed to have this facility in Georgetown to better serve the suburbs of North Austin.

We truly believe The Christi Center saved our family. We have shared this with many people and will continue to do so. We are so grateful for two special people, Susan and Don Cox, who are creating a legacy of LOVE AND HOPE that will live on in the many lives they have touched. Thank you and we love you!

There are thousands of real life stories just like ours, and, unfortunately, there will be thousands more.

CHAPTER

Charles Walters and Lisa Walters Brown

Loss of Daughter Lindsay to Criminally Negligent Homicide by an Impaired Driver

No parent ever expects to get a call in the middle of the night from a hospital asking if you are the parent of "_____," but it wasn't our daughter they were calling about. We were then told to call the police station only to find out there was a fatality on the scene of a traffic incident. No, it couldn't be Lindsay, only to get the call as we were driving to College Station that "Yes", it was our precious daughter Lindsay who was the fatality at the scene.

Lindsay was two months shy of graduating Summa Cum Laude in four years with her Master of Accounting degree from Texas A&M University. She had already accepted an auditor's position with one of the top four accounting firms in the world. She was excited about her future and looking forward to her next chapter in life.

The journey began. We embarked upon a life sentence. We lost Lindsay, our one and only child. God blessed us with an Angel Who Walked This Earth. We knew Lindsay's heart and her love for the Lord, so although we know she is Home with the Lord, it does not take away any of the pain, hurt, and missing that we must endure forever in this life.

It was almost a month before I returned to work and even longer for Lisa, her mom. I would make it through a work day and then crash. I eventually lost my job and ended up doing part-time jobs until I retired. We have PTSD from the trauma of Lindsay's death, and Lisa developed autoimmune health issues directly related to the effects of grief.

We both tried professional counseling but found that it was not beneficial for us. A very kind and generous couple, Jimmy and Mary Shields, introduced us to The Christi Center in Austin, and we started attending meetings six to seven months after Lindsay's death. They would drive us to the meetings in Austin every Monday night. They did this for us until The Christi Center opened the Georgetown campus.

Although we were raw and in the densest fog, we gained comfort from the knowledge of others who had been on the grief journey longer. It somehow brought comfort and perspective to hear a fellow griever tell his or her story. We realized that we were not crazy and that it was okay to cry and be angry. Friendships established through The Christi Center go beyond the walls of the building. We not only lost our daughter, but due to the circumstances, we were also facing a possible trial.

On July 13, 2011, at approximately 3:30 p.m., we were informed that the woman who killed Lindsay had accepted a plea bargain. We were to be in court in Bryan, Texas, at 9:00 a.m. the next morning on July 14, 2011 (that would have been our precious Lindsay's 24th birthday). There were approximately 30 people affiliated with The Christi Center at the court-house in Bryan that morning to support us. This is just one example of the understanding of fellow Christi Center members and how they reach out in support of their fellow grievers.

The Christi Center offers a peer-based support that allows one to just listen or to interact with others who are walking a similar journey. There is no monetary cost to attend the meetings; the cost is paid through the heartbreaking loss of a loved one. Although one is never the same, The Christi Center provides a safe place to share and learn that although a loss such as this changes one forever, one can learn to live a changed life.

We are forever thankful and grateful to Don and Susan Cox for their courage in establishing and continuing such a terrific organization as The Christi Center. The Christi Center is a true blessing and gift to those in the Austin, Texas, area that provides a free and non-prejudiced source for grief support.

8

Member Stories

CHAPTER

Olivia and Rolando Andrade

Loss of Son Silas to Hydrocephalus and Baby Daughter to Miscarriage

Rolando and I first met in 2001 and married in 2008. Our oldest son Vance, born in 2005, was the ring bearer at our wedding. Our family grew to four when we had Silas on November 11, 2009. Both our sons were born with a rare disorder called hydrocephalus, which is sometimes better known as water on the brain. Sadly, it has no cure. We made sure to give them a normal, happy life with trips to Port Aransas, video games, summer camps at the park down the street from our Pflugerville home, and playing with the family dog, a wonderful black Labrador named Boudreaux.

Silas had a love of hats, all kinds of hats—fedoras, baseball caps, you name it! He also loved trucks and his John Deere tractors. Silas was all boy, and since Rolando owns his own private landscaping company, Andrade Landscaping, Silas always wanted to go to work with Daddy. He had his own wheelbarrow and would follow Daddy around proudly wearing his company t-shirt and hat. He would get so mad if he didn't get to go with Daddy to his outdoor office.

Silas' fourth birthday was on November 11, 2013, and at the time, I was two months pregnant. For his birthday, Rolando surprised him by building him a monster truck track in our backyard. Less than one week later, on November 17, 2013, Silas died. Shortly after that, his dog passed, too.

On that Saturday of his death, Silas complained of having a terrible headache, and Tylenol wasn't helping relieve the pain. We weren't all that worried because he had recently had an MRI that looked fine. To comfort him, Rolando was holding him when he suddenly yelled, "Daddy, I see sparkles!" and collapsed in his arms. We called EMS, and I rode in the ambulance with Silas to the hospital. We called Rolando's mom and sister to ask if they would come to be with Vance, so Rolando could meet us at Dell Children's Hospital. We had about ten family members who had come to join us when we were told Silas was not going to make it.

The pain of losing Silas was unbearable. Had it not been for our baby girl, Sophia, in my belly, I'm sure I would have either been drinking or self-medicating. But in February 2014, within three months of Silas' death, I lost our baby girl at five months along. I will always be grateful for her. Within such a short time, we went from having two beautiful children and one on the way to just one.

I only took off three weeks of work after Silas died. When I lost my daughter, it was for much longer. I don't know how we've gotten through it all without going off the deep end. Our family needed something to survive, but we didn't know what. One day, a co-worker handed me a brochure about The Christi Center and told me to go. She knew them well as she had lost her whole family before she discovered the organization that saved her.

At first Rolando didn't want to go to The Christi Center, but finally agreed. We started attending meetings in Georgetown, but now we go regularly to the Hancock location where there are other parents who have lost children. They helped me understand the different stages of grief, how we all grieve differently, and how different my grief was from Rolando's.

At the meetings, we were told to write in a journal every day. For six months I wrote my feelings down every day, describing what I wanted to say to Silas or to just vent that he was gone. I was worried about what I would remember about him, but the facilitators told me not to worry; Silas and those memories would always be there. Reliving the loss is so hard, but we went to the meetings and shared our story with other parents who lost their kids, too. They really understood. We realized that if we hadn't gone to The Christi Center, we certainly would have divorced.

My pattern is to try and shut it out and just work hard. It doesn't work very well because I think about Silas all the time. When I get in my car and listen to music that he loved, I lose it. It helps, but it also hurts so much. It was rough at first because Rolando was so angry about Silas all the time, and I didn't understand how to support him. He just wanted to work in the yard. But we still had Vance, and Christmas was coming quickly. We had to move forward for his sake.

Sometimes, when Rolando would be really down, I would be feeling normal, or vice versa. Thankfully, we never were down at the same time. To this day, we both still grieve —but never at the same time. By attending the meetings, Rolando learned that his grief story was similar to that of Don Cox. All at once we were at the hospital early on a Sunday morning, and by dinner time, Silas was gone. Don had experienced the same sudden loss when Christi died, which left him floundering. Rolando told me that after that night's conversation, he realized he was in the same boat as Don was when Christi died. Both had to figure out what he was going to do each day, how to manage their businesses, take care of their wives and surviving sons, and navigate their grief.

Since Silas went to heaven, we do lots of things to remember him. In the December right after he died, my uncle and I went to The Christi Center Candlelight Remembrance Service and hung a heart ornament with his photo on the tree. One of Silas' favorite things to do was to watch the Pflugerville Christmas parade, so in December 2014, we created a float in his honor called The Silas Express. Around his November birthday and angel day, we sell t-shirts and wristbands with his name on them to raise money, so that other children get presents during the holidays. We have gone to Dave & Buster's, Silas' favorite place, to play games, have chocolate brownies with ice cream, and still buy him birthday and Christmas presents.

Because Vance has the same condition as Silas, we worry about him and what he is thinking. It's tough to think about his future, and he is scared that he might die, too. We took him to the Kids Who Kare meetings for a while, but he doesn't really talk about his brother's death very much. We try to make life as normal as possible for him, so we continue to take our Port Aransas trips. Silas, who was cremated, travels with us.

In our front room hangs a colorful quilt made from Silas' favorite t-shirts. Some of my friends from high school got together and pitched in to have the quilt made for us. It includes t-shirts from his dad's landscape business, along with Spider-man, Speedy Gonzales, and UT Longhorns. When Silas passed away, many, many people were there for us. I hadn't spoken with many of them in years, but they knew what we were going through (how devastating it was and still is), so they did something very thoughtful for us. It's the best gift ever!

Life continued to move on, and three years after the passing of Silas, we found out we were pregnant again! I was scared out of my mind to have another child, but as Rolando would say, "We can't live in a bubble." Due to our history, the doctors watched us very carefully and by some miracle (for which I thank Silas), we had a beautiful boy on September 13, 2016. He came seven weeks early, so he had to stay in the NICU, but he is very healthy.

Xander Quinn Andrade is a bundle of joy, and I love to see Rolando's and Vance's eyes light up when they see him. I know that Silas would have loved to have been a big brother, but seeing our beautiful baby boy smile when his daddy and Vance walk in the room makes me so happy!

CHAPTER

Cheryl Booth

Loss of Daughter Daisy to a Heart Anomaly

April 20, 2006, started off as a day like any other; in fact, it was a really good day. It was the Thursday after Easter, and we had spaghetti for dinner—Daisy's favorite. She knew all her spelling words for her test the next day. Bedtime was not a struggle. At 9:30 p.m., Daisy called from the top of the stairs that she needed help with something. She had gone into her high school sister Haylie's room and gotten a little box of her earrings. Daisy was putting them in the ears of all her Beanie Babies, but couldn't get this one earring in. Usually, I would have scolded her because she wasn't supposed to be in her sister's room and was supposed to be asleep. But that night I didn't. I put the earrings in the puppy's ear and then got Daisy into bed, surrounded by all her Beanie Babies.

She talked about her friend Jennifer and how she was afraid of storms, but that she wasn't anymore. I told her I was glad, and that she was always safe

182

in her home. Daisy was very afraid of the dark. She slept with a nightlight, a little flower lamp, and the hall light on with her door open. As I rubbed her back and stroked her hair, I thought how beautiful she looked.

At 10:00 p.m., I heard a swishing noise outside, and the moment I turned on the back lights, our electricity went out. Haylie and I walked up the 15 stairs, calling Daisy's name, Haylie with her phone light on and me holding a little candle, never thinking she was at the top of the stairs dying. Although we didn't know it at the time, the noise we heard was her last three breaths.

I learned later that Daisy's artery was concave and not round. She got scared running down the hall and didn't get enough oxygen to her heart. It was a condition we could never have known about. She had been a healthy little girl.

My life as I knew it ended that night. When people talk about a broken heart, I know what they mean. I thought my heart was actually broken, it hurt so much.

Haylie had a friend who was killed in a car accident a year or so before. I went to the funeral as support for Haylie and her friends. When Daisy died, I asked Haylie for the mom's number, just to talk to another mom who had lost a child, and because I thought I was actually losing my mind. Martha told me about The Christi Center where they had been going. I went for the first time in June. It was so hard that I couldn't even say Daisy's name for a long time when we passed the heart around at the meeting and said who we were there "For the Love of."

I went every Monday for many, many years. As hard as it was, I had to go and be around other moms. I don't go often now, but every now and then, I still need to be there to meet the new mom and hear her child's name, to show support. It's important to be able to say your child's name out loud.

Unfortunately, there are always new moms and dads there. I don't know where I would be today without The Christi Center and the love of Susan and Don. There, you can be with other parents who have lost children and not be judged or asked, "Aren't you over it yet?" We would often say we could write a book of all the stupid things people say—how they don't understand the greatness of the pain. I love hearing the stories of other parents' children, love hearing their names, and I love talking about Daisy and saying her name. The people I have met there have become my friends, and I would do anything for them. I know Daisy and all those kids are up there taking care of each other, and it makes me smile to think of it.

It's hard to find that "new normal," but without the love and support of Susan and Don, The Christi Center, and all the moms and dads I have met, I don't know where I would be today. Daisy is the first thing I think about in the morning and the last thing at night. I thank God every day for her. I miss her every day, but now I can think of those moments we had and smile. I know she is always with me. Where else would she be?

Daisy sends me lots of signs, like a penny when I need it the most. I know she would want me to smile and be happy, so I'm trying—For the Love of Daisy.

CHAPTER

Jenny Boyd

Loss of Mother Maxi and Brother Melvin to an Automobile Accident

I don't remember anything about the head-on collision that occurred on July 28, 1997, the day my mother, my brother Melvin, and I headed to my favorite beach on the Big Island of Hawaii. I was 11-years-old at the time, Melvin was 12, and we had lived on the Big Island since we were babies. My dad lived nearby but had not been a major presence in my life. Mom and Melvin were all I had, and Hawaii was the only home I knew.

I woke up in a hospital bed to a circle of relatives—my dad, Aunt Sue from Texas, and my Aunt Jane and grandmother from Michigan. They told me that the crash had killed my mom and Melvin, as well as the driver of the other car. Somehow, I had survived. They explained my injuries, which included two broken legs, a broken arm, broken nose, and whiplash. The doctor initially estimated that I would not walk for a year.

Aunt Sue showed me a picture of the house in Austin, Texas, where I would go to live with her. I had met her family only once, when they took a trip to Hawaii. They were practically strangers, and Texas seemed like a foreign country.

On August 15, I was wheeled out of the hospital and straight to the airport. My new life was exactly that—a completely new life. Shortly after arriving in Austin, I started seventh grade. Fortunately, Sue and Dennis registered me with their son at a very small and welcoming Montessori school of only 30 students. Since I was new to the school and on crutches, the teachers asked another student, Anjali, to help me out on the first day of school. She remains my best friend to this day.

Sue and Dennis took me to a therapist and to the Kids Who Kare weekly meetings at The Christi Center. I dreaded the therapist appointments and reluctantly answered her questions without really letting her in. But at The Christi Center, I sat with a group of kids who shared stories and feelings similar to my own. They were experiencing the same things I was. Not just the pain and sadness, but also the more confusing aspects of grief, such as guilt and emotional numbness. I was surprised that The Christi Center was not a sorrowful place. It had a cozy, loving atmosphere, even though everyone there was suffering from a terrible loss. We started each meeting by passing a purple glass heart, saying our names and "I'm here For the Love of _____."

In the beginning, that statement was enough sharing for me. Every time I said it out loud, it became more real. Some people were reticent, like me, while others talked openly and even got sidetracked into other topics. At first, I marveled at how they could chat casually about some insignificant topic. I wondered how they were not consumed by their grief. I was getting a sneak peek into how people who suffered similar tragedies and, with time and support, eventually start feeling normal again. As Susan Cox once said, you find a "new normal."

The Christi Center set up simple, yet meaningful, activities as a way to honor our loved ones and help us cope. I recall creating a Memory Box, painting it, and filling it with photos. Another time we made a grand quilt with a patch for each of our loved ones. Back then, the organization was just starting their teen group, and as I got older, I moved into those meetings. The annual retreats were very special, sharing a cabin with other girls in the group. One of the most powerful ceremonies I attended was their annual Candlelight Remembrance Service. Hundreds of people held candles representing the loved ones they had lost. After a moment of silence, we were instructed, "Blow out the candle when you are ready."

It was so simple, yet so hard to do, to let go. I was a teenager, convinced I was already over it and wouldn't feel anything over a candle. However, when I looked down at the flame, I realized I was not ready. It took me some time to face the truth of my relationship with my family, acknowledge that they were gone forever, and say goodbye to them. When I finally blew out that candle, I felt closure. I hadn't been able to go to the funeral, and even after several years of missing them and coming to terms with their absence, I had never actually said "Good-bye" until that moment.

When I entered the University of Texas, I continued to go back to The Christi Center to support others, helping facilitate the Teen Group or the Mother's or Spouse Groups. Some of the mothers who had lost a child told me they found comfort in seeing how I was healing and that it gave them hope that their living children would do the same. I am now 29, living with my husband Taylor and two dogs on a beautiful vegetable farm in Jefferson, Oregon. We met in the Peace Corps in Paraguay and spent a few years traveling and working throughout South America and southern Africa before returning to his hometown to start a farm. I work as a Bilingual Instructional Assistant and Program Coordinator at the local elementary school, where I also run a school garden.

We recently took a trip to Hawaii, my first time back since the accident. I could not stop smiling as we stepped outside the airport. The warm island air, the fragrant plumerias, the lush green all around—it was home. Even though I was separated from this place by a devastating loss and eighteen years of a different life, the memories that flooded back brought comfort more than pain. I took this to mean that I have reached my "new normal."

There is no doubt that after the immense loss I experienced as a child, The Christi Center provided me with something not available anywhere else.

They offered me a place of comfort with others who were going through similar pain and helped me to become better as a teenager, and now as an adult. In a culture that generally hides death and grief, they created ceremonies and rituals to honor the dead and help heal the living. They taught me that in times of tragedy, the greatest comfort can be the simple camaraderie of another person, someone who knows loss and who is willing to listen.

Robert Bryant

Loss of Mother and Father Irene and John Bryant to Homicide

My mother and father were murdered by a serial killer. This fit, active, retired couple in their early 80s had just finished a forest walk on a beautiful October day in western North Carolina. The killer beat Mom to death near their car at the trailhead. The autopsy stated that the weapon was likely a tire iron and that she had fractures on the front of her skull. The back of her skull was crushed, causing her death. Both hands and arms had broken bones, defensive injuries. Her killer dragged her body into the forest and covered it with branches. She wasn't found for three weeks.

The killer kidnapped Dad and held him for a day or two—we don't know. The killer had prepared his van with chains and locks to secure his victims. He stole $300 with Dad's ATM card. A hunter found Dad's skeletal remains the following February 2008, 100 miles away. The autopsy showed he had been shot once in the temple. His clothes were found months later at a third forest site.

Separately, on New Year's Day in 2008, a 24-year-old woman was kidnapped from a hiking trail in Georgia. After three days, a manhunt led police to her killer and his van. By a plea, in exchange for a life sentence, he led police to her body. His van contained evidence of other crimes. Police identified DNA from three other victims—my mother, father, and a woman from Florida.

The killer had abused the Florida woman for two or three days and stole $700 from her ATM. Hunters found her naked body covered with brush. The killer had cut off her head and hands and burned them with her clothes in his campfire. From the ashes, crime technicians recovered a bra hook, teeth from a zipper, and a few fragments of bone. He was charged and found guilty of murder. A Florida jury sentenced him to death, and he is now on death row.

Five years after murdering my parents, the killer made a deal and pled guilty to the charges and received an additional five life sentences for their deaths.

How does one become *normal* again after such horrors are committed against the people you love? At first, I felt numb. I couldn't sleep. I had recurring nightmares of those woods. I drank so I could *sleep*. I couldn't remember things; I wasn't mentally present. People would honk at my driving, and I wouldn't know why. I would lash out in anger without reason. I was anxious and fearful in public around strangers. I stayed in, becoming more and more isolated. Some months later, the memorial service was over, the estate was resolved, and the law enforcement and media activities wound down. When those distracting tasks were gone, I was left with only my grief. My friends saw my distress and wanted to help but didn't know how. My grief made people uncomfortable.

An FBI's Victim Services Representative in North Carolina called a colleague in Austin to find help for me. She gave me the contact information for The Christi Center. About nine months after the murders in 2008, I went to my first meeting. I felt so broken in that circle. When the heart was passed to me and it was my turn to speak, I shook as I told them my mother and father had been murdered. As I heard other stories, heartbreaking stories, of other peoples' losses and grief, I didn't feel so alone. When it was over, I was hugged. I had never met these people before, and they hugged me.

I started attending the Crime Victim's Group and told them all the bloody details, the sequence of events, the mounting horrors, my search for my father's body, going to the places where their bodies were found, nightmares, anxiety, and fear. After some time, I could talk about the media attention, the court proceedings, and the small kindnesses of strangers. I listened to the other crime victims' stories, and their stories led me to new insights about my own experience. Sometimes, I could even briefly forget my own grief as it was displaced by the compassion I felt for others in the group.

It has been a rocky road. There have been setbacks, new revelations, and new hurts. But things have gotten better. Now the facts are just facts. They don't stab at the heart as they once did. After eight years, I still go to meetings to hear other peoples' stories and, also, to talk about the echoes from the crime that well back up now and again. Through helping others in their grief, I have helped myself. Now when I remember my parents, I am no longer overwhelmed by grief. Instead, I feel their love. I am grateful to be part of The Christi Center family.

CHAPTER

Arron Cargo

Loss of Wife Janelle to Breast Cancer

Janelle and I met in the third grade in Capitan, New Mexico, a town famous for Billy the Kid. We never dated in high school and when she went to New Mexico College, I headed to Austin in 1998 to study engineering at the University of Texas. I subscribed to the work hard,/play hard philosophy. We kept in touch over the years, but it wasn't until 2008 that Janelle and I started spending time together. She would come to Austin or I would go back home to visit my parents and see Janelle. We also traveled together to Colorado and California. She always wanted to go places to explore history she loved. Janelle majored in history and art and she particularly loved South American history. If you look around my home now, you will see many pieces from her collections.

At only 28-years–old, Janelle did not fit the typical age group for breast cancer and so they did not catch it until the cancer was already at Stage 2. Over the next couple of years, she dealt with the radiation and chemo treatments, and then doctors declared her cured. She could now say she was a cancer survivor. During this time, we took a trip to San Juan, Colorado, and although Janelle thought the chemo had made her sterile, it was then that we conceived our daughter Bella.

When she and I went to the oncologist, the doctor suggested she terminate the pregnancy, warning her that pregnancy did a lot to hormone levels and could cause the cancer to come back. The doctor even said, "You don't want to die and leave him and a 10-year-old child." Terminating the pregnancy was not an option, and she did not like the comment, as well. I told her whatever she chose would be okay with me, and she said, "I got this." Nine months later, we welcomed our daughter Bella.

Because I had a good income and there were job opportunities for her in Austin, Janelle and Bella moved here. I never chose this for Janelle, but she decided she wanted to stay at home with Bella. We eventually bought our own home in Crestview with a huge yard for a dog. Moving was very stressful and while I was at work, she would be at home unpacking. We had been working hard, and I didn't think much of it when she complained about her back hurting.

The first night we were in our new place, we ordered pizza and then crashed. Janelle woke me up at 2:30 a.m. "I want to go to the hospital," she said. Her symptoms sounded like bad indigestion, but I took her to Seton Main where the doctors said her symptoms sounded like gallstones.

While Janelle held Bella on her lap, they did a sonogram. I should have known something was wrong because the tech took forever – taking repeated pictures and measurements of something. She then took her to get a CT scan, and when the doctor and tech came back into the room, the doctor said, "You have cancer in your liver and spine…and it's bad." Janelle lost it. In the ER, doctors focus on stopping you from dying. When the doctor followed that with "You just need to be made comfortable," it was the wrong thing to say. Janelle immediately said she wanted to go home.

Things are fuzzy after that. I didn't know a lot about cancer then, but feel that someone should have done a better job of monitoring her. We connected with Texas Oncology, and even though she was at stage 4, we were told they could give her a couple of years. The immediate concern was the tumors in her liver as they grow quickly; instead, they treated the cancer in her spine first. I am a software engineer and work with numbers, so my job was to help her understand the options and treatments. She does not work that way and did not want to hear about statistics, etc. When you have stage 4 cancer, you can't just go in and get rid of it. You have to try to stop it. With Janelle, at first, they gave her treatments that had easier side effects; but those cells are always mutating, and then you have to switch medications. It gets harder and harder until you have no choice but to do chemo.

She had told me when her cancer came back that she wanted me to allow her whatever time she could have with Bella. When it became clear that she no longer could be a mother to Bella, she wanted to quit. She had undergone two and a half years of treatment and decided to stop.

We got married when she was diagnosed the second time; I cannot bear to look at our wedding photos because I never wanted this for her or for her to have to get married that way. We had only been married for four years when it was clear the end was close. Janelle wanted to go back to New Mexico, but the doctors told her she might not survive the trip. Her sister Ashley, who was 15 years younger, lived with us for two years and never left Janelle's side. On December 15, 2014, we loaded Janelle into the car and took her where she wanted to be. Six days later, on December 21, 2014, surrounded by her family and home health staff, she died. No one had any gifts for anyone that Christmas, except for Janelle who had spent her last week running around buying gifts for all of us.

Bella and I returned to Texas on New Year's Eve, now having to learn how to be just the two of us. We had taken Bella to Wonders & Worries when her mom was first diagnosed. After losing Janelle and my dad to pancreatic cancer in the same year, they suggested I go to The Christi Center. For me, my personality type is to fix everything as soon as possible. I've just been through a couple of horrible battles with cancer and I am a single parent now, so I am going to knock these things out – anything on my list of things to make me feel better. But grief does not work that way.

I spent an enormous amount of time and regret in anticipation of grief. Fear can be a really bad thing, and you are so afraid that you miss what's in front of you. I was so concerned about how I would take care of Bella when Janelle was gone. Navigating Bella through the Hospice process, I had Wonders & Worries, a psychologist, and a PA who was also a very good mother. There were a lot of decisions regarding Bella, and my instincts were very different from what the experts were telling me, such as "Bella doesn't need to see her mother dying." I knew that was wrong; Bella sailed through it with grace and ease and was able to help take care of her mother, who was her world.

The last conversation Bella had with Janelle, who was not very coherent because of the ammonia inside of her, was about how it was time for Mommy to go to Heaven. A lot of people were stunned by the way Bella handled things. Bella was okay when so many adults were not because our daughter had no memory of her mom not being sick and had only a working knowledge that Janelle was going to die.

As the only person Bella has now, I knew I had to survive. I also knew that I needed to act on the suggestion that I go to The Christi Center for help. I soon learned there was no instant *fix*, but I also learned that The Christi Center would be there for Bella and me every step of the way.

CHAPTER

Andy Caswell

Loss of Sister Lauren to Asthma

Lauren was a great big sister—about three years older than me. She would calm me down a lot, as I was quick to anger. "Andy, you need to calm down, and we are going to do this or that," she would say to me. And, as if by magic, Lauren would take me somewhere else. You might say she was like having an older sister and a brother because we would do so many things together, like spend time on PlayStation. She was very tall for her 13 years, 5' 7", in fact, and was stellar at softball, soccer, and track, despite her struggles with asthma. As an eighth grader, Lauren also played the flute in the All Region Band. She held the first chair position. After she died on March 3, 2000, the band left an empty chair with roses in her place.

On February 29, 2000, I was fast asleep around 10:00 p.m. when I heard my dad calling her name. I walked to her room, and there he was administering CPR to Lauren, blue-faced and lying on the floor. My dad, a fireman, had won many Phoenix awards for saving lives, so I knew he could do anything. I was scared, but confident, as my parents told me to go back to my room. But the ambulance came and took her to the hospital where she remained in ICU on life support. I didn't want to believe that she couldn't get well. I thought surely there was something they could do. I went to visit her and would talk to her about what we were going to do when we got back home. On March 2, the doctors let us know that there was no brain activity and that Lauren was not going to survive. On March 3, she passed away.

No words can describe how I felt after the loss of my sister. I was in disbelief. I would wake up and go into her room, expecting to see her. But Lauren was not there, and I never really accepted that she was gone. No one in my family knew how to talk to each other about our loss because we had never been in this situation before.

People at school treated me differently. They would say "Hi," but it was different. One day, my mom, who knew I didn't want to talk about Lauren's death, told me about For the Love of Christi. I didn't want to go, but she kept encouraging me, gradually giving me more insight into their Kids Who Kare program. I finally thought, "Nothing worse can happen, so I might as well." I recall driving there and imagining being back in the car, and it would soon be over. When I arrived, everyone was so welcoming. Although I don't remember what we did at that first meeting, I do remember getting back into the van and telling my Mom I wanted to go back. She was glad and probably very relieved.

At home, we were all doing what we could, but it was like having a car with only three wheels instead of four—it gets you there, but it's not the same. We were impacted in many different ways. My parents lost a daughter, but it was different for me. When I talked about it to others, they didn't understand. At the Kids Who Kare meetings, however, everyone talked the same language. The facilitator and the kids had gone through what I had gone through, and it felt like I had known those people all my life. I originally felt it might be a mournful place, full of sorrow and sad stories, like going to the funeral all over again. But they were able to make it fun, while at the same time, interesting and healing.

My anger could have been bottled up after I lost Lauren. Every time I went to The Christi Center, I could breathe a little bit better and manage to carry on. The organization's very special facilitators were able to show me another side—never that my situation was okay, but that there were ways to deal with it, such as instead of being sad, remembering your loved one. I learned how to celebrate Lauren's life and to understand I was in a dark place, but there could be much brightness. You could laugh, but also talk very seriously and genuinely. In one exercise we imagined our families in Heaven together. We created artwork on a huge piece of butcher paper wrapped around the walls.

I loved the annual Kids Who Kare Retreat at Camp Champion. It was one of the most fun things to do in the summer -- a whole weekend with the same people I shared with during our weekly meeting. I enjoyed hanging out with Dave Seideman who had lost his son Charlie; it was so much fun to be with him. Maybe he thought of me like a son on those retreats. I went to Kids Who Kare regularly for about two or three years and then on occasion until I was 15, when I felt I had healed in a way that I was going to be okay. A good friend's brother died about two years after Lauren, and I was able to help her find the place that had helped me for so many years.

It is unreal to me that The Christi Center existed when I needed it. Although I didn't know Susan and Don for very long when they invited my family out to their New Mexico home, *Almost Heaven*, I knew they were angels on earth. They bring such a breath of fresh of air when they walk into the room. I will never get over the loss of Lauren, but I was able to go on. Every year, my family goes to the Annual Candlelight Remembrance Service at St. Edward's University, where we hang Lauren's photo on the beautiful tree. For a number of years, my family organized and participated in the American Lung Association Asthma walk, wearing our *Lauren's Team* T-shirts in her honor. Every June 23, on Lauren's birthday, we go to Olive Garden, her favorite restaurant. She was always such a caring person who always wanted everyone to be happy, like letting me decide where to eat out, even though it was her turn to choose. She was a very giving person and helped six different people live through her organ donation.

I cannot thank The Christi Center enough for all that they have done for me and my parents. I am a better person because Lauren was in my life. The Christi Center helped me see light in my life when I thought there was none left. I am enjoying my life now as my sister would have wanted.

CHAPTER

Norma Chapa

Loss of Son Ryan to an Automobile Accident

... and she loved a boy very, very much- even more than she loved herself.

— Shel Silverstein, *The Giving Tree*

The same could be said for me when I met the be-all, end-all love of my life on a miserably cold Tuesday in December 1989. The plummeting temperature was the big news story, but all I could feel was warmth -- the warmth of a love so profound, the likes of which I'd never known before. It was the day on which I received what will forever be God's greatest gift to me—my son Ryan.

For 21 years, three months, and two weeks, I spent my life dedicated to the blessing of being Ryan's mom. My love for my child is so intense that sometimes I wonder if my soul knew we were going to be limited in our earthly time together, so I tried to pack more love into our lives than most folks get in 80 years worth of life. Was I the perfect mother or Ryan the perfect child? Hardly, on either count. We were (are) perfect for one another. That's all that matters. Ryan, much like me, is a curious combination of love, laughter, and a bit of mischief. I've often said that Ryan lived hard, loved hard, and played hard. He was always my number one defender, my knight in shining armor as early as the age of three. Much of our years together were spent as a single mother to an only child.

There are definite challenges that come with such an arrangement. The perks of forming a unique and intense mother–son bond, for example, which make the challenges pale in comparison. That bond is everlasting. It defies any and all boundaries. It is a bond that continues to thrive between here and the hereafter. It is because of this continued connection that I thrive to this day. It is because of our everlasting connection that I generally speak of my son in the present tense. Truth be told, I rarely (if ever) speak of Ryan by way of the "D" word. Death (to me) signifies the end—a big, fat period at the end of the sentence that is life. Such is not the case. Ryan's signs of our continued connection give proof to the fact that he lives. Perhaps not in the earthly realm, but there is no doubt in my soul that my son truly lives. One Glorious Day, I shall be reunited with my child. When we're finally reunited, I shall live with him and be like him in the truest sense of the word. Until then, I will continue to attempt to have a little fun, do a little good, and, most of all, share Ryan's story, our story. My dedication to the blessing of being Ryan's mom did not end with *The Unthinkable*. Our connection is everlasting.

You may be curious as to how I ended up sharing our story in this book. Well, it was early April 2011, and life was going along fairly well when *The Unthinkable* happened. My son's passing came about after a single-car collision, which occurred at 2:00 a.m., just one-half mile from home. The impact was of such intensity that the thunderous boom woke me from a deep sleep. In fact, sometimes in the still of the night, I can still recall the sound. He was gone in an instant. No opportunity for goodbyes. Still I feel as though God was very merciful with Ryan and me in that swift departure.

My family and dearest friends all live hours away. Desperate to find a resource to aid me in their absence, my sister came upon The Christi Center (For the Love of Christi, as it was known at the time). I resisted at first, figuring that no one would be able to comprehend my specific brand of misery. I just knew that I was the only single mother in the history of the world to have lost her one and only child. At my sister's insistence, I read Marianne MacDonald's story on the Christi Center's website. I took one look at her son Dylan's photograph and was comforted knowing that my son had found a friend in heaven. Little did I know I was about to meet one of my dearest friends ever in Dylan's mom! Two or three weeks later, there I was, sitting in my first meeting of bereaved moms.

Miraculously, I was feeling a semblance of normalcy that I just *knew* I'd never feel again. These women understood me, listened to me, and shared their stories with me. They cried with me, and, yes, even laughed with me. To this day, I affectionately refer to my precious sisters-of-the-broken-heart as my *Christi Chicks*. I am eternally grateful to this incredible group of women who guided me (sometimes crawling) through the initial weeks and months of this cruel journey, often filled with agony and despair. They are the same women who continue to walk and even dance beside me almost six and a half years after *The Unthinkable*.

Thank God for signs from our children that prove our everlasting bond. Thank God for The Christi Center, and thank God for my *Christi Chicks*!

CHAPTER

Linda and Michael Christopher

Loss of Son Joey to Drug Overdose

Joey was the youngest of our five kids and the 16-year-old *baby* of our family. He was carefree and loved to spend time with his friends and family. Joey liked music and the Philadelphia Eagles. He liked to swim and let his mom and sisters spoil him. He loved his brother and nephew. He was a loyal friend, a loving son, and I don't think he ever had an enemy. He was funny, and he liked to make people laugh.

One night at a party, the mother of one of his friends gave her daughter and the other kids some prescription drugs. Joey was one of those kids, and he died in his sleep from the Methadone pills that she gave him. She would end up accepting a 30-year plea bargain, which translated to a bit less than five years total time served before she was paroled. Joey's family was given life sentences of living without him.

You never really recover from the loss of a child, but, hopefully, with help you learn a "new normal." We have spent years in peer-based counseling at The Christi Center in Austin. Don Cox, the co-founder, says, "I know one thing—we are not meant to grieve alone," and he is right. In the same way that other parents love their children for their whole lives, we love and miss Joey every day, and we won't forget him. Our family carries him in our hearts and with us every day. We all try to live our lives in a way that would make him proud. In the deepest sadness we have had, he sends us *signs* so we know that he still watches over us. Other people may not believe or may even think we are crazy, but we know he is nearby.

Joey's short life taught us to stay very close to God and to let the wisdom of His commandment to forgive others seep into our souls. He taught us to live in the present because we never really know how long we have. Our hearts are very sensitive to others who suffer the loss of a loved one. Joey's mom makes candles for members with pictures of their loved one, so that when they miss them, they can light them. We have learned that the only comfort you can find in the hurricane of loss is in the comfort you give to others.

Joey said, "Life is not about what gets you down. Life is about what gets you going." We never forget that fact, and we never forget our Joey.

CHAPTER

Judy and Larry Cooper

Loss of Son Craig Wilson Cooper to Jet Ski Accident

Two weeks after Craig Wilson Cooper, our 20-year-old son, was killed in a jet-ski accident on July 4, 1994, we began our journey with The Christi Center. In that first year, we participated in "The World Gathering on Bereavement Conference" in Seattle and served on a panel with Susan and Don Cox, Bob Dockerty and the late Pat Dockerty, who lost their daughter to suicide, and Beth and Steve Dorfman, who lost their young daughter to a brain tumor. Board members Patricia Stuart, Ph.D., late Larry Bugen, Ph.D. and late Reverend Will Spong, a professor of pastoral theology, Episcopal priest, and grief counselor, also participated in the conference. It was a 90-minute presentation on "How Do Marriages Survive the Death of a Child," rated among the highest attended sessions during the entire conference.

After another year of grief support meetings, I began volunteering at the Center, and that's when my real healing began by reaching out to others in their grief. I was honored to be named the 1996 Volunteer of the Year. Larry and I were board members and supported the organization with our time and efforts. Eventually, I began work at the Center as the Program Director for several years. We also attended the annual Men's and Women's Retreats held in Ruidoso for many years. These retreats were extremely beneficial for both of us.

We honestly believe Susan and Don Cox saved our sanity and, ultimately, our lives. Losing a child is devastating. To have never known the love of our precious Craig would truly have been the greatest tragedy of all, and we have often said that if this horrific tragedy had to occur, we were so thankful to have lived in Austin to take advantage of the love and support generated by The Christi Center. It became our extended family, a relationship that continues to this day.

CHAPTER

Leslie Cox

Loss of Brother Jimmy to Mid-Air Helicopter Collision

My kid brother Jimmy and I were very close. Although he was five years younger, I recognized a kindred spirit in him from the very beginning. He was, to be honest, a better version of myself. Like me, Jimmy was artsy, creative, and inquisitive, but he was also outgoing and brave—two things I am not. And he was a truly fun person (and *really* funny). He loved life and was passionate about so many things. And, oh, was he kind and loving, and so good to his family and his many friends. To this day, I strive to be more like him.

Our bond was forged as youngsters and continued throughout his too short life. I remember a conversation with Jimmy once while we were in Florida visiting our grandparents about what we would be and do when we grew up. I talked to him about living on the same street, just a couple of houses from each other. We told each other then that we would always live close to each other and would always hang out together. I think we always just thought it would happen eventually. We had time, and we would live in our "Cox Commune" together one day.

I have so many great memories of Jimmy from childhood: playing in the backyard pool with our sister Jenny, sledding down the big hill in front of our house in the winter, and going on family trips to South Carolina or Florida. And even though I moved to Chicago first, then Texas, while Jimmy moved to Arizona, we remained close and saw each other frequently for holidays, family vacations, or visits back and forth between Austin and Phoenix. I remember so clearly one of our last trips out to visit him in Arizona. Jimmy really went all out every time we traveled to see him. On that particular trip, when my son Nate was five, Jimmy rented an RV to take us to Sedona, Flagstaff, and the Grand Canyon. What an experience! Nate will never forget it, and while the Grand Canyon is a bit foggy in his memory, Uncle Jimmy's RV is not! He still talks about having beds *in a car* and being able to walk around in a *living room* while driving down the highway.

Some of my best, and, unfortunately, my last memories of Jimmy are at our family reunion in New York in June 2007. I remember him playing with my son and my sister's daughters at the lake house we rented on one of the Finger Lakes, and talking to our cousins, which we hadn't seen in several years. He was the playboy of the six cousins and regaled us with his career and life. I also recall sitting around a big fire late at night, down by the water, drinking and talking incessantly.

Jimmy was an incredible photographer and worked for more than 12 years at KTVK, (Channel 3) in Phoenix. From the very beginning, he loved his job there and the people he worked with. He was a great video journalist—probably the best they ever had. Everyone wanted to work with Jimmy. While he was demanding, a perfectionist, and as someone once called him, "crusty," he was also caring and wanted each reporter to give it his all and do the best work that he could. Jimmy even did a little of his own reporting, including a great, fun story about skiing. I loved the view from the camera as he skied down the hill, somewhere outside of Flagstaff. He also did a tribute to my Dad's military career as a B47 pilot.

When he was killed in 2007 in a mid-air helicopter collision, filming a car chase for his station, it didn't seem real for a long time. We went through the funeral, the aftermath of the accident, as if in a coma, or on autopilot. When someone is taken from you suddenly, without a chance to say good-bye, you just keep expecting them to show up one day or call you on the phone. In a way, I still feel that Jimmy is on vacation, and he will be coming home soon—even many years later. To deal with our grief, we started a foundation in his memory, The James Alan Cox Foundation for Student Photojournalists. It helped to have something good come out of this terrible tragedy. It also helped to have something *to do*. But equally important in helping us deal with our grief was discovering The Christi Center.

I was talking to a friend one day a few weeks after my brother's accident (the family still doesn't like to use the word *death* in relation to him) and mentioned how we couldn't sleep, we cried all the time, and we were basically still in shock. He told me about a group, For the Love of Christi, that he had read about in a newspaper article. I called my parents and told them we should go. My Mom said she would try it, but, initially, my Dad refused. That wasn't for him, he said. He couldn't see talking about his grief with other people. Dad, being former military and of an older generation, is very stoic and quiet about things like that. We didn't make him go that night; in fact, I thought he would never go. I just couldn't imagine my Dad opening up and talking to others about loss or sadness, or really anything emotional.

The first night Mom and I went to a meeting, I think we cried throughout the entire session. But that was okay—and expected. It was a completely loving environment, and you could be yourself. You were accepted, no matter what. And I'll never forget meeting Susan and Don Cox. I was so touched by their kindness and caring for everyone who walked through the Center's doors. To this day, I still get a card with a personal note on Jimmy's birthday and on his angel day. They have never forgotten.

Mom and I went home after that first night and told Dad that he had to go, at least try one session. Well, he went and then went again and again. He became The Christi Center's biggest fan. In fact, he joined the board, and Mom also became very involved with several events and fundraisers.

Probably, though, the most important thing that came out of The Christi Center was getting to know the people there and becoming friends— sometimes great friends—with the other *zebras* (we may look like horses, but after someone you love dies, you are forever changed and now have your stripes). Mom and I even walked with some of them on the Camino de Santiago in Spain. It was there that we saw one of the greatest signs we've ever had from Jimmy since his accident. After a tough morning of walking, with Mom struggling with some of the hills and almost giving up, we saw some graffiti that changed everything. It made Mom go on. It said simply, "Jimmy Vive." How perfect and so appropriate that our Christi Center friends could witness this with us.

CHAPTER

Markie Duncan

Loss of Husband Harve to Heart Attack

In the summer of 1994 I lost my husband Harve to congestive heart failure. Though his health had been declining in recent years, his fatal heart attack came as unexpected. I don't believe I ever thought about Harve dying before I did, even though he was 10 years older. I was a "young" widow at age 67.

My pastor lived across the street and was with me when Harve passed from a heart attack. Susan Cox had just set up a bereavement group at our church. Our pastor John Haller introduced us, and I began attending those meetings soon after that. Over the next two years, Susan and Don Cox became my close friends and confidantes. In 1996, Bill Duncan started attending The Christi Center after his wife of 50 years died. He was retired military, like my first husband, and shared so many common interests with me, specifically a love of travel and photography. Susan and Don knew we needed to get acquainted.

They introduced us at The Christi Center, and we immediately felt connected. We dated that year and were married in June 1997. Susan was my matron of honor.

For the next 12 years, Bill and I traveled extensively and enjoyed living in a high-rise apartment at the Army Residence Community in San Antonio. I was thrilled to have another loving companion who valued his first wife, in addition to being open to another exciting second chance at marriage.

In 2009, we both had physical ailments that kept us from taking trips again. We moved into Assisted Living In 2011, we chose to move back to Austin to be closer to my children and grandchildren. Bill died in the spring of 2017. He was 98 years old. We had almost 20 years together! I am grateful to Susan and Don for getting us together after helping us both work through our grief.

CHAPTER

Jessica Galfas

Loss of partner Mark who fell from cliff while hiking

Mark captured my attention when I met him in a yoga class in 2014. The room was hot, and he was shirtless. I placed my mat next to his, and we practiced together for the first time. Our movements and our lives were in sync from that day until Mark's last. On April 1, 2017, our day started like any other with breakfast and chit-chat at the dining room table. Mark decided to go on a hike with one of our friends while I relaxed at home.

Mark fell from a cliff about 100 feet above a dry creek bed. Fellow hikers stood a few feet from him, dumbstruck by how fast it happened and how helpless they were. One second he was right next to them; then, the next he was gone. Our friend called me at home and told me that Mark fell. We had no clue the trauma would be fatal. Over the next twelve hours, ER surgeons restarted Mark's heart multiple times and failed to stop massive internal bleeding.

When a surgeon officially announced Mark's death, I crumbled. My mind couldn't accept the situation. I kept arguing with myself, "This can't be real." I didn't know anyone who had lost someone so close to them unexpectedly. "No one will ever understand this pain," I thought. I've never felt more alone while surrounded by people who loved me.

The pain was suffocating. I moved out of the apartment Mark and I shared and took off looking for relief in California, Europe, and remote islands in the South Pacific. My grief traveled with me, even to Bali. I wanted to share that tender part of me, but I didn't know how. The few times I told people what happened, I was disappointed in their responses, mostly because I couldn't absorb what they were saying. I gave up talking to people about what happened and decided to write about it instead. It was a one-way conversation.

When I came back to Austin, I wasn't sure I'd stay. I would imagine Mark standing on every familiar corner. Austin didn't feel like home without him. I didn't want to feel haunted like this forever, but I didn't see things changing any time soon. I had cried every day for more months than I could count. Invitations to catch up fell to the wayside. I had the thought, "No one understands" so many times that I totally believed it. That belief took the pain I had around my loss and amplified it into suffering. Now I felt resigned, stagnant, and hopeless, all indicators of depression when sustained long enough.

Luckily, depression is obvious to mindful spectators. One close friend realized how disengaged I had become over the last year and emailed me a list of local grief resources. I called The Christi Center from my bedroom floor, literally pulling myself up on the side of the bed from a fresh bout of sobbing. Eyes swollen, head pounding, and dry-mouthed, I was tired of drowning in self-pity.

Telling my story to a group of strangers felt overwhelming. What would they say? Would they accept my sadness or try to push me to think happy thoughts? Would they even believe my story was true? My brain still hadn't accepted my reality, so my story seemed unbelievable, even to me. I attended my first support group the following Monday night, almost a year after Mark died. I spent the entire day convincing myself to show up. Thank goodness that I did!

Everyone in the group had lost a spouse or partner. Some lost their partners unexpectedly like me. Others took care of their partners for weeks, months, or even years before they passed. I couldn't decide what was worse, and I didn't have to.

What we had in common was more meaningful than what we did not. We didn't have to grieve alone. We rejoiced in being able to share what was true for us in that moment. Oftentimes, they were thoughts we couldn't share with anyone else, feelings that ate away at us from the inside out. We were present with each other, listening and responding and encouraging each other in ways that we couldn't on our own. The diversity of the group offered perspectives I didn't have before. We were all in different places on our grief journeys. I found hope listening to the people who were further along than me and began to think, "I could be okay some day, even if I'm not right now."

Each meeting closed with our facilitator asking us to talk about whatever helped us cope. I talked about the stories I wrote and shared them with the staff at The Christi Center. They asked if they could include my story about spreading Mark's ashes in their newsletter and I agreed. I started to own my story and choose what I wanted to believe about it. A new thought brought me my first touch of relief. "I can't change what happened—and that's okay."

A few months later, The Christi Center staff asked me to speak about my experience at their annual events. I was nervous just like before when I went to the group for the first time. I thought about how much I benefited from hearing others, and that drove me to take action in spite of my fear. It gave me hope to hear other people say the same things I was thinking and for them to hear what I had to share, too. At the first event, I told a story about what it was like to attend the grief group for the first time. I hoped this could ease others' nerves about not knowing what to expect. Maybe then people could find just enough peace of mind to show up and receive the same amazing (and free) benefits that I had in my time of need. At the next event I spoke to a few hundred members who had already gone to The Christi Center. I talked to them about courage and how it feels like fear. I wanted them to know how brave they were for showing up. People I'd never met responded with tears and smiles and handshakes and hugs.

I never realized how many people were dealing with the same thoughts and feelings that I had, mainly because I had already decided that no one understood. I had to change the way I thought about the world to see what was there all along. It was my mind that made me feel isolated, not my loss. So, when I am driving around Austin now, I see strangers on the corner, not Mark, and I wonder if they might know grief, too.

The Christi Center offered a time, a place, and a community for me to release those vulnerable thoughts that turned my pain into suffering. Through my interactions with other members I was able to choose new thoughts that serve me better. That's how The Christi Center sparks hope. They allow people to create a future they can believe in—one thought at a time.

CHAPTER

Dorcas and Gary Green

Loss of Son Phillip James Green to Being a Good Samaritan

Love is all things. It comes the instant you hold your newborn baby. The day Phillip was born, he filled a life-long hole in my heart. I always knew I wanted to be a mother. Our mother-son relationship began like a fireworks explosion and never subsided. Phillip was surrounded with love by his whole family, and he loved back deeply. He became the man mothers want their sons to be. He was generous and was always bringing home the stray dog or person who needed help. He died on March 4, 2004, at the young age of 27 because he tried to help someone.

Phillip saw a lady crying on the side of the road. Her dog had been hit by a car. The police report says Phillip went up to the lady and put his arm around her. He told her that he loved animals, too. Then, he did the unthinkable. He saw a car coming that was going to hit the dog again, and Phillip ran from the side of the road to retrieve the dog. He misjudged the speed of the oncoming car and was thrown over the car. I am told that my son died before he ever hit the ground. I'd like to believe that is true, but I don't know. I just know that the world changed forever for me, his dad, and our family. Moms are always trying to protect their children by telling them to be careful, look both ways before crossing the street, and hold hands in the parking lot to be safe. There are an infinite number of things parents say to protect the children we love.

How could this have happened to Phillip, my only son? He was my life, my past, my present, and my future. He was young, smart, and had so much life ahead of him. Phillip had recently married Michelle, his loving wife, and I envisioned beautiful grandbabies someday. For me, the world lost its color that day. It was now all black and white with ugly gray streaks. The beauty and innocence of the world was gone for me. I did not understand how the planets could continue to revolve around the sun without Phillip. My husband Gary and I were devastated. We held onto each other as tight as we could. Gary would continue to tell me that Phillip died trying to help someone, and that is the son we raised. Neither of us was surprised that Phillip would try to help someone in need, especially if a dog was involved.

Somehow, we got through two memorial services for Phillip, but the traumatic shock stayed with me for a long time. The shock slowly wore off, and shock's other friend—depression—set in. My husband's sadness was different, but still life-altering. Our grief was different as was our paths to find a way to cope. Gary became quieter and he would tell me that sometimes his eyes would *just water*. My journey led me to psychologists and psychiatrists, because I did not want to live in a world without Phillip. At times, it made sense that my death was a viable option. My family was scared for me, but they did not know what to do. My mother told me that she would take the grief for me if she could. Great friends, relatives, and co-workers all tried to help, but the avalanche of sorrow was nipping at my sanity.

I am sure many got tired of me trying to explain how Phillip was good and kind and that the world was a darker place without him. I could not accept the fact that I was left in this world without Phillip. They all knew what we had lost in losing our son. My friends looked at me with worried eyes, wondering if I would never get over this tragedy. With time and lots of love, my desire to live came back. Thankfully, my psychiatrist strongly recommended that I reach out to others who had been pushed into this hellhole I was in because they had lost children, too. I knew I had nothing to lose by going to a grief support group, For the Love of Christi. I was desperate and grasping for any help I could find. I knew that Don and Susan Cox had lost Christi, a daughter, after which they founded the organization. I was absolutely sure that no parent could love their child like I loved Phillip or miss their child as much. I thought I was the last person on earth who would go to a support group. Boy, was I wrong!

What I found was other moms and dads hurting and missing their child with the same intensity with which I was missing Phillip. How was that possible? I saw people hugging and crying, but there was also laughter and hope. The Mom's Group became my salvation and refuge. The other moms never tired of hearing stories about Phillip, and I loved hearing about their children. I have never had a bond so deep than the one I have with the other mothers who attended the group. It was easy to keep Phillip's memory alive because every Monday night there would be the moms and maybe someone newer to grief than I was to talk about our losses. It was the safest, most non-judgmental place on earth. I found my footing and sanity in the world again and knew this was a place that was special, unlike any other in the world.

My friends at The Christi Center are lifelong friends. Let's face it, grief is a life-long struggle, and facing this struggle with understanding, love, and friendship is immeasurable. I wanted to help ensure that the organization For the Love of Christi was there for other moms and dads. The Center needs to stay viable even after Don and Susan Cox go to Heaven to join Christi! I wanted to become involved and give back for the support and love I received. I served on the board six years and remain active on the advisory council. Because I am an attorney, I can provide what legal services the nonprofit needs.

Non-profits are not free and still require funds to stay open. I found ways to raise money for The Christi Center, and every time I made a donation, I knew exactly who would benefit—others like me. I made quilts and would raffle them off to raise money. When my friends ask what they can do for me, I always say that a donation for the "Love of Phillip" to The Christi Center would be great. I have to confess that some slot machine winnings were donated from time to time.

It has been more than 17 years since that tragic night that permanently altered my universe. Life changes us all and death even more. I live in gratitude and awe that I am Phillip's mother. I never see a firework go off that I don't feel closer to my son. The joy he brought his dad and me is immeasurable. The love and hope I found through The Christi Center is immeasurable. Next time you see a firework display, look up because Phillip is there somewhere smiling!

CHAPTER

Melanie and Jay Holt

Loss of Son Matthew Arellano to Epileptic Seizure While he Slept

Since the day he was born, two months early and weighing only 4 lbs., 4 oz., my whole world revolved around Matt. I left his biological dad when Matt was just four months old, and for the longest time, it was just the two of us. Matt had the funniest sense of humor, could get anyone to smile, and if he saw someone having a bad day, he considered it his personal mission to make their day better. He was kind and generous, had a huge, caring heart, and loved to help and serve others. When he was 5-years-old, he witnessed me injure my leg, which landed me on crutches and in a full leg stabilizer for two months.

221

During the recovery, Matt wanted to help any way he could and declared himself the man of the house and my protector! By age 11, his biological father was not very involved in his life anymore. It was about that same time that I met and started dating Jay. There were some bumps along the way, but it wasn't long before Matt was calling him "Dad."

Our son was healthy, strong, athletic, and had a full and promising life ahead of him. When he was 16, he had his first seizure. A series of tests, including a CT scan, found a spot on his brain; however, there was no way to know if it was there at birth or a result of a baseball head injury when he was nine. He was subsequently diagnosed with Juvenile Myoclonic Epilepsy (JME), and with medications, he typically had only one seizure a year.

On June 3, 2014, I was shocked to hear that my cousin, a deep-sea fisherman in Alaska, had died from an apparent heart attack in his apartment, and his body had been found by his girlfriend. My Aunt and I cried and cried on the phone that night. I had always known that should something happen to Matt, I would not be able to survive without him and figured my heart would just stop beating. In a cruel twist of fate, less than 24 hours later, this exact scenario would play out again with my son.

The following day at 5:02 p.m., Bekah, Matt's girlfriend, called me. But instead of her voice, it was that of her friend telling me that Matt had a really bad seizure, and the paramedics wanted us to come to his apartment in San Marcos right away. Looking back, a rational mind would have picked up on one of the many signs that Matt was already gone, but my brain saw nothing. Jay figured it out pretty quickly and was doing every-thing in his power to keep me calm during the long rush hour drive to San Marcos from Austin.

When we turned onto Matt's street and he saw no ambulance, only a police car, Jay realized that he was right. Matt really was gone. I, on the other hand, was so relieved to finally have made it there that I didn't see or notice anything until we drove up and parked in front of his building. That is when I saw two police officers—one standing on either side of Matt's front door — along with a lady in a bright shirt and Bekah sitting on the porch between them. (I would later learn that the woman in the bright shirt was a victim services advocate.)

I think the brain somehow tries to protect itself from impending doom because suddenly, I felt disconnected from everything. As if I were watching a silent movie of someone else's life, I sat there staring at them. I didn't even realize that Jay had already parked the car and was on my side helping me out of the car. All I remember thinking was, "Why are the police here?"

Then they were standing in front of me, and I noticed Bekah was sobbing and saying something over and over, but I couldn't understand her. The woman in the bright shirt was talking, too, but I was completely numb and had no idea what either one of them was talking about. Nothing was registering...nothing at all...until I looked at Bekah again and finally heard her say, "I'm so sorry, Mom! I tried, I really tried to save him!" I must have asked, "What are you talking about? What do you mean?" because the lady in the bright shirt clearly said to me, "I am so sorry, Melanie. Matt has died. He passed away, and Bekah found him in his bed."

Like a tsunami crashing to shore, the impact of their words finally registered. Apparently, I screamed "NO!" and my legs refused to hold me up. My collapse to the sidewalk would have been painful had Jay not been holding onto me because he anticipated my reaction to what he already knew. I don't remember much about the minutes, hours, days, months, and even years that followed. All I knew was that at only 23-years-old, my best friend, only child, and the light of my life had died overnight in his bed and had been found by his girlfriend—eerily similar to how my cousin had died the day before. I also found out that contrary to what I believed, my heart would keep on beating...even though his had stopped.

Three weeks after Matt died would be our tenth wedding anniversary, and Matt had walked me down the aisle in our wedding. But with him gone, everything was broken and I felt dead inside. Jay and I were both stumbling through life, having no idea how to survive without him. Five weeks after Matt died, we ended up walking through The Christi Center doors. What we found was something intangible that happens when you meet someone else who knows exactly what you're feeling. We built connections with other grieving parents who were dealing with the same pain as we were and who understood what it is like to bury your child.

At our first meeting, one dad (speaking about me) said to Jay, "The wife you knew and married is gone, and she is never coming back. If you want your marriage to survive, essentially, you two need to start dating and fall in love all over again." There were people whose children died one, three, eight, and 30 years before we lost Matt. Don and Susan told us, "Missing our loved ones doesn't get any easier, but ever so slowly, it does get different." Even though I thought I wouldn't make it like they had, because they must be so much stronger than I was, there they were -- proof that it *is* possible to survive and, with time find a new normal and learn to live with this debilitating pain.

At one Monday night meeting, about six months after Matt died, I was so grief stricken that I just sat there and cried, unable to say a word. Jay shared with the group that he was afraid I was going to commit suicide and that he couldn't survive losing both Matt and me. Don said something that has stuck with us since that night. He told us of another couple who had ben in the same situation and said to Jay, "Melanie doesn't want to kill herself. She just wants to die, and those are two very different things."

Just like that, after months of feeling like no one "gets it," he eloquently described <u>exactly</u> how I was feeling!

In our opinion, success is not measured by the number of zeros in your bank account, the cars in your driveway, or the things you have. We believe true success is making a difference in the lives of others. In our eyes, Susan and Don Cox are the epitome of success. Navigating the devastating pain of losing their beautiful daughter Christi, they wanted to honor her memory. So they found a way to give all the love they would love to give to her and freely give it to others who are walking through their own grief journey. They have turned their grief into a gift of love that has been shared with tens of thousands of people -- people just like us who were terrified of facing a future without Matt and having no idea how to survive it. I owe my life to Susan and Don Cox for their never-ending love for their daughter. Christi led them to start this place.

The waves of pain that would buckle my knees every second of every day have, over time, eased up and now hit me farther apart. During the times of calm, we try to live our lives, find ways to honor our son's memory, and give back to The Christi Center as best we can. We have served on the Board of Directors, volunteer at events, and made the organization part of our estate planning. We want to make sure that the doors stay open to greet the hundreds of new people who walk through the doors every year after the loss of a loved one. They will be welcomed into this "child loss club" of which no one ever wants to be a member.

Like Don and Susan did for us, we want to be tangible evidence for others who have lost a child that if we can make it through the most unimaginable pain, they will, too. Even if they don't think they will or want to. Just one day at a time, and sometimes, just one minute at a time, because love never dies.

CHAPTER

Benny Jasso, Sr.

Loss of Son Dennis to an Automobile Accident and Wife Alice to Medical Complications

The Charreada, a Mexican Rodeo, was an event for my whole family. I trained my sons, Benny, Jr. and Dennis, when they were young to participate in the rodeo's nine events. Alice and the other wives cooked and raised funds for the rodeo. Back then, many dignitaries like John Trevino were also involved. I loved sharing those times with my family, especially my sons, who participated in their pre-teen and teen years.

On August 26, 1988, life changed for all of us. After lying in a coma for five weeks, Dennis, 19-years-old, died as a result of injuries he sustained as a backseat passenger in an automobile crash.

Later, someone told us about For the Love of Christi. I went there primarily to take Alice, who suffered tremendously after our son's death. I sat in the background at the meetings and couldn't imagine how people could talk about something so painful. I spent most of my time, for close to six months, just listening to others in the group. In my culture, men don't cry or hug. (With Susan and Don, you get over not hugging *real quick!*)

Finally, I wanted the chance to talk about my son and began to open up with those closest to me. I wanted to remember the happy times with Dennis, even though we did have our issues because we were so alike. His death definitely challenged my faith, and I was mad at God. At The Christi Center, I learned that people cope with grief in their own way – differently from how I might. Just listening was helpful to me, but my wife, who worked with handicapped kids in Manor at the time, had a terrible time. The organization sent her to one of the Kübler-Ross workshops, which was so good for her. When I think of those days now, I realize I was focused on taking care of Alice and my job. I did not have time to grieve. It wasn't only my culture, but other things in my life.

Miraculously, less than a month after Dennis died, we got a call, which again changed our lives. The mother of Dennis' child with whom he had lost touch heard about Dennis' death. She was having complications with the birth and wanted Alice and me to be there for the arrival of our granddaughter. We even got to name her—Denise. She's now in her 20s and so much like her dad.

The baby and her mother lived with us for a while, and I know her birth really turned things around. I was mad at God for taking away my son, but He gave us the blessing of my granddaughter. Our other children were grown, married, off with their own lives, and we now had someone to concentrate on. Life as Denise's "Momo" and "Popo" was worth living again.

Alice used to say The Christi Center saved her life, and it certainly impacted mine because it helped her so much. It is such a unique organization; you can't help but benefit from being around others who have also lost loved ones. Don and Susan and all the facilitators make it easier to understand grief and how to act around those who are in grief. Alice and I volunteered in many ways. In the early years, we helped load up their office to move into new offices at One Westlake Plaza. We supported the garage sales, and I brought my famous BBQ chicken and other food. Alice, who operated Alice Country Crafts Store after she retired, handled the beautiful decorations at the annual Candlelight Remembrance Service at St. Edward's University. And I would make sure the organization's copier was always running smoothly!

I visit the cemetery to see Dennis and Alice, who passed away on November 26, 2006. I also go to the annual December Candlelight Remembrance Service. One day not long after Alice's death, I was having one of my down moments. I was walking out my door and looked up and saw this sign I had never seen before. It read, "You may live with sorrow, but you don't have to live sorrowfully." I know she was there with me.

CHAPTER

Suzanne Kennedy

Loss of Brothers Shawn, Jason, and Jeff to Muscular Dystrophy; Father Robert to Leukemia; Sister Kathy to Breast Cancer; and Mother Rose Mary to Stroke

We had a very big family: Mom, Dad, and nine of us kids -- five girls and four boys. The youngest three boys had muscular dystrophy. We turned heads everywhere we went—to church, outdoor concerts, etc.—and people often asked us what organization we were with. Growing up in a family with nine kids was fun but very challenging. There were lots of hospital visits, surgeries, and medical appointments, leg braces, special vans with wheelchair lifts, and exercises to be done every night. Many people asked us how we did it. We just did it.

We did lots of fun things as a family, such as beach vacations in California and Florida, and trips to the Olympics, Hollywood, Carlsbad Caverns, the Grand Canyon, the Smithsonian, the Ozarks, Epcot, and Disneyland. We had New Year's Eve parties, Hawaiian parties, and St. Patrick's Day parties. Our parents let the boys' friends turn their home into a haunted house every year for Halloween. One year we even had Christmas in July when we thought Jeff might not be here for Christmas. When Jason and Jeff, the twins, were teenagers, I took them to New Orleans for Mardi Gras. Many people on the floats noticed the good-looking twins in wheelchairs and cowboy hats. They got more beads thrown their way, and the kids had a blast!

Dad took the older kids camping, exploring, and bike riding all over Dallas on Sunday mornings. He got us all interested in exercise, too, especially running. One year, when dad was the victim of a violent crime and in the hospital, he was unable to run the annual Turkey Trot, which was a family tradition. So that year, six of us kids ran in his honor, and we had shirts printed for all of us with the words, "Jogging runs in our family...Thanks, Dad." Our family was featured in the *Dallas Morning News* that year for honoring our dad. Dad would often take the younger boys camping and swimming. One time, we carried them to the seashore when we couldn't get their wheelchairs through the sand.

Mom and Dad provided so many great opportunities for us to have a well-rounded life. We were encouraged to further our education, which most of us did, and even Shawn attended nearly two years of college before he succumbed to his illness. Shawn was the oldest of the three youngest boys. He was witty and had a dry sense of humor. He adapted well to the use of an electric wheelchair, which enabled him to be more independent, and he led the way for his two younger brothers. He was definitely a "Mama's boy," naturally spoiled because he was the oldest of the kids with MD, but he was also trainable, as we got him to think about his sisters once in a while! After I left home for college, he sent me a Valentine's card, "I love you, Sue, even though you think I'm a brat!" When Shawn died in 1984 at the age of 20, it was very difficult to grieve, as Jason and Jeff were still here, and we tried to keep our spirits up for them. We didn't want them to see us grieve, but then, they were grieving, too. We just couldn't help each other at the time.

The twins were stoic, introverted, and often silent, so the rest of us worked hard to be funny and silly and encourage them to do the things they were able to do. One of those was Muscular Dystrophy Camp where all three boys went for a week nearly every summer. Several of us girls volunteered as camp counselors during those years. The camp was a great opportunity for the kids to participate in *normal* activities like swimming, horseback riding, and staying up late—all things they loved to do.

Jason died three years to the day after Shawn at age 20. I think he planned it that way. I'm pretty sure I didn't grieve then either, as Jeff was still here and we, as a family, tried to make the best of things for his sake. It had to be difficult for him to keep on going, as he knew what was ahead. But Jeff did great. He had a spirit about him that loved the attention he received from family and friends. When he died almost a year later at age 21, it felt as if all three boys died at the same time. I had put my grief on hold for a long time and knew I needed something, somewhere and now, not later, as I thought my heart was going to break. My family members had their own ways of coping, and my friends really didn't know what to say to me.

That's when I turned to For the Love of Christi. I called Susan, and she was so kind. I told her I would be there for the Monday night group, then got cold feet and called her to cancel...three weeks in a row! Susan gently said to me, "We are here for you when you are ready." The Christmas Remembrance Service in 1988 was the first thing I did with the Center, and I have been a part of The Christi Center family ever since. I was a group member for two years. Every Monday night I was sitting in that room. We'd pass a small glass purple heart around, say our name, and tell our story to people who would listen. I quickly realized that no one would judge me or tell me I was taking too long to grieve. The group was a safety net for me, and I kept going back. I thought I would be in that room forever, but as time went by, I could hear my voice getting a little bit stronger, a lot less angry, and I cried less and laughed more. I made new friends whom I knew would be my friends forever. After two years as a group member, I became one of the facilitators of the grief support groups, which I did for many more years. I loved being able to give back to the community that which I had received at a very low point in my life.

When my dad was diagnosed with Leukemia in 2004, we were all so shocked. How could he be sick? He was so healthy and fit! He worked hard and played hard and had more energy than all of us. Seeing him losing his strength was difficult to witness. We, as a family, all knew what we were about to face again, and we tried to pull together and offer solace to each other. I connected with friends I had made through The Christi Center and with my family, and that helped me through a very tough time. Dad's illness was brief—just six weeks from the diagnosis until his demise. Time is so relative. I am sure my dad thought it was a long illness. No one wants to see their loved one suffer, so any time is too long. At The Christi Center, I realized that I was fortunate to be able to say goodbye to my loved ones. My heart ached for those who lost their loved ones suddenly. That is the wonder of a support group. We can share our grief, while we offer support to others, and we learn from each other what we have not experienced ourselves. When I have the chance to talk about my dad, I do. I honor my dad's life every time I run or ride my bike or recycle that plastic bottle that would be easier to throw away, silently thanking him for the lessons of good health, education, and protecting the environment.

Our oldest sister, Kathy, was like a mother hen, slightly bossy to all of us kids, but a great big sister. She played guitar and taught me a few tunes; mentored us in how to deal with life as we knew it. She listened to us when we wanted to gripe about Mom or Dad or all the work we had to do. She showed us by example how to stay calm in the midst of chaos, and she was kind to everyone. She and I started social work school at UT at the same time, and then she moved to Florida where she worked with children from broken homes. She and her husband adopted one of the foster kids she mentored, but then she got breast cancer, which she fought for six long years—always with the will to live and with a happy attitude, trying to love and raise a child when her own health was failing. We lost our loving sister two years after my dad. I miss her terribly. Sometimes I wish I could talk to her and hug her one more time. But I will always remember her for her example of patience and good will toward others, and I still try to be more like her.

I remember my brothers for their bravery to live their lives in spite of their disability. Sometimes, I wear Mardi Gras beads to remember the fun times, and I love to talk to people who have twins in their family. I know for sure that growing up with the boys has helped me to be more empathetic toward those with disabilities in my profession as a social worker. People don't have to hear my stories to know I understand. One very special thing we do sometimes as a family around the holidays is to place photos of family members we have lost in the center of our big round table as we share a holiday meal. That way, our loved ones will be with us in spirit as we celebrate the lives we have now.

After I thought I had finished my family story for a while, my mother, who loved to tap dance, fell and broke her hip just before Christmas 2016. The day after the surgery, she had a stroke, which led to her hastened demise on Valentine's Day. I was not ready to lose my mom; no one ever is. But I can tell you I will always appreciate the lessons she taught all of us kids— to be kind to others, forgive each other often, and have faith in God that He will never give us more than we can handle. Now that mom is tap dancing in heaven, I feel happy that she is reunited with my dad and four of my siblings. She missed them so much, as do we.

If you are grieving, let yourself cry, rant, and rave, or just sit quietly with a friend who will listen. And consider joining a support group. That is the best thing I ever did for myself to heal my heart. Hang in there, take it slow and easy, and before you know it, the days will turn into weeks, the weeks turn into months, then years. Along the way, you will meet people who will understand your grief and those who don't...yet. Share your stories. Tell them over and over again, if you want, to people who will listen, and hold on to HOPE. One day you will feel your heart lighten, and you may want to help others as they have helped you.

Volunteer to be that support to someone else. Over all these years, I have offered many thanks and praise to Susan and Don who have shown so much love to so many grieving hearts. With their love and kindness, and for the love of their daughter Christi, they have provided us with a sacred space to grieve, and for that, I will always be grateful.

CHAPTER

Julie and Ken Kirk

Loss of Son Joseph to Accidental Drug Overdose

On September 14, 1987, Ken and I were blessed with our third child and only son, Joseph Michael Kirk. We have two older daughters, Carrie and Emily, who were equally as thrilled to have a baby brother. He came into the world and brought so much love and joy to our family for 24 years. Joseph was a charmer -- kind, witty, artistic, smart, a published poet and sensitive boy. He continued to be so up until his death on January 31, 2011, of an accidental drug overdose, not long after leaving his fifth rehab on December 22, 2010.

We just never thought he'd die. We had no idea about the deep pain he was experiencing, and we were, and continue to be, devastated. Our beautiful boy was gone. It was a blur for the next week with funeral arrangements, out-of-town relatives, and so many dear friends who were there to support us through this tragic time. But when they all left, we knew we didn't know how we could ever go on without Joseph. Within a week following his death, I received a phone call from Sharon Balcezak, a fellow parishioner who lost a son a few years earlier to suicide. She urged Ken and me to go to The Christi Center and be with other grieving parents who knew our pain and who would give us hope. She gave me Susan and Don's home phone number. I called the next day and spoke with Don. He extended his condolences and told me that while he and Susan could not be there the following Monday, he would have another couple waiting for us.

With heavy hearts, Ken and I went to the Monday night meeting at The Christi Center. Larry and Sandi Rebecek were waiting for us with open arms. It was the hardest thing we had ever done because we didn't want to be there. We just wanted our beautiful boy to be with us. We were broken and didn't know how to get better. The love and understanding in that meeting were so strong, we both felt that we were where we needed to be to heal and to gain hope we needed to carry on. We were in a group with four couples who had lost children and were further along in their grief journeys. They spoke of their children and would cry, but in the next breath, they told us that while we will never be done grieving, it would be different. They said our lives would eventually find a "new normal."

We truly believe that Don and Susan are angels sent from Heaven to all of us who have experienced loss. They share wonderful stories about their beloved Christi, and watching them extend their love and care for others is a miracle. And yes, they still grieve. We will never get over it. We will never stop loving our Joseph, but we will find our "new normal." I served on the Board of Directors and am honored to be a part of this wonderful organization.

Don and Susan have continued their passion to be there when a person loses someone dear to them. They have given us the most loving and kind gift at the time of our grief—themselves! God bless you, dear friends. Thank you both for being there for us, and know we love you forever!

CHAPTER

Debby Krueger

Loss of Husband Garry to an Automobile Accident

When I accepted the offer to contribute my story to this collection, I was excited and flattered until I sat down and started to write. How do you tell a story about an event that hits your life like a bomb out of nowhere? A bomb that shakes the foundation of your life and challenges and changes all the assumptions under which you have lived to the point that the bomb explodes and nearly kills you? Even now, more than 10 years later, the power to hurt is still there, and the wounds that I believed had healed can still surface out of nowhere.

A good friend of mine saw a draft of this story sitting on my kitchen counter and read it. He knows me well and offered to proofread and make some editorial suggestions. I accepted the offer. A few days later, he called and asked me if I remembered the scene in the movie *Forrest Gump* where Forrest explained his view of life. "Life is like a box of chocolates. You never know what you're going to get." My friend suggested that I use that scene and life view to establish a context for my story's beginning. Much of my life had been a series of good chocolates, full of pleasant memories and good feelings. Then, there was one so bitter and nauseating, so horribly nasty tasting, so bad that I supposed I would never really get over it—somehow, it became a part of who I am. I thought about his suggestion for a day or so.

I told my friend that I didn't like comparing my story to a box of candy. How could I compare a horrible-tasting chocolate to an event that changed my life in an instant to something indefinable? His response was, "Debby, it's only a literary device to help you get a handle on your story and communicate with your readers. It's your story, your truth to tell in your way."

I didn't pick this piece of chocolate. It was forced into my mouth and down my throat. Yes, I participated in the process. I had to chew it up and swallow. I had no choice about that part. Spitting it out was not an option. Sometimes life offers no options. You can stand still, staying stuck in a moment of grief-stricken immobility or move forward. It is in the moving forward that real options, real life-sustaining choices appear. I chose and choose life!

Life is a journey. Many times, you get ready for a trip, prepare for it, look forward to it, and can't wait for a great time. Then there are trips you wish you could just skip or never take at all since you didn't ask for them. That was grief for me when my husband Garry died in a car accident. It was an unwanted trip into which I was thrown. I would never have chosen to take it, but I was there. This unexpected trip became a journey inside of my life's journey. The grief journey is long and affects every part of your life. It is a journey that can't or shouldn't be taken alone.

I am a problem-solver, and my path includes a personal walk with God. In the early months I was in shock or, at least, denial. I thought I could just work my way through this. Oh, how so wrong I was. I had no idea who I was or what I was to do. I would go through hell before I would be whole again. I didn't know the journey would be so long and arduous. When Garry died, I realized I didn't know who I was by myself. Everything in my life changed. My heart was broken when half of it was torn away. My heart hurt every time I drove through the intersection where Garry died. I had no control over it. My breath would be taken away, and I would reach for my heart. I was hurting so bad that my mind was like the fuzz on a TV. You hear and see something, but nothing makes sense. On TV you just turn it off, but in grief, you never stop thinking. Nothing makes sense. Living through grief is worse when you feel you have no control over your body or thoughts.

It didn't take long for me to figure out I was either going crazy or needed to get some help. I could not see how I would be whole again. I made a choice to move, which offered me options. I went to The Christi Center, a place I knew about even before Garry died. As part of a Christian Caring Ministry, I had helped others going through crisis and was accustomed to doing this. I knew it was important to get help, but when life changed in an instant, I had no clue what I was in for. Even though I thought I would be okay because I knew some things about helping people, it did not prevent me from experiencing hell and extreme pain for years.

At The Christi Center, I met people who did not let me walk alone and helped me realize that I wasn't crazy but in grief, which is physical, mental, and spiritual. Walking through this grief with others gave me strength to go on. I continued to grow and move until one day I realized that I didn't need The Christi Center as much. That didn't mean my healing was done because that continues. I can say I am a whole person who loves who I am and my life. I have joy again. I still talk to and about Garry, but I can do that now because I didn't walk alone down the scary and unfamiliar road of grief.

One of the things that helped me heal was a vision I had two years after Garry died. I knew my grief was bad, but I had resources, family, and help, while others didn't. I carried this idea for 10 years before it was realized and became a reality because of Susan and Don and The Christi Center. First, Susan and Don's weekly and constant devotion to the organization and the people who came there was inspiring. I wanted to do something, so I came up with the idea that I saw as a vision of hope. I would help others some day by planning a one-day retreat called a

"Breathe Retreat," named after my poem *Breathe*, in which I shared the way I was living, healing, and opening my life to options as I moved forward. The "Breathe Retreat" would be a way to help others recognize hope and work towards it.

Early on I knew I was not ready to help others, and I needed to take care of me first. I wasn't healed enough. So I continued the journey and worked with The Christi Center in different ways until the time was right. Another opportunity opened. I spent the next three years renovating our family's historical, more than 110-years-old Victorian home. As I continued to heal through breathing new life into this old home, I was doing the same for me—breathing new life into a grieving soul.

The old house that had once been the location of movies like the "Best Little Whorehouse in Texas" was now my home and the perfect place for hosting the "Breathe Retreats." The hope of carrying through with the retreats kept me going. After many changes in my life and the rough journey, it was finally time. The Christi Center partnered with me, and on February 10, 2018, almost 10 years from the inception of my vision in June 2008, we had the first successful "Breathe Retreat"—so successful that we had a second one. May this partnership and program continue as The Christi Center has through the years. Thank you, Susan and Don.

Breathe

by Debby Krueger

Be Still

Remember who loves you

Each day talk to God

Accept help

Thank God for your blessings

Heal thyself

Enjoy the rest of your life!!

CHAPTER

Mary Locke

Loss of Daughter Jessica to an Automobile Accident and Husband Cliff to Advanced Stage Lung Disease

I Love Easter time, always have. Since 1989 I tend to get very emotional around Easter. My daughter died on Palm Sunday, March 19, just three days after her eighth birthday. My husband was driving, I was in the passenger seat, and Jessica in the back seat, just like any other day. We were so happy. Cliff had just been accepted to Wartburg Lutheran Seminary in Dubuque, Iowa. However, that happiness was met with much negative feedback from Cliff's parents regarding a move from Texas.

Miraculously, we found that Wartburg had an extension in Austin called Lutheran Seminary of the Southwest. We were thrilled. So after church we planned to get picnic food together for our trip to Austin the next day. Jessica was so excited about seeing the Capital and looking at the possible new home for our little family. The accident happened on our way back from shopping, and, ironically, we were about two to three blocks from the entrance to our subdivision. Jessica had told me that she was very sleepy and asked if she could lie down in the back seat. Reluctantly, I said "Yes," since we were so close to home.

Just minutes before turning into our neighborhood, we were hit. We were hit with such force we flipped and skidded upside down into ongoing traffic and hit again. I remember the metal and concrete sound. I will never forget that sound. All I kept thinking was I had to reach back and hold her. We came to a stop upside down wedged in a ditch. Cliff could not get out but my window blew and I was able to get out to find her. It was utter chaos, people running toward me, telling me to sit down. An EMT came to me, and I begged him to let me find my daughter. I must have been in shock. He told me I could not help my daughter. I knew then she was gone. That morning our little girl, dressed in a pretty little dress, had gone to Sunday school and church. By 1:30 she was gone.

Twelve weeks after Jessica's death, Cliff and I went to Austin. I found a job, and Cliff started his Seminary studies. It was very hard to focus on anything but our loss. I remember tricking my mind, thinking Jessica was with her grandparents for the summer. Reality would always come back to bite me. A member of our church slipped a business card in Cliff's hand. Don and Susan Cox had just started a wonderful group, For the Love of Christi. Don and Susan plus the small early group of people saved our lives.

I remember the early days meeting in an office off of 360. I felt so warm and safe. We were not alone; we were with people like us. Sharing our raw pain with these beautiful people was the only thing that helped us in those early days. I will always cherish those days like the planting of trees along Town Lake in memory of our loved ones. Our For the Love of Christi group was there when Cliff and I welcomed James Anders born October 17, 1991.

There is no manual written about loss, and parents should never have to bury their children. But Cliff and I were blessed to be a part of a group that brought hope in the midst of great sorrow. While I was struggling with the emptiness of my daughter's death, I was also struggling with the "What Ifs." What if I told her not to take off her seat belt? Would she still be alive? When I looked at my husband, I knew he was struggling with the same thoughts. What if he had taken a different route home or made a split decision behind the wheel to avoid the collision. Those are the thoughts that drove us to despair, especially early on. Sharing at the meetings our deepest thoughts of sadness helped us to start forgiving ourselves. The healing process started in that one meeting room on that sofa, holding hands with strong courageous people who were grieving their own great losses.

I think of those days often and especially when I said goodbye to Jessica's father, my husband in October 2015. I am forever grateful that I had a place to go to cry, laugh, get angry, and share my grief. Thank you, For the Love of Christi. You showed me I was not alone.

CHAPTER

Kathy and Bob McCleskey

Loss of Daughter Shannon to an Automobile Accident

The Beginning

The first day of the rest of our lives began on February 4, 1998. That was
the day our daughter Shannon was killed in a car accident. We knew from
that point forward our lives would become very different—
full of firsts, full of questions, full of *whys*. Bob and I remember vividly
what we were doing when we received the news Shannon had been
killed. A Texas Department of Public Safety Officer reached me on my
cell phone while I was driving to Fort Worth. He kept asking me where I
was and saying that I should pull over. I did pull over into a gas station in

Lorena on I-35. A local policewoman showed up, helped me secure my car, and took me to the police station. To this day, I don't know who called her or what her name was. What I do remember is that she looked at me and said that she, too, had lost a child, and that I would survive.

While at the gas station, I tried to reach Bob and my dad, but Bob was at a dinner meeting and my dad didn't answer. I finally called a dear friend in Fort Worth. Jo Corbett was able to reach them both. Bob answered his phone in the restroom, because he couldn't hear in the restaurant. When he learned what happened, he felt like someone had physically struck him and had to grab the wall to keep from falling down. He remembered how Jo said Shannon had been in a fatal accident. Bob drove home, while my dad came and picked me up in Lorena. His friends from the Texas A&M Corps of Cadets brought Pat, our son, and his girlfriend home. The Corps also called Shannon's fiance and got him to Austin. Our grief journey had been set in motion.

The Evolution

I always likened this journey to being forced to get on a bus that pulls up at the door, to take a trip you don't want to take. The grief journey, especially after the loss of a child, is one no one wants to take. It is so out of order of what everyone expects. You do not know what the rest of your life will look like. You have to build your new life one day at a time. You learn things about yourself and others that no one should ever have to learn. You put on a public face and say "Yes, I am fine" when you are not. The journey forces you to a "new normal."

Intuitively, we knew we would be treated differently when people found out. We still remember when the cards, letters, flowers, calls, emails, and visits dwindled. After all, we were supposed to be okay. What we did not realize is that there would be flashbacks—sounds, songs, and smells that would trigger the feeling of loss for the rest of our lives.

I knew we had to find some help. I had colleagues who had lost children and divorced. We did not want to become another statistic, so we found The Christi Center and began to attend meetings. The Christi Center confirmed it was fine to feel a little crazy because when you lose a child, you do go slightly mad. Through the peer-to-peer support groups we began to reach the "new normal" and learned that men and women grieve differently. We learned there would be ups and downs, and that, too, was normal. We were lucky because when one of us was up, the other was down, and vice versa.

Today

The difference today is the primeval cry does not come from my lips like it used to. There are some people who still call or email on February 4, even though it is more than 20 years now. We find things at the cemetery that people have left. There are messages on Facebook from her friends that help us know others remember Shannon.

Years after losing Shannon, Bob and I both served on the Board of Directors at The Christi Center. We are still on that bus, but now we look through the windows and see brighter days, thanks to this organization. We laugh, remember, and we still cry. We sign Christmas cards "With Memories of Shannon."

Shannon's memory is sealed firmly in our hearts. Bob and I continue to strive to reach our "new normal" in a world without our child. We realize how blessed we are to have a wonderful son Pat, our daughter-in-law Erin, and two beautiful grandchildren, Molly and Delaney. We are continuing our journey, but we are not alone because The Christi Center is still there.

CHAPTER

Tracy Moreland

Loss of Son Anthony to Motorcycle Accident

No doubt the loss of your child is an abyss, the unfathomable. For those who have lost a child, I know the anguish; for those who haven't, I understand the thought is incomprehensible—beyond impossibility. This I know. On July 16, 2008, my life, my family's life, changed forever when Anthony, lovingly called "Ant," left this earth. After crashing his motorcycle, just that fast, in the blink of an eye, our world changed forever.

Ant and his younger brother Tanner have been my world since the day I was blessed to be their mom. They were very close, just fourteen months apart. They shared a lot, playing sports together, school classes, and friends. During Ant's high school senior year, he walked into my room as I was completing his application for student aid and announced, "Mom, I joined the Air Force!" I couldn't quite respond—the Iraq War was in full swing. He hurried on, "I've thought this over, Mom, and I figure most

247

kids at school have more chances than me, driving new cars and having parents who can afford for them to try new things. Not me. I feel this is my chance to make a difference."

As a single mom, it's one of the many reasons I am a proud mom. I got to raise my hero. Ant's family, friends, and his deep country roots mattered to him, and if you were lucky enough, you were in his circle. Ant had your back, and you were certainly loved. So on January 13, 2004, his 19th birthday, Ant boarded his first plane and headed to Lackland AFB in San Antonio for basic training. From basic he went to tech training at Sheppard AFB; spent a year in Korea; based out of Alamogordo, NM; was deployed in February 2007 to Kuwait, lasting just short of a year, which completed his four years of service. Ant was ready to come home, and he did for Christmas 2007.

In April 2008, Ant purchased a Kawasaki crotch-rocket motorcycle. He called me one day and said, "Mom, it's pretty, matches my eyes." I asked, "But I thought you wanted a Harley?" He said, "No, I will get a Harley when I am old." Yeah, how I wish! Ant worked for Thyssenkrupp and lived in a two-bedroom apartment with Colby, his best friend. He was driving a new truck he purchased in February, and, of course, his new, very fast, "pretty" motorcycle. He got home from work that Wednesday, July 16, about 5:00 p.m., showered, and drove to On the Border for dinner with a friend Katie. When he got home, Colby was headed over to his friends on a motorcycle, so Ant hopped on his and off they went. Ant never made it back home. His body left earth, and Heaven called him home.

We went home to Sulphur Springs in East Texas, our boy's birthplace and home of our family. We had to plan our son's funeral. Once his ashes were buried next to his papa in Horton Cemetery, I headed home to Austin where I found myself unable to function. On the first morning, I found myself on my knees. My world was shattered, and I had no direction. My dear friend Janice gave me the name of a counselor in Georgetown, so I went. He was pleasant enough; however, he didn't have answers and provided no comfort. He did give me a recommendation for a place in Austin—For the Love of Christi.

It was a very warm Monday night in August when I walked through the Christi Center's front door. Marianne met me as I came through, and we sat and visited. She listened as I cried while introducing myself, letting her know I had lost my world and needed a purpose. She assured me that she understood. You see, she had lost her only son Dylan just two years earlier on my birthday—May 22, 2006 (the day her life became two parts: before May 22, 2006, and after that date.) I mention this because life is now more precious than I could ever imagine. The signs and connections matter, and they are part of the heart connections, which allow me to be grateful for everything. I mean *everything*.

At the meetings, we start in a large room, sit in a circle, and pass a beautiful purple glass heart around. We share who we are and the loved one's name for whom we are there. "I am here for the Love of." We then break out into smaller groups, and I found comfort in those small rooms. Moms like me shared our pain, our love through tears, and even laughter.

Love doesn't die—the physical has changed, but love lives on. Walking with others like me, sharing and encouraging each other, gave me the hope to keep moving forward. Before you know it, weeks and months have passed, and you don't realize how far you have come until a new mom or dad walks into that room, and you are now the one reaching out to give comfort.

In 2011, a movie, "Rabbit Hole," came out, and some of us moms went to see it. The young mother in the movie had lost her son in a tragic accident, and her own mother had lost a child earlier. At first, the young mom thought it was two different losses, but, no, she learned it was not. She asked her mother, "Do you ever get over it?" Her mother answered that at first it is a heavy boulder sitting on your chest, making it impossible to breathe. But as time passes, the boulder becomes a brick you carry in your pocket. Occasionally, you take it out and feel its weight. No, we never get over it, but we can get through it.

The Christi Center gave me hope. July 16, 2018, marked ten years since Ant's death. There is no way my heart or the heart of my family would have survived his physical loss without The Christi Center and the heart connections made with others. Still to this day, The Christi Center, Susan, and fellow moms remember my son and celebrate his life with me. Love never dies, and the heart always remembers.

For the Everlasting Love of my Sweet Ant
Always and Forever—Mom

CHAPTER

Danni and Pete Morford

Loss of Son Travis to Disease of Addiction

July 8, 2007, our son Travis died from the disease of addiction. He was 25-years–old and the eldest of our three boys. Travis had a great sense of humor, a beautiful smile. He was handsome, smart, kind, a great athlete, and loved his family. He was a good son and brother.

Soon after his death a friend suggested I should go to a grief support meeting at The Christi Center. Three months after Travis died, I attended my first meeting with other moms who were in different stages of grief. Several months later my husband Pete met with the father's support group, which was the beginning of our new normal. Listening to the others' stories, we found out that we were not going crazy, that others were not sleeping well and had experienced memory loss. We heard the statistics about the high divorce rate among couples with the loss of a child. Most couples who come to The Christi Center have stayed married. That was a positive for us.

Losing Travis has been the hardest thing we have ever gone through as a family. The sadness and emptiness were unbearable at times. In our grief meetings we learned that everyone grieves differently. I could see this in my and Pete's relationship and with our boys, Eric and Caleb.

Pete's way of grieving was through physical work, building pools and clearing acres of cactus and mesquite on some land we owned. I founded a grassroots organization, DOA (Disease of Addiction), with the help of several friends. My passion was to raise awareness about addiction. Eric flew to Canada and rode a bike down Highway 1 all the way to Mexico. Caleb worked hard to open a gym, Guerilla Fitness.

Painting became another way for me to work through grief. In all, I've completed 21 paintings and two mosaics. Art has helped me feel the emotion and express it on canvas.

We have some property near Lockhart, Texas, that we enjoy as a weekend getaway and for celebrating holidays. We have enjoyed hosting weekends and sharing country life with other parents from The Christi Center.

Over the years our family has found many ways to honor Travis. One year we built a fire pit, another year a labyrinth. We do crazy, silly things. We laugh, we cry, but most of all, we talk and share "remember when" stories. There are some nights we watch for shooting stars. We write messages to Travis on sky lanterns and send them to Heaven.

The friendships that developed at The Christi Center provided me with an opportunity to share a dream of walking 500 miles on the Camino de Santiago with Kate and Elda. We were able to honor our boys in May 2014 when we completed those 500 miles with 22-pound backpacks. The last night before we finished our walk, we received a video text from a smiling Don and Susan Cox, telling us how proud they were of us. It made our day to see their faces and hear their voices. It's a memory that I will cherish forever.

We went to The Christi Center seeking help, and we stayed because we found hope and strength in the meetings and new friends with which to journey. We have been honored to serve on their board. We hosted a dinner at our home when "Space Between Breaths," a documentary about grief, was presented. I went through training to become a facilitator with the moms' group.

Pete made himself available to help with the general maintenance of The Christi Center facilities.

Susan and Don embraced us from the moment we walked in the doors, and they continue to keep up with what is happening in our lives and be a part of our journey. They have worked tirelessly for over 30 years sharing their story and what they learned about grief. I can only imagine how proud Christi must be of them.

We are grateful for Susan and Don loving us, giving us a Plan A and Plan B, and suggesting that we not drive while grieving, plus the wonderful yearly remembrance ceremony, their phone calls, and their handwritten cards. We appreciate your grace throughout the years and your sharing of Christi with us. We are forever grateful.

CHAPTER

Muhammad "Mo" Muhib

Loss of Wife Carol to Pancreatic Cancer

We often see people who live in many corners of the world get bogged down and fight wars because of religious and cultural conflicts. Carol and I, on the other hand, were able to prove that two people could take the gems from two different cultures and religions and increase our collective treasury. We proved that it is possible to be different yet be madly in love with each other. In our case, it lasted for 40 years on this God's earth, counting two years of courting. That is unusual and exceptional at the same time. We raised two beautiful and successful children. We thought the future of our lives was all planned out.

We retired from our respective positions and moved to Georgetown, Texas, in December 2015, leaving behind all of life's familiarities and not knowing a single soul in town. Then the bottom fell out. Carol, my sweet love, was diagnosed with pancreatic cancer on that Christmas Eve, less than two weeks after the purchase of our house. She fought cancer with all her valor, but her once strong body was not any match for this nasty disease. We lost her eight months after her diagnosis. A few days after the funeral, as expected, all retreated to their respective normal lives. I sat in the house and said, "Now what?" I'd come to the realization that my best friend and my soulmate had left me forever. I was all alone now, which was a totally new thing for me. My hardest journey, into the unknown, had just begun. In a time like this, I felt totally lost and frightened like a little child who could not find his mom in a market full of people. Then a very best friend came to my rescue and asked me to find and attend a related grief support group. And that is where I began the next phase of my life!

On a Monday evening, I came to The Christi Center for my grief support. I met many people on my first day; Larry, Jimmy, and Mary are among those who stood out from the pack. A week later, I joined The Christi Center in Austin where I found Peg, El, Beth, and Be, who also became my guides to recovery. All these people and more have had a tremendous effect on me and helped to ease the tension of those first time visits. We sat down for our usual ritual and then came the hard part, telling my story and the reason why I was there. There was no pressure, but it needed to be said and done. Sharing my inner secrets or private issues and opening up to a bunch of strangers were overwhelming to me at first. I went home angry, angry at myself, because my bad situation compelled me to do so. I am a man and am supposed to protect myself and my family, and I had failed to do that on that day.

I have always been a very private person, and privacy was the most important factor of my life. I continued to feel angry that night because I felt my privacy was gone forever. I never wanted to go back to The Christi Center again! Then I recalled Jimmy's advice, "Come to at least three consecutive meetings before making any decisions."

I came back to our next meeting. And thank God that I did! I have now been going to The Christi Center for several months, and I believe The Christi Center may have helped save my life.

255

The Christi Center is a support group for all kinds of grief-stricken people, led by people who have had years of life experiences. Almost all are not certified psychologists, psychiatrists, or mental health workers. Instead, they are peers who carry a lifetime of pain from a tremendous loss they suffered and convey their experiences on how to cope with life after such loss. Some lost a loving child, their dearest spouses, or other loved ones. Some chose to dedicate their time for more than 20 years. The center is structured to function properly and provide what is needed to deal with my grief and the grief of so many others.

After I started going there, I realized that my attitude and my way of thinking began to change from hopelessness to looking forward to another day. I was alone in a dark place with sadness and despair, but by joining this group, I could see that I was not alone in the battle of grief. There were many who were struggling and tackling the same issues as I was. While I admit that there were days when I was so overwhelmed with my own grief that the mere presence of another person's grief or emotions was too hard for me to bear. I would feel frustrated because I was not getting fixed right away. I felt like a man being torn apart, but I had no clue how to stop it.

Even after all that, somehow, I found strength. I started to meet people and talk with them—very little at first, but more as time went on. Soon I realized that telling others my life story or inner secrets lightened my burden, the excruciating inner pain, and I found hope in the midst of everything sad around me. I started talking more and noticed that each passing day my sadness was slowly being replaced by hope for a better day. Instead of fearing death or dying alone (suicide is forbidden in my religion so that was never an option for me) as the only future choice for a grieving spouse, I felt like I wanted to live again. And keeping this thought in mind, the discussions and exchange of ideas started to flow among us, and more positives started to transpire because of that.

Even though I was alone and scared, I learned to deal with these two emotions in a positive way with the help of The Christi Center. They helped me to be emotionally strong throughout the last 11 months. This was possible because we were repeatedly and respectfully told during every meeting that what we said there stayed there, and our words and thoughts were not subject to any judgment by or from anyone. Our facilitator, who experienced a similar loss, helped us understand some of the complexities of grief by being there and helping us navigate the jungle of bad emotions roaming in our minds. We learned to listen to others, which, over time, helped shape our future healing. During our group discussions, we learned from each other about coping with grief.

Some friends who had been there at the center for a while provided words of wisdom, which gave us hope for the future. I reminded myself that Rome was not built in a day. The most important part of my learning was that of not fearing the unknown, such as being alone. I found friends here who, in a sense, have become a part of my family. Now I can laugh again, joke again, and talk again without crying most of the time. I feel that The Christi Center has been the beacon of light for me in my recovery, and it has shown me how to have a spirited life full of hope for the future. I can dream again of having a happy life someday.

As my friend stated, "My goal in life is to leave this earth a little better than when I came into it. Carol made you a better person and gave you unlimited love (not many of us are lucky like that), lots of pleasure in life, and happiness to last a lifetime on this earth. She left this world a better place, among other things, by taking very good care of you, than when she came into it. She was very special to all of us. Cherish the memories of her. She will be with you until you die!"

CHAPTER

Dina O'Brien, Ph.D.

Loss of Sister Dana to Leukemia; Mother Faith to Colon Cancer; and Father Steve to Brain Cancer

It is such an honor and privilege to share my story. It is one of profound loss and grief, but also of healing, resilience, and immeasurable love. As I reflect back on the tragic events that shaped so much of my adolescence and young adulthood, I am struck by how far I have come and how much I have learned along the way.

My introduction to grief started when I was just days away from my 16th birthday in July 1987. My only sister, Dana, was diagnosed with Acute Lymphoblastic Leukemia. She was just 11-years-old. I realize now that because of where I was developmentally at that time, I could not really

258

appreciate how serious that was. I did not and could not believe that my sister might die. It would have shattered my world and the sense of innocence I still had to think that was even possible. But it was possible, and Dana died on February 22, 1988, just three days before her 12th birthday, with us unconsolable at her bedside.

Being almost five years apart, our relationship had been a typical sibling one—we loved fiercely and we fought fiercely. As I moved into my teenage years, my focus naturally became more centered on my own interests and obligations. I certainly helped when I could or when I was asked to, though I spent less time simply talking with and playing with her. What I would have given to really understand that she was going to die and that my time with her was so limited. After her death, I struggled for years with deep feelings of guilt for not being more present, for not telling her how much I would miss her, and not spending every possible minute I could with her. I still grieve the fact that we did not have the chance to come out on the other side of things—to develop and strengthen our sister bond as adults.

My mother and I talked openly about missing Dana and memories shared, but deep down I could not fully understand her pain over losing a child, and she could not fully understand mine over losing a sibling. There were no organizations for grieving children at that time, and although we went to a Compassionate Friends meeting together, I felt different from them. I *was* different from them. I was now an only child, and I had no idea how to navigate that. My mom was my rock, and although her heart was just as broken, if not more, she never failed to be there for me in every way I needed. Her love for me and pride in me was never something I questioned, and she always inspired me to reach for my dreams. In June 1989, we celebrated my high school graduation, and in some unspoken ways, it seemed like we had come out of the fog and despair enough to truly enjoy some things again, even though life was forever altered. We talked about college, enjoyed lunches together, and were reaching a new level in our relationship with me approaching adulthood and independence.

But in July 1989, just two weeks before my 18th birthday, my mom was diagnosed with colon cancer. She was only forty-four. I left for college that fall at my mom's absolute insistence, and my youthful and innocent thinking again prevented me from believing she could die. I fully believed that since it had already happened to me once with the death of my sister, "God" couldn't let it possibly happen again! It was that naive thinking that allowed me to leave for college, do well my freshman year, and survive during her illness. It was always incredibly hard to walk through the door at home, as I never quite knew what to expect. The physical changes were so profoundly noticeable, and I watched a strong, active, beautiful woman I always viewed as invincible literally wither away one week at a time.

Two weeks before the end of my freshman year in May 1990, my stepfather told me that I needed to come home, and he was clear that, prognostically, things did not look good. I honestly still didn't believe she could die. I think that denial is our brain's way of protecting our sanity and innocence, but it comes with a cost. That Mother's Day was the last one I spent with her. No amount of praying, begging, or bargaining could change the fact that the cancer had spread to her vital organs and that they were shutting down. She died on May 15, 1990. I vividly remember screaming at her bedside for help, though the nurse calmly said 'just hold her hand." It bothers me to this day that I was unable to just be with her in that moment. I was angry for so long that no one explained what was happening or helped prepare me for those final minutes.

College got me through after the loss of my sister. It was predictable, and I could pour my energy and focus into my studies. But after losing my mother, I was so lost that even the escape back to college that fall could not fill the hole in my heart. A UT counselor told me about For the Love of Christi and suggested I attend a meeting. I called and scheduled a face-to-face intake with Susan. We formed an immediate and indescribable bond on that fall day in 1990. There we both were, I a motherless daughter and she a daughterless mother. We saw our own grief through each other's eyes and stories. I saw how incredibly painful it was for her to lose her child. She saw how incredibly painful it was for me to lose my mother. As a result, we, along with her husband Don, have lovingly filled the holes in each others' hearts for many years. She left me with a sense of hope that it would not always be this hard.

I began to attend meetings religiously every Monday night, sometimes sharing and sometimes just listening, yet every time leaving with that important reminder and realization that I was not alone. I was getting better through the support of others who were grieving, too. I truly was not at the beginning anymore, and that was a turning point for me. I started volunteering with the organization, facilitating some workshops, and helped start the Kids Who Kare program, which I felt so passionate about. The grief of children/teens is so different from adults, and it was incredibly meaningful for me to help get that program off the ground. I saw myself in the faces of all the other children and teens I worked with, and felt like helping them was a way to honor the memory of my sister and mother.

All these experiences solidified my long time professional goal of becoming a child psychologist, and I received my Ph.D. in 2000. Oftentimes, my patients will come to me with issues about recent deaths they have experienced or someone in their life battling a chronic or terminal illness. Although it hurts my heart to know their struggles, I don't believe it is a coincidence when we are brought together. I look at serving on the Advisory Board and as a permanent ambassador for The Christi Center as ways to help give back all I have received.

My father Steve was diagnosed with Stage IV Glioblastoma Multiforme in October 2013. I was old enough and mature enough this time to know the reality and the severity of his incurable situation. I also knew that just because I had already dealt with losing two of the most important people I loved, I was NOT exempt from it happening again. I didn't know how long my dad had until he would die, but I knew this time I wanted to accept the reality of the situation and be a part of the process. I wanted to face this "elephant in the room"—death—head on, and not let the naive denial I understandably had as a child show up again. I sought the assistance of a professional counselor trained in working with terminal illness and caregiver issues. She helped me make the time we had left together meaningful and identify the role I wanted to play during that time. Given that I lived in Texas with my husband and four young boys and my dad lived in California, it was even more challenging. My dad and I talked openly about his illness, our fears, and, perhaps even more importantly, our regrets. We talked about 44 years worth of shared memories, my mom

Section Eight: Member Stories

and sister, and the relationships we had with them. We talked about what we meant to each other and what we hoped for each other. We expressed our love and asked for/gave forgiveness. Nothing was left unsaid throughout the two years he battled with this horrible disease. I spent nights in the hospital with him, participated in conversations with his medical team, helped interview caregivers to provide assistance, walked with him, sat quietly with him, and did anything he needed me to do. All of it, as hard as it was, was an absolute honor for me. As the decision was made for Hospice services to begin, I sought out and soaked up knowledge on what to expect, how to help him have a "good death," and how to do what no one ever wants to do—watch someone you love slowly die.

On February 12, 2015, I was by his side as he took his last breath. It was devastating and just as deeply painful as the times before, but I am so thankful that I was able to hold his hand and tell him I would be OK. It repaired all the other times when I felt guilty and inadequate during and after my sister's and mom's death. I was able to forgive my younger self and recognize that I could not have done it any differently at the time. I was able to find some peace with that. My life has been filled with loss, and it undoubtedly has colored the lens through which many of my experiences, perceptions, and feelings are viewed, even now. I have to work hard to not live in daily fear of it happening again to someone else I love, especially my husband and children, or to let that fear prevent me or them from living life to its fullest.

With the help of The Christi Center and Don and Susan, I found a new level of self-sufficiency and a deep realization that I am a survivor. It has allowed me to be the best wife, mother, and psychologist I can be, as I do it with love in my heart and appreciation for the fragility of life. Not a single day goes by that I don't think of my mom, sister, or dad and wish I could talk to them or have them by my side as I continue to navigate life. Many days I still feel like that 16 and 18-year-old child and just wish I could hug my parents or ask them for advice. And many days I just wish I could call my sister and share the journey of parenthood with her. But having Susan's and Don's support and love as "second parents" for me (and as "Nana and Gramps" for my four sons) is a true blessing. They took their pain and so unselfishly transformed it into a permanent gift to countless others through the creation of The Christi Center. I know that Christi, my sister, mom, and dad are up there together somewhere smiling down on us—grateful that we found each other, and that they are at peace knowing we are there for each other until we all meet again. Love never dies.

CHAPTER

Pat Ortega

Loss of Husband Christopher to Stage 4 Colon Cancer

Grief – It's Not Something You Get Over, BUT It's Something You Get Through. Willie Nelson recently released a new song with these lyrics in the chorus. I discovered the video on YouTube, clicked on it, and as it unfolded, felt as if my heart was singing to me. I lost my husband Christopher Ortega on January 26, 2018 to Stage 4 colon cancer when he was 46-years-old. He was diagnosed on December 7, 2017 (you never forget the day), and he remained in the hospital until he took his last breath. I am grateful for the time we had together alone in the hospital for 52 days. We talked about everything. It was the closest we had ever been to each other and God.

Losing him was like having my breath leave my body slowly. My body went into automatic pilot. I did everything without being present and moved forward out of habit, really. The more my body moved forward, the more my mind and heart fought to just stay still. I really just wanted to sleep and wake up and find out that all of it was just a dream. I began to feel like I was losing my mind. I felt lost, angry, empty, confused, sad, and overwhelmed, all at once. Days started to blur into each other.

Then a co-worker gave me The Christi Center's *Coping with Grief* booklet she found online. I decided to go to a group session. I didn't know what to expect, but I knew I needed to attend. The day came, and I kept giving myself a pep talk all day - "You can do this. You NEED this." I got there early to fill out some general paperwork and then went to the big group room. I was surprised to see so many people. Everyone there was grieving, and everyone there felt what I felt. They welcomed me, and I especially was touched that Don and Susan Cox were there in person to greet everyone. They led the big group session and told us how they were there for the love of each of our loved ones. I felt it.

Then we separated into smaller, specific-loss groups. There we could talk about how we lost our spouse, how we were coping, or pretty much anything that was on the forefront of our minds. You also could just attend and say nothing. Although I am an extrovert, something about sitting in a room full of strangers talking about my feelings was not something I looked forward to. I told myself I wasn't going to say anything. I was determined to just listen—until my turn came. I started with when my husband passed away, then how he passed away, how we met, how long we had been together, then how we married. I just couldn't stop talking, or crying, for that matter. The "sitting back and observing" plan did not last long. I learned that how I think things should go doesn't necessarily end up happening that way. I learned my grieving process was normal. All the different feelings (the out-of-control feeling, most of all) was, in fact, normal. What a relief!

Now I look forward to going. I wonder who I am going to meet this time. I often wonder how a particular person is doing throughout the week, and I pray for them. I look forward to the last 10 minutes where we go around the room and tell each other ways that help us cope with the loss. For some it's having a routine, for others it's music, and for most (not me) it's exercising. For me personally, it's God.

I have attended since April 16, 2018, and everyone who attends these support groups can relate to all that I am feeling. It's like joining a family you never knew you had. I'm so grateful for the loving support of Don and Susan Cox. They took their grief and made a way for others not to grieve alone. The Christi Center is truly a blessing.

CHAPTER

Maureen and Fred Patrizi

Loss of Daughter Meghan to Lung Cancer

Our daughter Meghan was the second born of our four children and the first to marry and have a child. She was a beautiful, energetic child and grew to be an outgoing and compassionate adult. She struggled academically due to a learning disability, yet went on to earn a Master's degree from the University of Virginia. She did not excel at skilled sports, but was a serious competitor in track and ran cross country track in college. She had no training in gymnastics, yet learned how to do a back-hand spring in order to try out for high school cheerleader as a freshman. Even though it terrified her, she made cheerleader. She loved to dance and later became the captain of her high school drill team. She was tenacious in spirit, embraced others socially, and adopted an attitude of loving kindness as her guiding life principle.

267

We lost her to lung cancer on February 18, 2011, on her 30th birthday. Charlie, her son, turned one-year-old only six days later. Meghan had begun complaining of pain in her back shortly after Charlie was born in February 2010, but, because she was so healthy in other ways, we attributed it to her being a young mother. She was living in Northern Virginia at the time, and we were living in Temple, Texas, where we had moved in 2009. We had lived in Oklahoma for the previous 30 years and still had a house there. Meghan, her husband, and Charlie came to Oklahoma to attend our other daughter's graduation from the University of Oklahoma in May 2010, and we all gathered at our Oklahoma home.

Meghan stayed in Oklahoma after her husband returned to northern Virginia, and due to her increasing back pain, we took her to our local doctor who ordered an x-ray and then a CAT scan of her lungs. She was diagnosed with lung cancer and referred to Oklahoma City for further testing. Those tests revealed that she had Stage 4 cancer. Her cancer was in her lung, liver, pelvis, and brain. With the rallying support of family, we were able to have her admitted to M.D. Anderson Hospital in Houston for immediate treatment involving chemotherapy and radiation.

Maureen and I had both grown up in Texas, and the majority of Meghan's family and support network were there, and we also had strong support up the road from the community where she had grown up in Ada, Oklahoma. We felt fortunate in being able to get her into M.D. Anderson so quickly, and she was assigned a treatment regimen of chemotherapy every three weeks with radiation therapy as needed. She and her husband first rented an apartment in Houston for June, then moved to Meghan's uncle's Austin house in July where she was able to be surrounded by more family members. This arrangement continued until Meghan's husband moved back to Virginia in late summer.

Maureen and I moved into the Austin house and provided care for Meghan and Charlie along with the help of her sister, two brothers, and many other family members and friends. The outpouring of help and support was tremendous and greatly needed and appreciated. We are blessed with a large caring and supportive family, a family in which Meghan was always heavily involved and which was a significant part of her life.

As her treatment progressed, different medications were tried without good results. Meghan and everyone around her attempted to remain positive and hopeful, but her health continued to decline. There were numerous times when we had to make trips to the hospital in an effort to get her pain under control. Meghan even had to make an emergency trip to the hospital the day Charlie was scheduled to be christened, so he ended up being baptized in the hospital chapel in an impromptu service instead of in the church ceremony that had been planned. Always upbeat, at the end of the day as she was being wheeled out of the hospital, Meghan said, "Well, I think this has been a pretty good day, don't you?" She said that because any time family gathered together, it was a good day.

Up until Christmas Eve, Meghan's husband, Tim continued to live and work in Virginia and would have Charlie come for periodic visits. When he arrived Christmas Eve, he realized that her condition had deteriorated to the degree that a recovery might not occur. Several months before, Meghan's doctor had said that unless a new medication was found to stem the growth of her cancer cells, she might have only months to live. No medicine was working, but Meghan remained positive. She did not want to talk about dying, so we did not bring it up. There were two occasions in which I tried to broach the subject, and she questioned why I would want to talk about that, so I dropped it. During this time, I was commuting from Austin to Temple, about an hour commute, and I would have many tearful trips to work and back.

Tim decided to stay in Texas and remained by her side until she died. We had, by that time, gratefully accepted the care of Hospice Austin, and they were instrumental in guiding and assisting with her final journey. They accepted her as a patient while allowing her to continue her treatment. In February 2011, while Meghan was waiting to return to Houston for more chemotherapy, she made another trip to the hospital due to pain and a persistent cough. In the emergency room, the doctor informed Meghan and us that she had untreatable pneumonia and had a week to ten days to live. There was no more denying what we were facing.

In a state of shock and horror, we made arrangements for Meghan to be admitted to the Christopher House, a residence for the management of the terminally ill prior to their death. Even in these circumstances, Meghan was hopeful of some kind of turnaround. She was not in complete denial, but just choosing to take a positive route, given the options. On one of our previous trips from chemotherapy in Houston in route back to Austin, out of the blue, she said, "Well, I guess if I don't make it, I'd choose to be cremated and to have a service in Ada."

Meghan died after twelve days in Christopher House. For the last few days she was mostly in a non-responsive state. When she died in the morning, on the day she turned 30, she was surrounded by her loving family.

Life changed the day Meghan received her diagnosis and went into a state of no return after her death. I now think of my life as being Before Cancer (BC) and After Death (AD). It's hard to put into words the range and depth of emotions one goes through with the loss of a child. Needless to say, it is an intense, exhausting, painful process. I have learned that grief and mourning are necessary processes and believe, as a general rule, the more one allows oneself to experience the range and depth of the emotions that accompany loss, the better off one tends to be in the long run.

That's where The Christi Center comes in. Maureen and I participated in a six-session grief group offered by Hospice Austin and learned of The Christi Center. We began attending their groups in December 2011. It's hard to imagine how either of us would have handled our grief process without the help of those at The Christi Center. The love and support that have poured forth from Susan and Don Cox following the loss of their daughter in 1985, and from the other helpers and fellow grief travelers, is beyond measure. The suffering one endures with the loss of a child is immense; yet, The Christi Center has lessened that suffering for us and for so many others. Maureen and I are, and will always be, extremely grateful for their help and friendship.

CHAPTER

Deb Pilcher

Loss of Daughter Anna who was Stillborn and Husband Wally Killed by a Drunk Driver

We have all experienced grief. The quote, "Grief is the price for loving others," rings so true. Wally, my husband, and I are no strangers to grief. In September 1999, our first child, Anna, was stillborn. We had to say "hello" and "goodbye" in the same moment—one that will last a lifetime. We grieved the loss of Anna in different ways, but, ultimately, we found healing, grew in faith, and grew as a family with Jacob, Matthew, and Rebekah.

In September 2015, Wally was killed by a drunk driver. He and Jacob, who was 15 at the time, were headed to San Antonio early that Sunday morning for a soccer game. Around the same time, a driver with a blood alcohol level almost three times the legal limit and a large amount of cocaine in his system headed north on the southbound lanes of the tollway. Both Wally and the driver died in the head–on collision. Jacob survived with broken bones and a traumatic brain injury. As I reflect back on those first few months, it's a blur. Jacob's recovery was the focus. Learning how to get through each day logistically was a huge challenge, and we were functioning in survival mode. We were so lucky to have family, friends, neighbors, and our church to support us.

By December, Jacob was back in school and doing well. We had all started counseling, and I felt the fog begin to lift. The grief I felt and the pain of losing Wally was almost unbearable, but I began to notice a pain that was far worse. It was the pain of watching my children grieve their father. I couldn't save them from the heartbreak. I couldn't take their pain away. I had to face the grief with them and teach them how to feel it. I wasn't sure how to do that. In the spring, Matthew's counselor suggested I visit The Christi Center, and so Matthew, Rebekah, and I started going to Kids Who Kare, the children's grief group.

I am so happy the kids enjoyed going. These children around them know what it is like to lose a mom, a dad, or a sibling. My kids see that they aren't the only kids grieving a tremendous loss. Rebekah, age 10, once said, "It is a place where I can talk to other kids who know how I feel. I also feel welcome at The Christi Center, and it's very fun." The kids talk about school and things going on in their lives. They play games and practice ways to release stress. They make memory boxes and posters and create art to express their feelings.

In one of our first weeks at Kids Who Kare, they painted. I'll never forget what Matthew told me about his painting. There were two boats in a stormy sea with two silhouettes, one person in each boat. He told me he was in one boat, and his dad, along with all his hope, was in the other. No matter how hard he tried, he couldn't reach the other boat. I'm not sure he could have expressed those feelings without painting them. Matthew, age 13, started attending the teen group recently. "I can be with other people just like me," he said. "I know I'm not alone, and there are people around me going through the same thing."

I will be honest. I am so tired. Most days, I'm lucky I haven't misplaced a kid, much less found time to provide creative ways for them to express their feelings. So I am very thankful for The Christi Center and all they offer my kids. I am also grateful for those who work for and with The Christi Center. They step into our grief—our uncomfortable, unpredictable, and complicated grief. They truly are here for the love of our loved ones.

I came for the kids but quickly found The Christi Center was there for me, too. I met some of the most courageous mothers, fathers, and grandparents who were grieving. Seeing their strength and growth gave me hope and inspired me. I had the great honor of speaking at a Heart Connections fundraiser luncheon in 2016. And Jacob and I have had several opportunities to talk to teenagers about the consequences of driving under the influence. By sharing our story and reaching out to others, Wally's death matters just as much as his life did.

Grief is truly a journey. The road ahead is long and daunting, but there are good days among the bad. And one day, you will see a light at the end of the tunnel, and it isn't the light of a train speeding toward you. It is an idea of how to spend your 21st wedding anniversary without him. It is a picture created by your child expressing his fear, sadness, or hope. It is a new name for the anniversary of the accident, which we now call *reunion day*, the day Wally and Anna were reunited in heaven. That light at the end of the tunnel is the opportunity to make our loss matter, as Susan and Don and The Christi Center have done since 1987.

I am grateful for The Christi Center. And I am most thankful for the inspiring people who honestly and openly share their grief journey in hopes of healing, growing, and being a light for someone else.

CHAPTER

Sherry Smith-Meyers

Loss of Son Michael Scott Smith to Automobile Accident; Brother Scott Smyers to Lung Cancer; Sister, BJ Smyers to Breast Cancer; Dad, Clint Smyers to Diabetes and other Health Issues; Mother, Susan Smyers to Breast Cancer

February 3, 1988, would end up being the worst day of my life, the day of the worst thing that could possibly ever happen, and the day my life as I knew it irreparably changed forever. I had just separated from my second husband after a short three-year marriage because of his problems with alcohol and was near the end of my day at my very stressful job as the business manager for a busy medical practice. My beautiful, intelligent, kind, funny 16-year-old son, Michael, who was at cross country track practice was to ride home from school with my stepson who was attending a tutoring class after school.

Michael called as I was finishing a final task before leaving for the day. He couldn't find his stepbrother and wanted me to pick him up. I said okay, but reminded him that with the 5:00 p.m. traffic and the distance from my office to the school, it would take a while for me to get there. A couple of minutes passed as I hurriedly finished the task, grabbed my purse, and prepared to leave my office. Those couple of minutes would haunt me forever and become a constant *if only* in my mind, as they gave Michael just enough time to call me back and say he had found his stepbrother. He asked if they could go to Barton Creek Mall (a short distance from the school and our house) to get his stepbrother a pair of shoes. I said okay, but just buy the shoes and come home, and I would take them to dinner. If only I had dropped what I was doing and left immediately, he wouldn't have been able to reach me (no cell phones back then) so he would have had to wait on me to get to the school.

As I am driving home, I hear on the radio news about a wreck on the road leading from the school to our house with a *fatality*. An uneasy feeling immediately came over me. As I passed the road where the accident had happened, I could see a crowd of people and the emergency vehicles but not the accident. I drove the other couple of blocks to my house. The boys were not there. My heart sank, and my anxiety level rose. I drove back to the scene of the accident, asking the teenagers who passed by me as I walked closer if they knew who was involved in the accident. With their heads hung low, looking at the ground, they shook their heads. "No." I asked, "What kind of car?" "A white Daytona."

My stepson's mother had a new white Daytona, and he had spent the previous night at her house. Fear gripped me as I ran up to the police officer, pleading to myself, "Not my Mikey," over and over. He thought I was my stepson's mother because of the last name and told me they had taken my stepson to the hospital. That meant my Mikey was the one who had died. I fainted. I was in total shock and in the worst pain I had ever felt. I had been a single mom for ten years before my second marriage.

Michael was the light of my life, and we had a very strong bond. Now I felt completely alone.

My own mother had died of breast cancer when I was 20. I was not close to my father and stepmother who lived in another town. My sister was a learning-challenged person, and neither she nor my brother lived close by. My marriage ended, and I had no home. Friends didn't know what to do with me and soon dropped off. My one blessing was that before one friend abandoned me (I never heard from her again), she had found out about an organization called For the Love of Christi and dropped me off at their evening meeting at the Cielo Center. I have no idea what would have happened if not for Don and Susan Cox and the other members I would come to know. I've always felt like I just wouldn't have made it, wouldn't have survived. I really had no other support system and felt like I didn't belong in the world anymore. My life felt surreal as I struggled to make it through each day. Going back to work was a nightmare. I felt the stares; people didn't know what to say, and although I know they didn't mean to, they often said things that were very painful. My only safe places were closed up in one room in my apartment and at For the Love of Christi. In the beginning, I mostly just sat and listened to other members' stories and cried.

Eventually, I felt safe enough to tell my story and express my feelings, too. We could tell each other the same things over and over (something I think our minds just do to come to grips with what has happened), and could express whatever emotions we were feeling— anger, sadness or hopeless-ness. Everyone listened in a supportive, caring way without judgment.

Now, more than 30 years later, Don and Susan remain dear loving friends. Over the years, there have been many events, such as the annual Candlelight Remembrance Service over the holidays, tree grove planting dedications, and retreats for me to attend and at which I could assist. I was happy to serve a term as secretary of the nonprofit. I have also been blessed to be able to make many financial contributions to support the group activities, which have helped so many new members over the years.

There have, of course, been more losses among our original group of founding members, and we have continued to be there for each other.

Several of our members have themselves passed away, and each of us have lost more of our family members. Susan and Don have been there to help plan and be a part of many, many funeral services. In 2002, my only brother, age 51, died of lung cancer. Susan and Don visited him in the hospital during his illness. Don was a pallbearer, and Susan read the beautiful poem (I call it the *Group Poem*) she actually found in Christi's writings, "To Those I Love and Those Who Love Me."

In 2013, my only sister passed away at age 67 from breast cancer. Susan went to the funeral home with me to help me plan her service and contacted several of the group members who were kind enough to attend her small service. My sister lived in another city, so no one had actually met her, but they came to support me. Susan and Don also drove me to Dallas to collect her personal items, photographs, and other belongings from her apartment, and to take care of her personal matters. Three weeks after my sister passed away, my 95-year-old father passed.

So, all of my original birth family is gone, and Susan and Don have been there for me through all of these losses to offer love, support, assistance, and hope as they have done for so many, many others. Once, many years after I had lost Mikey, Susan came to my office so we could go to lunch. When I returned, one of my co-workers said, "You know, whenever I look at Susan, it always looks like there is a light all around her." I replied, "Yes, there is. She is an earth angel for sure!"

CHAPTER

Daniel Sustaita

Loss of Brother David Benavides to Head Injury

Daniel Sustaita, a freshman at Austin High School, frequently checked his mirror to monitor his muscle strength after years of playing basketball. "Am I as big as David?" he would ask his mother Samantha. David Benavides was Daniel's big brother, known for going to the gym for hours after work while in the Marines. David had gained the nickname "King of Muscle-ups" for the impressive amount of muscle/pull-ups he could do.

Daniel's brother, his hero, died in March 2014 from a head injury. While Daniel was in Texas with his father and sister, his mother flew out to California to be at David's bedside. Daniel always looked up to David, who often served as a father figure while their father worked overtime around the clock. From shooting hoops in the driveway to a trip to Universal Studios during David's Marine station in California, the brothers had an unbreakable bond. A favorite pastime between them was playing Madden NFL Football.

"He loved the Dallas Cowboys, and I was for the Saints," Daniel said. "We played against each other, and I always won. When I won, David would say, 'This game is cheap!' I had a feeling after he died that maybe he let me win."

David died on a Friday, and Daniel was back in school the next Monday because he couldn't miss the STAAR testing. He said his teachers and classmates were supportive, coming to visit that tragic weekend and writing him notes, but his return to school was difficult.

"When I got there, I was still in a daze, trying to process what had happened over the long weekend. That day, the counselor and I decided to talk about my loss in front of the class. I agreed, so I wouldn't be in a bad mood, and they would quit bugging me! They knew he had been in the hospital and would always ask how David was doing," said Daniel. "There were two classes. I had to let the counselor talk during the first one, because I could not express myself, I was so upset. She felt I could speak with the second class, but I was wailing."

Two months after David's death, Daniel's mother took him to the Kids Who Kare meeting. The first visit was uncomfortable for the nine-year-old. "I was a little nervous because I didn't know what to think or say. But by the second time, I clicked with the others."

Daniel, who eventually participated in the Teen Group, recalled a few Kids Who Kare art activities, which had an impact on him. "One was a collage that represents your loved one. I put David's Marine photo in the middle, surrounded by other Marines," he said. "Others expressed their emotions with colors and words. I drew a heart that was black (my sadness) and red (my love) with heartfelt words and feelings about David."

Daniel still has all these remembrances for David on a Memorial table at home. He noted there are numerous occasions when he most deeply feels the loss of his brother. One happened at the start of high school.

"Every year, you get to know the other students, and they pass out a survey. The one question that gets me is, 'Do you have any brothers and sisters?' Well, I have two brothers living and I have David, so I answer that I have three brothers. It's hard to process that."

At the Teen Group meetings, after Erin Spalding opens the meetings with a check-in about where all the teens are that night, Daniel said they might just relax and play "Sardines," where everyone hides around The Christi Center. During discussion time at other meetings, Daniel might refuse to talk about certain areas.

"What I really can't handle is David's funeral. The night it happened and then his funeral. I would always say, 'Pass.' Now, when I am able to attend the Teen Group, I am more open to sharing."

David was born on the Fourth of July, and the family would always celebrate at his favorite restaurant, Buca di Beppo. After his death, they continued the tradition, taking a candle with David's photo on it, made by a mother at The Christi Center, to the Italian venue and to other family gatherings. However, nothing can replace the weekly occasion that Daniel used to always look forward to—David's phone call.

"When he was away in the Marines, he would call me every Sunday night to ask me how the past week went. We would have a conversation about my life and his," said Daniel. "He would always tell me he loved me and to have a good week before we hung up."

Daniel wants to follow in his brother's footsteps and join the Marines right after high school. He used to feel anger all the time. Now his anger is mixed with sadness and disbelief. He looks forward to the times he can share his true feelings with others who understand.

"Sometimes at school, you think you are the only one, but at The Christi Center, others are going through the same thing. You are not alone. They definitely helped me get through the rougher times – those days when I was having a breakdown and would cry."

After being away for most of one summer, Daniel told his mom when he returned to The Christi Center, "It feels like going home. They always go with the flow and let you be. They have been patient and helped me get through what needed to be gotten through."

CHAPTER

Nancy Thayer

Loss of Daughter Hayley to Automobile Accident

I had just arrived home from work on Tuesday, April 25, 2006, when my telephone rang. It was my son telling me that my daughter Hayley had been in a wreck and taken to a hospital in San Antonio, Texas. I couldn't believe it because she had just been in a wreck two weeks earlier. I thought this couldn't be happening again! Hayley had stopped by just a few days earlier and watched videos of her growing up. I remember asking her, "Did you watch them because you had seen your life pass before your eyes when you wrecked your car?" She just gave me a smile and walked out the door. I will never forget the look on her face as she left. It was like she was in a trance.

Hayley and her boyfriend had traveled to Del Rio to meet her Grandpa to go fishing. She loved all her grandparents and would visit them often. She cared so much for her family. We are not sure what happened on their way back home to Austin, outside of Fredericksburg, but her boyfriend ran off the road, and his truck flipped several times before coming to a stop. Hayley was pinned in. Her boyfriend and a man who stopped to help had to pull her out of his truck. They laid her on the ground. A woman who had also stopped to help, told me that Hayley kept trying to stand up, but she was hurt so bad, they were holding her down. Air Flight transported her to University Medical Hospital in San Antonio.

It seemed for all that night, Hayley was in surgery for a broken back, ruptured spleen, and a horrible injury on her right foot. They also gave us the devastating news that she would be paralyzed from the waist down. I was devastated knowing that she would never walk again. She loved to dance and play volleyball and was also going to be a hair stylist. How could this be? The following night, as we were leaving the ICU, because no one can stay overnight with a patient over 18, Hayley asked if she could go home with me. I told her no, because she was hurt and needed to stay there. She was so sweet and asked if they would mind her staying there.

Never did I think things could get any worse. It seemed day by day, hour by hour, for the next two weeks, things just kept turning for the worse. Hayley's organs were shutting down—her lungs collapsed, her kidney's failed, and she was on dialysis. And then her liver died. After three weeks, Hayley's heart gave out, and she was gone. My girl had died.

I have never felt a pain like the one after losing Hayley. My heart felt as if fluid was flowing out of it—like it was crying, which now I know it was. There was a hole. I did not know how I was going to survive. People would say, "Well, at least you have two other children." What did that mean? That I just forget about Hayley?

I returned to work three weeks after she died, still numb and in shock. No one knew what to say to me. I wanted so bad to talk with someone who knew how I felt. I didn't know where to turn, so I started searching the internet and found The Christi Center. I called and a very nice lady named Susan answered the phone. She was so sweet, telling me that I had called the right place and inviting me to come to a meeting the following Wednesday at noon. When I arrived and was walking up to the center, another woman was walking up, too, with the same dazed look I had. Her name was Marianne, and she had lost her son exactly one week after Hayley died.

We walked in and Susan greeted us. She talked to us, listened to us, and gave us hope that we could survive this nightmare of losing a child. We would learn to live a "new normal" life. I attended the meetings for about a year and met some amazing mothers who I now consider my best friends. I am so grateful to Susan and Don Cox. They created a place where you can go and someone will listen to you talk about your child without feeling like you are crazy.

It has been more than 14 years since my daughter died, and I am living the "new normal" Susan spoke about. I think about Hayley every day, sometimes more than a few times a day. I still get sad and cry, but most of the time, I smile and think of the good times I had with her.

CHAPTER

Sonora Thomas

Loss of Sister Eliza Hope Thomas to Homicide

When the police came to our house at 1:00 a.m. on December 7, 1991, they asked my father whether he had a daughter who drove a green Karmann Ghia. The police officer said that there had been a fire at the yogurt shop where she was working. Four bodies had been found, but none of them could be identified. I spent the next few hours fantasizing that my sister had been kidnapped or had run away, and that she would show up in a few days. Nobody slept that night. On the 6:00 a.m. news a picture of my sister and three other teenage girls was shown next to the caption, "Murdered at a Yogurt Shop."

Though I was only 13, everyone told me that I had to take care of my mom. I tried. I cleaned her house, knowing she would have visitors. Though this seems strange now, I vaguely remember calling our family to tell them what had happened, that they would not need to fly down for the funeral, that we didn't quite know when that would be.

284

When I finally went to bed the following night, I thought I would never wake up. There had not been a day that I had been alive and my sister had not. For two more days, though, I kept alive a fantasy that my sister had somehow survived. That fantasy ended when we were asked to go to the Police Department to identify some of Eliza's belongings. They showed us her charred jewelry. Her remains matched the imprints my father had gotten from her orthodontist. The years of her painful and embarrassing braces now seemed like a waste.

Confusion, media, and chaos followed in what, at the time, was the small city of Austin. Four teenage girls murdered in a neighborhood yogurt shop. My neighborhood. I lived not six blocks away. I would often bike to the shop for free yogurt and a hug. When I went back to eighth grade a week later, the shock in the local community was palpable. Teachers didn't know what to say. Students were even more at a loss. One brave 12-year-old came up and said, "Was it your sister that was shot?" My math teacher, who was also one of my sister's favorite teachers, came to my desk and said, "I'm so sorry. Your sister was a wonderful person."

I began to feel a loneliness that week, which has not left me for almost 30 years. At least back then, wherever I went, people knew what had happened, even if they didn't know what it was like. Even if they couldn't possibly know what it was like to walk alone in the halls of the school, then home to a house that was strangely silent, to a mother who was unable to leave her bed. At some point in those early years, some women showed up and started taking us out to eat and shopping. I knew they had also been through horrible things. They were the first rays of hope that I had that life could be—never normal again—but more than just bearable. My life could again include people, laughter, and meaning.

My mom started to go to For the Love of Christi. She would get out of bed, shower, and dress. In the beginning, people picked her up, and eventually, she was able to drive herself. Although I wasn't there, I imagined she was often silent, crying, or getting angry at God. She was often tortured in a way only a mom could be—by the reality that she couldn't keep her child safe. At For the Love of Christi, she found nice people who were a few steps ahead of her on the journey of horrific loss. Sometimes, they went out to dinner, and sometimes, I was invited. I had mixed

285

feelings about being introduced to someone whose story was that her daughter was run over by a construction truck at the site where they were building a new home. Our tragic stories became like calling cards, the main ways we identified each other and related to each other. At least, they were honest stories.

Though I didn't know it at the time, my sister's murder was an event that would inform every decision I made going forward in my life. It was a relief to be around people who knew my heartache. They walked through life, numb for years, before they started feeling their agony and rage. If they stayed with those feelings for long enough, they could develop a level of appreciation for life that others might never experience. The survivors at The Christi Center were seen by outsiders as strong. The Christi Center gave us strength through good food, knowing hugs, and, surprisingly, more laughter than tears.

In this journey of traumatic grief, we need beacons to show us that we can survive and one day be happy again. For the Love of Christi was that beacon for me and my mom.

CHAPTER

Teresa Thompson

Loss of Three Children Illián, Ivan, and Sasha to Homicide

On May 29, 1989, at 5:00 a.m., I woke up to panicky screams coming from the bedroom where the children slept and smoke seeping through the doorframe. My cries and efforts to open the door proved futile. I ran to the yard, and standing outside the window, I beheld the inferno inside and I understood. Firemen and policemen arrived. I was a suspect. Four body bags were carried out of the half-burned home. Firemen came out weeping. Since the Sheriff found the door to the bedroom blocked from the inside, I was no longer a suspect.

The father had killed his own children—my children—and then himself. A gun was not used. We didn't own guns. Days later, I was told that it was a blow on the head with a hammer that had killed my three children, nine, seven and five-years-old. Then he had lit the fire, which killed him.

287

I had met John in South Africa as he was planning a worldwide fundraiser for cancer research in which I became involved, and soon after we married. John the Walker, as he became known, walked across South Africa, New Zealand, and Australia with me acting as driver of the support vehicle, contact, P.R., chronicler, cook and bottle washer. After the New Zealand leg of the walk, the project was interrupted by my advanced first pregnancy. We traveled to Mexico for the baby to be born near my family, but then moved to El Paso, Texas. There a beautiful baby boy, Illián, was born, and my nomadic life gave way to a greater love of motherhood. In four years, I had two more children—a second boy, Ivan, and a girl, Sasha. We moved to Austin where John and a partner opened a business in retail sales of sheepskin car seat covers. Life looked good, and the children flourished, healthy, intelligent, and likable.

However, a recession hit Texas, and the young business faltered and was eventually closed. This affected John greatly, having set out to conquer the world and to prove his father's low expectations of him wrong. Although I worked in the store and took portrait commissions, while caring for three children under five-years-old, I was somehow blamed for our financial woes. Friction escalated and John moved out twice only to eventually seek to return. I agreed, still clinging to the idea of a united family and the children growing up with both mom and dad. A third time he moved out, this time back to South Africa, leaving us in a rather precarious situation from which I soon recovered, free from stress and enjoying peace of mind.

After seven months, he returned, again seeking a reconciliation, which I now didn't believe possible. While he sought employment and visited with the children daily, he took up a newspaper distribution route at the end of which he would come to the house and wait for the children to get up. It was then, that early morning, when he ended it all. The day dawned. Monday, Memorial Day, a bad weather make-up school day, but the children were no more, the home was no more, the mother was no more.

I moved to my close cousin Becky's home temporarily, while I cleaned up the mess and tended to legalities. During this time, Leslie Webb, who had suffered a similar loss (one child), came to visit and talked about For the Love of Christi and how much the group had helped her. At her prompting, my cousin and I attended a meeting, met Don and Susan, and learned of the terrible loss of their beautiful daughter and the beginnings of The Christi Center. I also became acquainted with those early members of the group. My participation at meetings didn't last long because I soon left Austin for good and settled tentatively with my parents in Chihuahua, Mexico. Little did I know that the short-lived acquaintance with Susan and Don and their mission would mature into a solid friendship that endures to this day.

I continued to drive to Austin often and participated in the first tree planting in April 1991 on Town Lake, and with two other members took part in a workshop with Elisabeth Kübler Ross in Virginia. At this time I received many portrait commissions from people in Austin and was inspired to draw a portrait of Christi for Susan and Don. This led to many other requests by members for portraits of their deceased sons and daughters. These requests were highly meaningful to me as their appreciation for the very life-like portraits of their loved ones.

Through incredibly providential circumstances I acquired a cabin in Cloudcroft, New Mexico, a village in the Sacramento Mountains to which I moved without any plan, agenda, or expectations beyond attending the local Catholic Church and hiking in the woods. My main source of healing had been a return to the faith of my youth through God's Divine Mercy, prayer, and finding Jesus in the sacraments within the Catholic Church. Thus, I was led to the trustful acceptance of suffering and to forgiveness. I found new purpose through my involvement in the life of my parish, which took a new dimension in Cloudcroft. Besides participating and taking on responsibilities in the life of the congregation, I began making stained glass windows—first for the church I attended and then for many other churches in the Diocese. One of six windows placed in my own Sacred Heart Mission depicts a smiling Jesus with three children, my children, their likeness represented quite faithfully.

When Susan brought groups of women on retreats to Ruidoso, I sometimes joined them for a day or so, but soon they began planning a trip to Cloudcroft instead. These visits began at Sacred Heart Church where the center of attention was always the window of "Jesus with the Children." We talked, prayed, and then moved on to The Lodge's restaurant for lunch. The trips to Cloudcroft were repeated for many years. Later, the men's group also started doing retreats in Ruidoso, including the day trip to Cloudcroft. As in the case of the women's retreat, the visit to Sacred Heart Church has become a precious occasion for sharing the recent losses, the long journeys, the pain, the struggles, the wisdom acquired at great cost, and the love, mercy and providence of God, followed by the customary leisurely and even joyful lunch at The Lodge.

The mission of Don and Susan and the whole Christi Center extends beyond the walls of a building and city limits, as my own experience shows. We, the bereaved, have all experienced the well-meant, but sometimes shallow expressions of comfort and sympathy, so the friend-ship I enjoy with Susan and Don that allows one to be bereaved, to remember our loss, to feel the grief, is a true gift. Add to that the sincere love they have poured out on us all, which has touched so many hurting souls, and the practical help they are always ready to provide. Thank you, Susan and Don.

Although much fruit has resulted from our *heart connection*, this story is not finished. More chapters are still to be added. God, in His Divine Providence, has abundantly provided for my healing journey to Him through various instruments, some of which are no doubt Susan and Don and the many people they have brought into my life.

CHAPTER

Linda and Peter Thune

Loss of Daughter Andreanna to Suicide

It's hard to know where to begin—the story of the end of my child's life. Andreanna Irene Thune was named after my dad Andrew, who died of cancer two months before she was born, and Irene, his sister, who was much like a mother to me. We had no idea of the impact the fever and illness she had when she was nine-months-old would have on her life and ours.

At age one, Andreanna was diagnosed with a profound hearing loss due to that illness. Also affected was the limbic area of her brain, an emotional center. Her nickname became Annie as a way to make it easier for her to say, but she learned to say Andreanna quite well. She was exposed to total communication. My husband's parents connected us to Gallaudet professors and a former president regarding Cued Speech; she received a

291

Cochlear Implant at age eight; and, her immediate family learned sign language. She had wonderful teachers who explored techniques I brought to them. The schools gave parents support, offered sign classes, and more.

But what Annie wanted most was what I couldn't give—she wanted to hear. She wanted to be like her sisters. She wanted to be like most other young adults. She wanted friends, a real boyfriend who treated her kindly and with respect. She wanted to belong. She wanted to know what people were saying. She wanted to be self-sufficient. Something was making her hurt, and she wanted the pain to stop. Sadly, nothing could stop the pain. No amount of living with her big sister for a while before moving back home with mom being her interpreter. Or getting her into art classes or hippotherapy sessions because she loved horses. Or helping get services that led to her having a job at a vet hospital where she had a wonderful employer who treated her well (and where she even found her little Princess, my grand dog, a Chinese Crested-Yorkie). Or no amount of her dad's loving support was enough to make her feel like everyone else. No amount of therapy or medication helped her feel better or less alone.

On Easter weekend in 2010, Annie looked at pictures of my dad on my computer. She said she would have liked to have known him. I told her how much he would have loved her. He was a great soldier, but he was a quiet man. I loved him. I told her that he died just weeks before she was born and that the moment I saw her, it was like seeing my dad's face (he was as handsome as she was beautiful) and reminded her that her name is the feminine form of "Andrew" in Italian. He would have had a good laugh at her "hijinks" and would have kept her safe. Easter Sunday, April 4, Annie took her little sister to church for the first time in a very long time. Someone who saw them visited me later that week and said they seemed happy.

On Monday, April 5, 2010, at age 24, Annie took her life at home. I had forgotten my phone and was teaching. Peter received texts from her and ran home. I met him and one of her sisters at the hospital. Another sister had just landed in Miami for a meeting, so Southwest Airlines put her on another plane, and immediately she was headed back home. One sister was being driven down from Dallas. Her little sister, who had gone to church with her the day before, was a sophomore at school and wondered why she had to go home on the bus when Annie said she would pick her up. I watched her walk toward me from the bus stop, wondering how to tell her.

Without The Christi Center to go to that following week, the next year, off and on after that for several years; help in dedicating a tree to her; being in touch with my "loss moms" ever since at any time and in touch with Susan; knowing that there is a house with a door just for me, waiting just for me whenever I need to go in—without all of that, I may have followed Annie. Because love of family is not always enough, or Annie would be here. I love my remaining daughters as much and more than the day they were born, my new grandchildren, my moments of joyful memory, but they don't replace the emptiness left by my lost child. I have to allow the overwhelming ache that builds over the days and months to have its release — to flow over me and hold me for a few days or weeks until I feel it's time.

The Christi Center and everyone connected with it never get tired of hearing about your child or your pain. They are ready to just be there. I don't want to make my family or friends sad, although friends don't realize how much I'd like them to remember her or simply ask about me or Peter or our girls and mean it. I understand lives move on. They just don't understand that mine can't in some ways, but there's a place and people who understand that just fine.

CHAPTER

Susan Trammell

Loss of Daughter Dee Ann to Automobile Accident and Husband Tommy to Bipolar Depression

One day in 1995, I was reading the *Austin American-Statesman* when I opened a page to one of the most beautiful young girls I had ever seen. This Beautiful Girl looked into my eyes. She looked deep into my heart. She had been born less than a month before my own daughter. It was her obituary. I cut out her picture. I laminated her picture and placed it in my daily planner. I looked at her picture each and every day for a very long time. *I didn't know why I did this.*

But this Beautiful Girl had somehow touched and spoken to my soul. That Beautiful Girl was Christi Lanahan. Many months later, my best friend lost her son in a freak accident. She was devastated. I wanted to help her—actually, I wanted to *fix* her. I pulled out Christi's picture and the information about The Christi Center. My friend balked. I offered to go with her. Still she refused, and I eventually gave up. Life moved forward for us both whether we liked it or not. My friend lost her other son to disease. I still wanted to *fix* her. She still resisted. Life again moved forward.

Then on February 4, 2003, my own world came crashing down. My beautiful daughter Dee Ann, the one born within a month of Christi, was killed in a one-car accident. *But this isn't a story about Dee Ann.*

Many, many months went by as I struggled with grief and shock. Tommy, my husband, watched helplessly. I know he wanted to *fix* me, too. One day he announced, "We're going to The Christi Center." In my state, at that moment, I did not connect Beautiful Girl with The Christi Center. I went with Tommy the next Monday night to The Christi Center. I went kicking and complaining. I went crying and pleading. But I went. I then saw Beautiful Girl's picture at The Christi Center. I know there are no coincidences.

We went for many months until eventually I was the first one dressed and ready to go each Monday night. I was the one who insisted we leave home in plenty of time for the 40-mile, one-way drive. I began to absorb the stories and love and hugs from others just like me—ZEBRAS! I learned from everyone. Everyone helps each other at The Christi Center.

Tommy began volunteering there. He had always been engaging, gregarious, charming, and a charismatic leader. He was invited to join the Board of Directors. He loved The Christi Center and Don and Susan Cox. He teased Susan unmercifully about their ages. He loved going on the retreats to Ruidoso and at Charlie's Place and always came home with more stories than I could ever listen to about their adventures and misadventures. He was particularly fond of the retreats held in Ruidoso where the men spent a week together hiking, eating, sleeping, and especially sharing personal memories about their kids. He loved the camaraderie. Tommy also loved the Round Rock tree grove where we planted trees in remembrance of Dee Ann and Tommy's mother and father. He always attended the

December Candlelight Service and often during that service would notice and scoop up anyone he thought needed an extra hug. He loved so many people from this group. I know that Tommy believed that his years at The Christi Center were some of the best of his life.

Now you see that this is also a story about my husband Tommy Trammell. Sadly, Tommy lost his battle with bipolar depression on April 4, 2011. Most days my grief over these losses can look like the ocean. Peaceful and ebbing in coves where unconcerned children splash and play. Nearby, sporadically crashing and bubbling upwards through crevices and holes in the rocks. Rolling and building in the distance where surfers are paddling out and positioning themselves for the perfect wave. But, overall, peaceful.

Some days I see those same waves, rolling and building, and just like those surfers, I begin to jockey for position, because I know those crashing and thrashing moments could possibly come. Other days—and, mercifully, they are few and far between—I see that same ocean and remember the signs posted along the beach highway: *Tsunami Warning*. And I know that the tsunami is there. Ever there in the distance. Unseen, unheard. Waiting to rise up. Waiting to rise up and overpower me and wash me away. But with the help of The Christi Center, I feel like today I am more prepared for that inevitable grief tsunami. *Or, at least, I like to think I am.*

CHAPTER

Misty Valenta

Loss of Grandmother Vicky to Cancer and Mother Margie to Multiple System Atrophy

I come from a rare family. My Mama, my Mom's mother, missed the death of her eldest daughter and the birth of her first great-grandchild by less than a year. After beating cancer twice before, Vicenta ("Vicky") Barrera Collins, the matriarch of our family, the laugh that could be heard from a block away, the maker of pumpkin empanadas, the one who always left with "I love you more," became a spitfire of an angel on June 19, 2013.

I attended Mama's funeral with her great-grandchild growing in my belly and without my Mom. The physical pain from the two and a half hour drive from San Antonio to Del Rio would have been too hard on her failing body. Before FaceTime was a common family activity, my husband managed to discretely stream the ceremony to my parent's home television so my mother had the opportunity to watch the service from miles away. My mother missed her mother's funeral because she was slowly dying herself.

My mother was diagnosed with an extremely rare and degenerative disease affecting five people per 100,000 called Multiple System Atrophy (MSA). The diagnosis itself was long and confusing. Not only is there no cure for MSA, there is no route of diagnosis. A patient reaches the MSA diagnosis when no other treatments from previous diagnoses work. MSA is a disease of theft—a disease that robs not only time, but also you from your body. Her mind was completely coherent as each of her bodily systems collapsed and her muscles painfully contorted. As her brain cells were shrinking and taking with them her speech, walking, writing, swallowing, and breathing, my belly was growing with my last gift to her, her first grandchild.

But I come from a rare family. My son was born after an emergency C-section to stop my acute fatty liver disease (AFLP) of pregnancy. Of course, I'm not as rare as my mom. Potentially fatal, AFLP affects approximately one in 10,000 to 15,000 pregnancies. Baby Jude, named for the saint of impossible causes, now brought new joy to the world. I whispered to him, "Hey Jude, take this sad song and make it better."

Six months later, on the day Jude turned six-months-old, my Mom did not wake up from her sleep. On April 18, 2014, after four days in the hospital, I lost my mom, Margie Valenta, to the MSA monster. I lost the great caregiver, the maker of nighttime hot tea, the one who told me as I was looking at Jude, "Now you know how I feel about you." I was a new mom and a motherless mom. The matriarchy of our family had officially collapsed.

I used each crumbling thought, insensitive comment, and grief-coated moment as a brick to build my protective wall. I focused all my attention on my beautiful boy and let the wall set in. I was the first of my close friends to be a mom and one of the very few who had lost a parent. I felt rare and alone. I was feeling like "a zebra in a crowd of horses," until I arrived at The Christi Center and started attending the peer-based Mixed Loss Grief group at The Christi Center for the love of my Mom and Mama. Early on, as I listened to the stories of my grieving peers, the bricks in my wall began to vibrate loose.

I began to feel normal and understand. I never thought I would smile again, but after finding hope here, my grief journey seemed not so daunting. Instead of looking up from my deep pit watching the world pass by, I began to feel grounded, rooted in what The Christi Center calls "the new normal." With the help of my fellow zebras (and a very watchful doctor), I had my second son without complication on his due date—my mother's heavenly 60th birthday.

CHAPTER

Kate von Alt

Loss of Son Garrett to an Automobile Accident

I am a bereaved mom. For more than twelve years now, that title has defined me and the person I am now. My firstborn son by two minutes, Garrett, was considerably large for a twin at 8.5 pounds, 20 inches. Duncan, his brother, delivered at 6.7 pounds, 21 inches, and both were healthy, beautiful full-term babies. Their dad Nigel and I had spent more than five years trying to have children after dealing with infertility problems. These were our miracles, our perfect, wonderful baby boys.

As relationships go, Nigel and I were able to be better parents as friends than as husband and wife. When the boys were three, we officially parted ways, although we always remained close and supportive to one another. We were often held up as divorced parents who co-parented very well together. Nigel was a musician and a wood worker. Born in Scotland, he held an extremely creative and free-spirited soul, one that did not do well being bound by schedules and routines. For that reason, we did not have the typical divorce pattern of kids going over to dad's house every other weekend, Wednesday evenings after school, etc. Instead, what worked best for our family was that the kids lived full-time in my house. Nigel would stop by fairly often and visit. We would share dinners together as well as holidays. He would come to some of their sporting and school events. Nigel would take them on vacation for a couple of weeks in the summer up to Canada where he grew up to visit with family and friends. The boys loved their dad, and their dad loved them.

Although being a full-time single mom had its difficulties, I always loved this arrangement because it meant that I was blessed to spend as much time as possible with my sons. I treasured every second and still hold those wonderful years of raising my two sons as the absolute best years of my life. At least up until February 17, 2008, when Garrett's full and vibrant happy life ended in an instant at 4:35 p.m. due to a car crash while on his way back home with friends. It was a beautiful sunny day, he was wearing his seat belt, and even the air bag didn't save him. The driver was in a rush to get to work and passed a slower driver on a doubled lined curve, meeting up with a huge truck coming the other way.

Garrett was not lucky, yet, thankfully, no one else in the car was permanently injured. That day Garrett and Duncan were 15 years, four months, and two days old. Duncan is now almost 28.

I know that I'm not the only mom who has had a twin (or multiple) child die, because I have since come to know of several others. It is, however, rare, thankfully, and a bit unique as far as grief goes. At the time of learning of Garrett's death, while my own heart was shattered, the one and only thought going through my mind was my Duncan. How in the world will this young man ever survive the devastating loss of his twin brother? The bond they shared since conception made Garrett his soulmate, his world, his everything. It was literally amazing that they were not together on that day of the crash because they were rarely ever apart.

The way anyone ends up surviving such devastating loss is a very slow and gradual process. Time doesn't stop for us even if we think it should. Our old world literally does stop. At first, it was breath-by-breath, then minute-by-minute, hour-by-hour, and eventually, day-by-day—leading to years. The truth is the slow and extremely challenging process of living within the pain of grief unfolds whether we like it to or not, over time. The irony of grief is that the Love we hold, making the loss and missing so devastating, is the same Love that ultimately keeps one going and carries us day by day. Love holds such amazing power. Like most parents who have experienced child loss will tell you, "I actually didn't think I would make it in the beginning. The pain was so all-consuming that I couldn't even imagine it would ever lighten up."

This felt true for Duncan, too, although he did his very best to be "strong" for his mom and dad. Nigel's' grief was beyond consoling. He needed to medicate his grief. He was carrying a huge burden of guilt because on the day of the crash, Garrett had left from his house, his supervision, with his permission to get in a car with a neighbor friend to drive Garrett back home. I held absolutely no blame for Nigel. I knew to the core of my being that he loved his son deeply and would do nothing to put him in harm's way. I do recognize that feeling guilt with grief is crippling. Grief is filled with complications and mixed emotions. Guilt can become a number one challenger that cannot be taken away by another person's forgiveness. It can literally be a person's downfall. Exactly one and a half years from Garrett's death, Nigel died in his sleep from a seizure. At the age of 16, Duncan had now not only lost his twin, the other half of his heart, but now his Dad as well. I had lost my son and now his father, my very dear friend.

I could not help myself from looking up to the heavens and asking, "Really? Really? What in your divine plan can make any sense out of giving my son so much pain to bear at such a young age?" I think that trying to create a "plan" out of chaos is a "normal" reaction to sudden and especially compounded losses. Now, with time and lots of reflection spent with others who share grief, I feel that bad things just happen randomly (not planned). It's what we choose to do with these random and some-times awful life events that can help to define their "purpose" or, at the very least, help us to bring good things from the bad. The Christi Center exemplifies this in so many ways. Garrett's friends used to refer to him as "Gare-Bear" like the Care-Bears, because he was such a kind and caring friend. For several years now we honor Garrett's memory by giving away

302

"Gare-Bears" to children in need of some extra love. We have also helped a foundation that protects penguins in Garrett's memory, because he loved penguins. Many people create scholarships, feed the hungry, volunteer with hospice, run races, etc. The world becomes a more beautiful place from all the Love brought forth from grieving hearts.

I am not sure when I realized that Duncan and I would actually be okay. Like I said before, it is a slow and gradual process. I still worry about Duncan, but that's just part of being a mom. He moved to Vermont to be closer to family, his dad's side and mine. He really wanted to get away from where he and his brother grew up. At first, Duncan worked as a carpenter, like his dad, which felt like a good way for him to process his grief. Recently, he decided to go back to school for phlebotomy and Laboratory Science, like his mom, and also what he was leaning toward before Garrett's death. Duncan is an extremely kind and compassionate soul. He has certainly taken his pain and turned it toward kindness and caring. I have been blessed with the most amazing group of friends from The Christi Center. I have walked the Camino Santiago, a 500-mile spiritual journey across Spain, with two other moms I met in a support group. I got married in 2018 to Stan, a beautiful man I had dated for three years after Garrett died. He waited, extremely patiently, for thirteen years until I could fully open up my heart to the possibility of it getting broken again.

I can now embrace that grief comes from the amazing gift of Love. I confidently and boldly say, "Love is well worth every single drop of pain." To love and be loved is what this life is all about. If I'm blessed to have more decades unfold, I will fully embrace all of the grief that comes along with that. I will continue to honor Garrett's memory, and I will help others who are lucky enough to feel that Love as well. It's love, and love alone, that breaks the cycle of pain. The time will come when we can reach back and find the hand of someone else who is just beginning.

CHAPTER

Leslie Webb

Loss of Daughter Melinda to Homicide and Ex-Husband to Suicide

I remember a sleepy Sunday morning, reading an article about a three-year-old boy who fell to his death from a sixth floor balcony of a local hotel. Sorrow filled my heart. For a moment I experienced a wave of intense pain and compassion for the parents. I dropped the paper and picked up my precious child, rocking her, crying, and praying, "Please don't ever let anything happen to Melinda!"

I will never forget the knock on the door at 4:30 a.m., August 24, 1988. I was so relieved that my daughter Melinda was home that I flew down the stairs in my nightgown. I threw open the door to find two men in uniforms looming in the doorway. I was embarrassed that I wasn't dressed. So I turned and went to go put on a robe, but they abruptly stopped me with a firm "No!" They spit out the words: "We have located your ex-husband and daughter," and without taking a breath for a second of hope to cling to, they stoically declared, "They are both dead." I discovered later that this is protocol, to be firm, direct and blunt in order to keep the bereaved from retreating into denial. I prayed for those men. It had to be hard for them to deliver the message.

In the fog of trauma, I remember shallow words about his truck, a hose connected to his exhaust into the cab, exhaust fumes. His soaking up Jack Daniels until he passed out, our three-year-old daughter asleep in his lap until my daughter and ex-husband both died.

Two weeks after my world had crumbled, my sister Kathy was desperate to find help for us. She read a story in the newspaper about Sherry Smith-Meyers, a woman who had lost her son Mikey in a car wreck and the support group helping her. Kathy made a call to The Christi Center to arrange a meeting. When we met Susan Cox, she rose from her desk with her dog Angel, a beautiful soul in a dog's body, at her feet. Susan wrapped her arms around me and gave me my first "Susan hug." Her eyes and her heart welcomed us. She was gentle, compassionate, understanding, a beautiful soul in this woman's body. We visited for a while, and I took a brochure. I recalled being relieved that they met every week, but I asked if I could come every day. She sympathetically smiled in understanding, and Angel's tail wagged good-bye to us.

My first group was a dinner meeting and as we arrived at the restaurant, I hated having to be there. I was unable to find or experience pleasure. I was so very empty and lost. I pulled out a vacant chair, sat, and blankly occupied it. The woman next to me recognized my symptoms. She sweetly introduced herself as Sandy Krueger Seng and shared how she lost Bradley, her three- year-old son who fell to his death from a sixth floor balcony at a local hotel. Suddenly, I recalled the newspaper article and the pain I had felt in my heart for her. I was not alone. I could only now truly understand her pain and she mine.

I believe there were about 10 of us meeting in the beginning. Week to week varied, depending on who was able to make it as some days were better than others. As Susan shared, the rest of the world moves on except the heartbeats of our children. The "normal" people (those without loss) didn't understand, and many didn't want to. So many of those individuals wanted us to move on also and be "normal" again like them. Many just wanted to protect themselves from our pain, and so they judged or ignored us. As my coworkers talked about their children in the lunchroom, they would freeze when I brought up Melinda. It was almost like she died every time I had to stuff a memory, so as to not make anyone uncomfortable. Not only had we lost her in life, we also lost chances to share her memories.

The Christi Center was my refuge. We were free to talk about our children, to talk about our pain, and to feel each other's pain. It was a haven where we could cry, scream, be angry, cuss, or sit blankly—it was safe there. It was a Fraternity, not one I wanted to belong to, but one for which I was so thankful. Life was hard those days, but we were blessed by the wounded, yet beautiful, sojourners along our way.

Depression became resident and unbearable. I was suicidal, and it became too painful to live. Susan and Don and others from the group came to visit me in the hospital. They were always "there" for me when it counted. Seven months after joining, they sent some of us to an Elisabeth Kübler-Ross workshop with the help from generous donations and grants. It was there that I discovered I was expecting my Lindsay, and life was hopeful again. Due to the wisdom learned and modeled, I now had tools to help me survive and to eventually thrive.

I have three grown children now. None of them are Melinda, but Melinda was not them, either. Each child is unique with unique gifts to give. We had to squeeze a lifetime with Melinda into three short years, but she gave us a lifetime of love. I have volunteered with The Christi Center occasionally over the years. I found jobs, such as assisting Susan with her loving birthday and angelversary cards, printing, organizing, and answering phones. According to II Corinthians, God gives us comfort so that we will be able to comfort others. That is the only way through grief.

My heart will always be grateful for The Christi Center, Susan and Don, and the love and support they gave me in time of my deepest need. They loved us back to life!

CHAPTER

R. O. Williams, Jr.

Loss of Wife Patsy to COPD

Our story began in the 1940s when both my wife-to-be, Patsy Mayberry, and I were attending high school in Beaumont, Texas. I asked her to the Prom. She accepted, and she was beautiful in a long, ruffled white gown. We continued to date after graduation, and I finally decided that she was *the one*. We were married the following August 8, 1953. Since I had two years remaining at the University of Texas, we moved to Austin. I was often asked by my fraternity brothers, "How did you get her?" My answer, "It wasn't easy!"

When I graduated, we moved back to Beaumont where I worked in the insurance business, which my dad had founded, for the next 42 years. Our son, now a professor at UT, arrived, and three and a half years later, our daughter Suzanne made our family whole. God blessed us with two marvelous children, and they have given us four outstanding grandchildren. We sailed along enjoying virtually everything life had to offer from

UT football games to great travels, including a trip to the Holy Land, a highlight of our lives. We were both active in our church, all our children's activities, and the community as well. Patsy was a fantastic mother, a most loving grandmother, and without a doubt, a very encouraging and loving wife. Not to mention, she was also a great cook and made for us a beautiful home that was always open to everyone.

Some 25 years ago, she was diagnosed with rheumatoid arthritis (RA), and we fortunately got in to a local doctor who was aggressive in her treatment. From the beginning, we always thought we were managing it well. As the years passed, it became more and more difficult for her to navigate normal days. RA is a dreadful and unrelenting disease, but we always felt blessed with good doctors and excellent treatments. Unfortunately, Patsy smoked through the years, not a lot, but I did everything I knew to persuade her to stop, even offering that she find the best rehab place, at any cost, and go to break the habit. My daughter continued to tell me, "Daddy, it is an addiction, an illness."

Finally four years prior to her death, Patsy admitted the same. She continued to have a cough and congestion, which led us to a pulmonary specialist who diagnosed her with chronic obstructive pulmonary disease (COPD). They started her on infusions of Remicade, a fairly new treatment, which eventually led to an infusion every six weeks. It seemed to hold the disease at bay; however, our son, who is a Ph.D. in Pharmacology and involved in studies with the lungs, told me, "Daddy, it never gets better, it only gets worse."

That is exactly what happened eventually, she was on oxygen all the time. We tried to make the best of it. I remember one particular evening so vividly. It made it very difficult for her to get around, and she only managed a few steps, had to stop and get a breath, and then move another few steps. I said, "Let's go get something to eat." Her response was, "You don't understand that everything I do is a struggle." She felt that at times I simply did not understand — and, maybe. I didn't. I thought I did, but maybe not.

We had moved to Austin, but I continued to maintain an office in Beaumont, so she and I would make the trip each month. She still loved to

308

go to her beauty operator of many years, and we both enjoyed going across to Louisiana and pulling a few casino slots. Eventually, the trip was too much for her. On the last Saturday in April 2015, we had just returned home to find our daughter and her husband Gary had come to pay us a surprise visit. We all, except for Patsy, attended our older grandson's baseball game at UT. I, a cancer survivor for 14 years (thank you, Lord), took our granddaughter and attended the annual Cancer Walk. That evening as we were getting ready for bed, Patsy began to have trouble breathing. She was taken to Westlake Hospital. There we were told: At this point most people would say *enough is enough*. Or you can choose *aggressive treatment*, to which my daughter replied, "Absolutely!"

Patsy was on total life support for several days and then moved to the ICU at St. David's North Austin Medical Center. We went through four hospitals, rehab centers, and finally to a nursing facility that helped her get some mobility back. While in the ICU, Patsy had told me several times that she did not feel she was going to make it and that if she was going to die, she wanted to die at home. When they had done everything they could, we were told that she could either go home or to Assisted Living. We chose to take her home, and God sent us the most angelic caregivers who treated us like family. As time passed, Patsy became weaker and weaker.

Someone asked me if I had grieved through all of this, and my response was "Yes." I had since the day she went down. I later learned this is called *anticipatory grief*. You know something is going to happen, but you just don't know when.

With each change to stronger and stronger medication, I realized that Patsy was getting closer to leaving. I also realized that God was truly walking hand-in-hand with me. My prayer for her and me each day was, *Lord, you know who we are, you know where we are, and you know our needs each day. So, I call on you again. I know your line is open 24/7 and I will never get a busy signal.* I still hang on to that after her death. I put a small Christmas tree in her room, knowing that it would probably be the last one she would ever enjoy. The tree still stands several years later as my monument to her.

It came time for my monthly trip to Beaumont to tend to business. I told the caregivers that I would not go if it looked like she wasn't going to make it, but they felt she had more days, so I went. The next day Bill called to tell me that Mother was not responding. She died January 4, 2016, and even though I knew it could happen, I was devastated. Patsy and I had always lived by the message that *to whom much is given, much is expected, and that means more than just money, but our gifts, our services, our whole being.* The minister incorporated this into her service, a magnificent one with a large group of those who loved her and love us in attendance.

I first attended a series called "Grief Share" at my church, but while visiting the gravestone office, I was asked by a gentleman if I was aware of a place called The Christi Center. I wasn't. Then I received a letter from the hospice folks recommending the same place, so I knew I wanted to go. Oh, what a blessing it has been! What I loved about it most was that on those Monday nights, we had all ages and circumstances in those Loss of Spouse small groups. We had outstanding facilitators who really understood our hurt and our struggle with understanding it all. It helped me to understand that grief has no length or depth and is unique to each and every person. We all shed tears and learned that it is okay to let them flow. They are liquid love.

I am sad that I was not there when she died, but am convinced that God puts us where we are supposed to be. The caregivers told me (more than once) that Patsy waited until I was gone. Knowing that Bill and Maddi, her caregivers and hospice nurses who had come to love her so dearly, were standing next to her bed has convinced me that God knows best.

I have been invited to several Christi Center gatherings and am always grateful. I help financially whenever I can and recommend The Christi Center to anyone who is hurting from the death of a loved one. I know that Patsy is with me all of the time and is saving a place for me in heaven. We had a wonderful life together in our over 62 years of marriage.

I truly thank Don and Susan for asking me to write my story. I have shed some tears writing this, but as we have learned, sometimes writing our thoughts is very therapeutic. Once again, it has been. God bless The Christi Center and all it does for so many. Bless its founders, Don and Susan, who are truly a Godsend!

SECTION

9 Appendix

THE EXPERIENCE OF GRIEF

Most people are not prepared for the grief journey, which at times can be devastating, frightening, and lonely. It may also seem as though there is no respite, and no end to the intense feelings that you experience.

The grief journey has been compared to enduring a fierce storm at sea. The waves are peaked and close together. Eventually the sea becomes calmer, but occasionally the storm regroups, strengthening without warning. For several hours, days, or weeks, you may not experience grief; then grief resumes. At times it may seem as though you are taking one step forward and two steps back. You may think, do and say things that are very uncharacteristic. You are not alone in feeling this way.

People who are grieving have some experiences in common, but they also experience grief uniquely. Although grief is a universal experience, no two people grieve alike- even within the same family. Different losses can each be grieved differently, even by the same person. Like a fingerprint, each person's grief experience has characteristics all its own. Just as there are no instructions on how to grieve, there is no timetable we can follow. You will adjust to a new life, taking it one day at a time. Grief is often compounded by the stigma and discomfort surrounding death. Even well-meaning people in your life may want you to "get better" or "get over it." You may feel pressure to suppress your grief instead of acknowledging it as a natural and necessary process. Your life is forever changed so you will not "get over it". But you can find hope for healing, new meaning, and a new normal in your life after the death of a loved one.

COMMON RESPONSES TO GRIEF

While grief is a typical response to the death of a loved one, it sometimes causes reactions that can be unlike your normal behavior. These
responses are understandable and do not indicate " insanity." Pain may
surface in the following forms:

Emotional

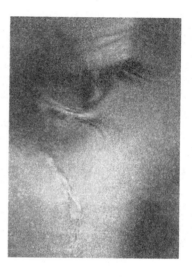

- Shock and disbelief
- Sadness and yearning
- Numbness
- Feeling disorganized or confused
- Wanting to be alone and yet
  feeling lonely
- Resentment towards those who
  have not experienced loss
- Anxiety, worry and fear
- Feelings of guilt or sense of failure
- Helplessness/hopelessness
- Irritability and anger at
- The situation
- Others
- Your loved one who died
- God/your higher power
- Medical personnel

Physical

- Change in sleep that may include bad dreams/nightmares
- Change in eating habits
- Pain with unknown causes– headaches, stomach problems, muscle
  pain, etc.
- Fatigue/lack of energy
- Sexual difficulties

Behavioral

- Lack of motivation
- Difficulty concentrating and/or remembering things
- Crying often
- Emotional out bursts
- Isolating self or avoiding others
- Abusing substances including alcohol, prescription medication, or
  street drugs as a way to cope
- Unnecessary risk taking

These are all common experiences of grief and may take an immense amount of energy to confront. If left unresolved through avoidance or denial, they can lead to prolonged or complicated grief. This in turn can significantly impact your health, marriage, friendships, job, or other areas of your life. Sharing with those who are on a similar journey is  often a helpful way to recognize and avoid falling into a pattern of complicated grief and to begin to find a new normal.

If you are concerned about the number or intensity of your reactions, you may find it helpful to consult a professional who can help you in your grief journey. To help you find this support, we can provide you with a referral list.

COPING WITH GRIEF

Each grief and healing process is unique, and people cope with grief in many different ways. Here are a few things that might help you:

Accept Support
Seek out support and help from friends, family, support groups, professionals, or religious leaders. People may ask you, "What can I do?" or "tell me what you need". Make a list and when the occasion arises, find someone who is able to provide the type of support you need (just being there, listening, talking, socializing, etc.) When someone offers you help, don't be afraid to accept it.

Be Active
It can be helpful to schedule activities or make plans to have something to look forward to. Remember that you are healing and in doing so, you are allowed to have enjoyment in your life.
- **Exercise** - Can improve your overall health, mood/energy level, sleep quality, and is a safe way to release emotions.
- **Volunteer-** Do something to help others - in doing so you can often help yourself.
- **Socialize** - Share a meal with friends or spend time with others who have also experienced a loss.

- **Yoga** – Can help calm your mind with meditation and active practice.
- **Gardening** – Provides benefits such as relaxation, exercise, meditation, and connecting with nature.

We offer ongoing opportunities to participate in these activities at The Christi Center. Please contact us or visit our website for a current list of activities.

Self-Care

Be kind to yourself and do things you enjoy. Rediscover past interests or learn something new.

- **Read** – There are many helpful books on grief and loss. You could also find quotes or poems that are helpful to you. The Christi Center has a resource library filled with many books that our clients have found helpful in the grief journey and shared with us. You are welcome to stop by and borrow materials even if you do not attend groups at the Center.
- **Journal** – It may be helpful to reflect on thoughts and feelings to increase understanding of your grief reactions.
- **Health** – Adequate sleep and nutrition are important for healing.

Commemorate

Many people find comfort in staying connected to loved ones by honoring their memory. There are many ways you can do this:

- Pass on an heirloom of your loved one.
- Plant a tree or other living monument.
- Try a new creative activity for a memorial such as; making a quilt, mosaic, painting, sculpture, stain g lass, etc. that allows you to create a memory of your loved one.
- Create a memory box filled with objects representing your loved one.
- Collect favorite stories about your loved one and put them into a book.
- Write a blog or develop a memorial page/website.
- Put your online photos in a slideshow with their favorite songs or songs that mean something to you on your grief journey.
- Make a playlist of your loved ones favorite songs.
- Enjoy your loved one's favorite food.
- Write or say a toast, meditation or a prayer for your loved one.
- Write a letter to your loved one.
- Light a candle in their memory.

WHAT TO SAY TO A GRIEVING PERSON

Sometimes when people are trying to be helpful or are unsure what to say to a grieving person, they make statements that are not helpful. These types of comments can dismiss the emotions associated with grief. It is okay for a grieving person to feel a whole range of emotions, and it is important to acknowledge them. Since each person grieves differently, there is no one right thing to say or do, but consider the following:

Common well intentioned remarks	Why they're not helpful	Alternatives to consider
Saying nothing at all.	This is actually one of the worst things you can do because it ignores the grieving person's pain	I'm not sure what to say, but I want you to know I'm here for you.
It was God's will, God will never give you more than you can handle, maybe God is trying to teach you something, God needed an angel, God needs him/her more than you do, etc.	Even if the person's faith includes God, they are relying on their own perception of faith or may even be struggling to reconcile loss and faith. Don't complicate things by presuming to know God's intentions.	This must be so hard for you. It's hard to understand why these things happen.
I know just how you feel.	Even if you've experienced a loss, each person's loss is different so you can't know exactly how the person feels.	I can only imagine how you feel. Can you tell me more?

ONE JOY SHATTERS A HUNDRED GRIEFS
Chinese Proverbs quote

Common well intentioned remarks	Why they're not helpful	Alternatives to consider
He/she wouldn't have wanted you to be sad.	Sadness and anger are difficult enough. Don't introduce guilt into the grief process.	I can see you are sad and you miss him/her so much.
It has been three weeks/months/years since he/she died. Aren't you over it yet?	You never really "get over" a death. The pain subsides and you begin to heal. The time frame for this is different for every person, so do not impose time frames.	I'll be here for as long as you need me.
He/she lived a good, full life and it was his/her time to die.	Knowing that someone lived a full life does not make it any easier to say goodbye.	He/She will be missed.
You should be grateful for your other children, You'll get married again, etc	One person cannot replace another. Making these statements discount the unique love they have for each individual.	I can tell how much you loved him/her.

If you need help with grief support, contact The Christi Center at (512) 467-2600 or visit the website christicenter.org

Order Form

For the Love of Christi: Death and Grief Met by Love and Hope is available from Amazon or directly from Almost Heaven Publishing.
Email Orders: susan@christicenter.org
Postal Orders: Send this completed form to:
        Almost Heaven Publishing
        6506 Huckleberry Cove
        Austin, TX 78746

Name: _____

Address: _____

City: _____ State: _____ Zip: _____

Phone: _____

Email: _____

Number of Copies _____ @$15.00/book $_____

                             Subtotal $_____

Add $5.60 for priority shipping in the U.S. Shipping: $_____

                                Total: $_____

**Make check or money order payable to
Almost Heaven Publishing**

For questions about a book order, call (512) 426-1920

If you wish to make a donation to The Christi Center, you can do so by visiting the donation link at christicenter.org

Made in the USA
Coppell, TX
07 June 2022

78580994R00184